Christian Counselling
An African Indigenous Perspective

OASIS
INTERNATIONAL
PUBLISHING

Gladys K. Mwiti and Al Dueck

ISBN 13: 978-1-59452-787-6
ISBN: 1-59452-787-3

Published by Oasis International Ltd, in partnership with Gladys Mwiti. Originally published in 2006 by Fuller Theological Seminary. To find out more about Gladys Mwiti, visit www.oasisafrica.co.ke.

Oasis International is a ministry devoted to growing discipleship through publishing African voices.
- We *engage* Africa's most influential, most relevant, and best communicators for the sake of the gospel.
- We *cultivate* local and global partnerships in order to publish and distribute high-quality books and Bibles.
- We *create* contextual content that meets the specific needs of Africa, has the power to transform individuals and societies, and gives the church in Africa a global voice.

Oasis is: *Satisfying Africa's Thirst for God's Word.* For more information, go to oasisinternational.com.

Printed in India.

21 22 23 24 25 26 27 28 29 30 BPI 10 9 8 7 6 5 4 3 2 1

To the current and future

mental health workers of Africa

Preface

In 2004, the Fuller Theological Seminary Board of Trustees approved a proposal to develop three courses that we anticipate could become part of a longer series leading to a Certificate of Christian Studies for evangelists, counsellors, church planters, pastors, and leaders in the two-thirds world who have previously not had the privilege of a theological education. The vision guiding the faculty was to create courses that utilize the best visual, textual, and verbal instruction to provide a basic theological education in areas and on topics not readily available to these leaders.

The funding and vision for this project came from a businessman, and friend of Fuller, whose call to ministry has led him to support evangelism and leadership training in Africa and Asia. In response to the leading of the Holy Spirit, this friend has instructed Fuller that these courses must be made available without charge (1) to anyone in the world who can access this knowledge through DVD, Internet, or other electronic means, (2) to church leaders seeking basic theological education, and (3) to Bible schools and seminaries.

Dr Gladys Mwiti of Oasis Africa and Professor Al Dueck of Fuller's Graduate School of Psychology have worked for more than a year to prepare the materials for this course, "Christian Counselling: An African Indigenous Perspective." Their partnership has resulted in an exceptional series of lectures and illustrated case material presented in the DVDs for the course and the comprehensive instructional manual that supports those lessons. We rejoice in the offering that Dr Mwiti and Dr Dueck have given to the Lord and to Christian leaders in Africa and the rest of the world.

We owe a special debt of gratitude to Remi Lawanson from Nigeria, and to Paul Cornelius from India, who conducted a survey of Christian leaders on their respective continents to learn more about their perceived need for support in training leaders for their churches. From their reports, we learned of the critical need for training around the world in the basic skills of pastoral counselling. We therefore rejoice in the completion of this first course in the series, which focuses on counselling in Africa.

I am also grateful to Grant Millikan, Chief Information Officer at Fuller Theological Seminary, who has served as manager of this project, providing administrative oversight, and to William Moffitt Associates which has done an outstanding job of filming, editing, and producing the DVDs for distribution. Most of all, we thank God, who provided the vision, the resources, and the gifted people to complete this work. We pray that God will take these gifts and multiply them for God's Kingdom and glory.

Sherwood Lingenfelter
Provost and Senior Vice President
Fuller Theological Seminary, 2006

Acknowledgements

If it takes a village to raise a child, similar wisdom holds true in the writing of books. Many individuals made this book possible. First, we wish to thank the Fuller trustee who envisioned this project of making theological education accessible to non-Western students by means of a learning package including both DVDs and a book. We appreciate the support of the Fuller Theological Seminary administrators who managed the production of the DVDs and the publication of this book. Along the way, the help of William Moffitt Associates was invaluable. Their suggestions, creativity, and encouraging spirits made the filming and writing of scripts a most rewarding experience. We thank the pastors, leaders, and therapists from Ghana, Kenya, Rwanda, Sierra Leone, Sudan, Tanzania, and Uganda, who met at Brackenhurst Conference Centre, Kenya, in August 2005 for the filming of material from this book. Your willingness to share proverbs, stories, and even some traumatic experiences changed us all and, hopefully, will change those who watch the DVDs and read this book. Thanks go also to the professors in the Fuller School of Psychology who provided helpful comments on the chapters. We are grateful to Angelina Ray and Randall Cole who assisted in the original layout and cover design of the book. Barbara Bell provided significant editorial help while Rachel Hall and Kathryn Streeter assisted in preparing the final manuscript. Lastly, we thank our spouses, who supported us joyfully throughout the project. Gershon Mwiti and Anne Dueck believed in this project so fully that they graciously granted the long hours of writing and editing.

Notes: Spelling in this book is consistent with the conventional usage of United Kingdom English, common in various parts of Africa. All persons mentioned in stories do not represent real people.

Table of Contents

CHAPTER 1

Africa: Dis-membered and Re-membered

South African artist, layman, and Bible reader Azariah Mbatha captures the African experience in a woodcarving that graphically presents the predicament of his own Zulu tradition and culture. Each panel is filled with characters, all with African faces and costumes. This is the African community – many people together engaged in a common enterprise. However, what is the enterprise? In each panel, a human is being exchanged for money. Joseph's brothers sell him to the Ishmaelite/ Midianite traders. Later on, the traders sell the young man to Pharaoh's Egyptian officer. Many years later, Joseph, now an official in the Egyptian government and unrecognised by his brothers, forces them to leave Simeon behind so that they can bring Benjamin to Egypt. In another panel, Mbatha depicts Jacob in sorrow as he is forced to let Benjamin go as a ransom for Simeon, and in exchange for food.[1] All this happens within community: suffering, plots, ransoms, pain, and brokenness. Just like any other African Bible reader, Mbatha accepts the Bible as God's word to him and to Africa and tries to "make universal signs speak to particular realities."[2] Mbatha meditates on the perspective of African community and the way this positive element of kinship has been abused, suggesting that the very strength of Africa has been used against her.

This is the dis-memberment of African culture. Agents for this dis-membering of community come from both within and beyond the community. Simon Maimela, a South African theologian, discusses this dis-membering of a people's culture. He states that after many centuries of oppression and white supremacy, black South Africans felt ashamed of their Africanness; it became synonymous with helplessness. He notes that this "humiliation was calculated to highlight the relative uselessness of our African cultures, religions, and gods, which failed to protect us against European military assault, our eventual subjugation and consequent oppression."[3] Community dis-memberment leaves vacuums that result in the loss of the values that usually root people and give them identity.

The challenge is to re-member and reconstruct African identity and theology. Maimela observes that degradation and domination made "South Africans suspicious of the inculturation approach in the reconstruction of African theology."[4] The author defines African theology as an emerging attempt that "tries to marry the essential core of the Christian message with the African worldview, so that Christianity could at last speak with an African *idiom* and *accent*"[5] to the African people. Openness to reclaiming African culture came slowly to South Africa, raising the consciousness of African liberation among the blacks of that nation and giving rise to people like Nelson Mandela, who, although imprisoned, brutalized, and dehumanised for almost 30 years, responded with true African hope. Without bitterness and with an African dignity that never bowed down to his oppressors, Mandela retained his nobility and survived the prison term to become a world-renowned leader, modelling the road from slavery to freedom for the oppressed and downtrodden around the world. Mandela's African resilience captures the essence of what it means to be African. He pointed to meaning that recaptured and nursed back to life the African culture that can be re-membered, revitalized, and reclaimed to repossess what was lost. This way, Africa can rise from her dust and ashes to become a continent of glory to the praise of her Maker. This is the role of Christian counselling in Africa: to re-member the dis-membered. In this chapter, we will explore the challenges and opportunities that Africans face, and then reflect on counselling in Africa. Finally, we will sketch our approach and illustrate it with the New Testament conversation between Jesus and the Samaritan woman.

Challenges

Africa hobbled into the twenty-first century covered with wounds from genocide in Rwanda, war in Sierra Leone, and ethnic cleansing in Darfur. HIV and AIDS in Africa kill even more people than war. The year 2001 began with 24 million Africans infected with AIDS – who will all die by 2010 unless a cure is found. In some countries, life expectancy will decrease by half by the year 2010. UNICEF reports that "eight out of every 10 children who have lost parents to HIV/AIDS live in sub-Saharan Africa."[6] Although the majority of Africans live today in rural areas, it is projected that by 2025, 60% of Africans will live in urban areas.[7] With poorly planned cities, the village is simply transferred into poorly planned neighbourhoods in the city, resulting in overcrowding, unemployment, insufficient sanitation and garbage collection, poverty, crime, prostitution, and children living in the streets. Drought due to poor environmental protection and deforestation produces undernourished populations and famine.

Chains of corruption mark many governments in Africa, as well as heavy burdens of national debt. At the time of this writing, Africa as a continent owes $293 billion and pays $15 billion per year in interest and fees.[8] This means that some poor African nations spend more on servicing foreign debts than on health and education. The result is declining economies, even though the African continent receives a total of $75 billion in aid each year.[9] In spite of massive aid, per capita income decreases each year in some nations. Doubt and helplessness are being felt all the way from government seats to village caucuses as people seek for hope and stability, whether in national leadership or in families. Those of us who care for and serve the needy seek help in understanding the challenges that they face and what to do about them.

Africa is a land "in between" – standing between the East and the West, the past and the future, colonialism and freedom, democracy and dictatorship, slavery and freedom. Africans often live in a *values vacuum*, straddling discarded traditional cultural systems and a Western value system that is unaffordable. The church struggles to define herself among a people supplanted from their traditions but never adequately planted in their new faith. This confusion has landed us in a crisis.

Vacuums in Africa are reflected in a loss of values that are supposed to root people and strengthen their identity. How did Africans get into such a crisis? Peter Mwikisa, an English professor at the University of Botswana, states that the modern African mind recognizes the presence of two forces that can be described as "Old Gods" and "New Worlds." Modern Africa is a creature of two legacies: one African, the other Western. Due to the deliberate suppression of African values and traditions, what it means to be African is veiled. This veiling was not always so, but it was a disguised strategy that re-labelled African humanity so as to make room for colonialism and Western manipulation. Mwikisa cites Chinua Achebe's depiction of colonialism:

> Colonialism is a very complex affair. You do not walk in, seize the land, the person, the history of another and then sit back and compose panegyrics to him. If you did, you would be convicting yourself of banditry. So, instead, you construct very elaborate excuses. The man is unfit to run himself and his affairs. Perhaps the man does not even own these things you are carting off . . . finally, the man cannot be, like you, fully human.[10]

When one is not fully human, that person's culture and indigenous value system is declared inferior and put aside, to be replaced by something labelled as superior. His dance and music are called primitive, as are his traditions and rituals. Her poetry is replaced with what is considered more elegant, and it is determined that his proverbs cannot be so wise. Africa ended up with a subsumed culture and an attempt to write over her traditions that were unacknowledged and subtly denied.

Mwikisa uses the word *palimpsest*[11] to describe the state of mental vacuum in the African mind, as masses swing between the two worlds. The author defines a palimpsest as "a piece of writing in which the original text has been partially erased in order to make room for a new one. Since the original is still decipherable beneath the new one, a palimpsest is necessarily a bivocal document."[12] When the morals that make people human are subsumed under an alien system, and the same people worship in churches that often do not utilize what the individuals know and love as teaching vehicles of the Christian value system, the result is a vacuum, an empty space without belonging or rootedness. This, in essence, is the African *values vacuum*, and the church must no longer be the instrument of this alienation.

Can we turn to the church? An alienated church is poor in wisdom, in culture, in guidance for its young, and in advocacy for its downtrodden. An alienated church has no message for its national leadership. It has ceased to be the conscience of the nation. In their novel *I Will Marry When I Want*, Ngugi wa Mirii and Ngugi wa Thiong'o call for a church that is burdened with what burdens her people. They caution against a church that does not care for the poverty of her people – referring to any kind of material, mental, or spiritual poverty. The authors write:

We cannot end poverty by erecting a hundred churches
In the village
We cannot end poverty by erecting a hundred beer halls
In the village
Ending up with two alcoholics
The alcoholic of hard liquor
The alcoholic of the rosary.[13]

The authors' point is that Christianity has the obligation to engage with society's heartaches, hearing the people's cries for wholeness and uniting them to find solutions for their problems. An alienated church has no message when storms of immorality blow across the land, corruption reigns in government, children as young as four begin using drugs, marriages are shaken, refugees colour the landscapes, and masses of land go untilled because of broken ecosystems from the Atlantic to the Indian Ocean.

Africa is in great trouble: the culture is broken, the children live in a vacuum, and personal faith has hardly touched the core of the culture that shapes Africans. Most resources lie untapped, and the few that are exposed have been vandalized, devalued, and stolen. Faced with a broken continent, Africans can respond with anger, striking out at agents of colonialism, or they can choose to utilize their energy in identifying rich resources that still remain in the land and use them to empower a richly blessed people. The calling of the Christian counsellor in Africa today is to reclaim the discarded, to rebuild the broken, and to re-member the dis-membered. Africa can rise up to take a place in the world community; this rising up depends on both the inner power of the African people and the rebuilding of African communities. The Christian counsellor can serve as God's channel for this healing and rebuilding of Africa.

Resources

Africans are blessed with many gifts, including the sense of peoplehood, an abundance of natural resources, deep faith, a love of education, and concern and care for the family. Africans pride themselves on the presence of a strong community element. Kinship survival is embedded in the communal sense of what it means to be African.

Africans are blessed with people. At the time of this writing, 12.5% of the world's population lives in Africa (749 million people). More than 60% of these are young. In sub-Saharan Africa, for example, 45% of the population is under 15 years of age. While some continents can be described as "dying" because of too many old people, in terms of youth population, Africa can be described as rising. In spite of deaths from AIDS, Africa is a young continent with 2.4–2.5% population growth. The United Nations Population Division projects that by 2025, one billion people will be living in Africa. Indeed, projections indicate that by 2050, "Africa's population is expected to surge from 900 million to almost two billion, while South Asia's is projected to swell from 1.6 billion to nearly 2.5 billion. Europe's population is expected to shrink from 730 million to 660 million."[14]

Africa is also blessed with some of the world's top leading natural resources. The continent produces 60 metal and mineral products, among them gold, diamonds, uranium, manganese, chromium, nickel, bauxite, and cobalt. Indeed, Africa holds 30% of the planet's mineral reserves, including 40% of the Earth's gold and 60% of its cobalt reserves.[15] Africa has unknown quantities of oil and diamond reserves. Indeed, some of the top diamond-producing nations are in Africa: Botswana, Angola, Central African Republic, Democratic Republic of the Congo, Gabon, Ghana, Namibia, Sierra Leone, and South Africa.

Africans celebrate their sense of community, *umuntu*, the fact that each individual's survival is linked to the other, with God as the centre of life, and everything else in cosmic relationship to the order that his presence creates. This is the African's understanding of community "whereby nature, divinity, and humankind live in harmony."[16] Most African nations have not legalized abortion, not because Africans don't care for the health of their women, but because they value their unborn whose voices go *unheard* when decisions to abort babies are made.

Africans celebrate their faith. Some of the fastest growing churches are in Africa.[17] Africans love God and acknowledge that they are because he is. Africans are religious people. There is no separation of spirituality from family, politics, education, or business. In Africa, too, education is so loved that people sacrifice to go to school and encourage children to excel in school. Education will be the foundation for advancement in all areas of research and writing.

Despite the challenges described above, there are new signs of hope. Throughout the 1990s, African theology has seen a shift away from a liberation theology that sought to lay the blame of the poor status of the continent upon colonialism and a Westernized Christian faith. Now African theologians and contemporary thinkers have moved from anger and pessimism to hope for social transformation and reconstruction. The point is that whereas Africa has been raped repeatedly and is still being ravaged by external forces, there still remains a resiliency that can serve to rebuild what is broken. Professor Mugambi, theologian of African realities, argues that this shift from projection to reconstruction and rebuilding:

> Involves discerning alternative social structures, symbols, rituals, myths, and interpretations of African social reality by Africans themselves, irrespective to what others say about the continent and its peoples. The resources for this re-interpretation are multi-disciplinary analyses involving social scientists, philosophers, creative writers and artists, biological and physical scientists.[18]

Discerning alternatives; rediscovering meaningful symbols, proverbs, rituals, and myths; reclaiming the lost; and legitimizing African experience through the Christian faith – these are the tools with which we can rebuild and reclaim. These are the vitalities still alive in Africa waiting to be reclaimed so that after re-membering the broken, African vitality can be restored. Christian counsellors within the church in Africa will play a significant role in filling the vacuum and bringing restoring life to the people and families of Africa.

The sons and daughters of Africa who answer the call to care will liberate those who cannot help themselves, contributing to the collective good in the true spirit of *umuntu*.[19] Thus enriched, the people of Africa can sit back and exclaim, in the words of this Meru proverb:

Ngaturua ni mwana ja
M'Itinyai Muthara.
Watorerwe ni mwana.
Ngakua na ncengerio ya iria iri rwaru.

I shall enjoy my son's riches like
M'Itinyai son of Muthara who,
although he did not have cows of his own,
enjoyed the cows brought by his sons.
I shall die with a gourd of milk under [my] armpit.[20]

Our greatest challenge is that Africans walk around like paupers and beggars when in fact they are rich and blessed. Over time, one comes to devalue or under-utilize resources, yet there are vitalities still present in Africa waiting to help rebuild and re-member African existence. The Christian counsellor can become the connection between vacuums and vitalities. Vacuums exist alongside unrecognized vitalities and resources, especially in Africa. But vacuums can leave the counsellor overwhelmed and discouraged when required to do too much with too little. This is why Christ is essential to any reconstruction and re-membering of Africa. He opens our eyes to see the many resources that can be used to rebuild and reclaim – resources such as meaningful symbols, proverbs, rituals, and folk tales. With these resources, Christian counselling becomes not merely another rescue operation, but the opportunity to rebuild the broken in partnership with the Master Architect.

African Identity and Holism

One of the greatest hindrances to the creation of "African knowledge" is the oral tradition in which wisdom and ways of life have been passed from generation to generation orally, without written documentation. In that way, a voluminous amount of information has been lost, opening the continent to the adoption of systems of learning from societies that have been based on written information for generations.

For example, within Africa, one of the few documented records of organized knowledge, philosophy, concepts, definitions, and models of practice concerning the nature of the universe and human functioning is the record of the Kemet, a black civilization that occupied the Nile valley before Arabs conquered their land. The records of the Kemet, which predate European civilizations,[21] resonate with a basic understanding of human psychology in the rest of Africa. For instance, whereas Western psychology elevates an individual and empowers the self to dominate over mind and matter, African psychology teaches a communal sensitivity, embedded in a societal motif. Africans perceive the individual as part of a web that stretches from God in heaven to humanity on earth, enveloping all nature and creation from generation to generation. These assumptions colour the mode of psychotherapy or counselling, and also dictate the resources that the therapist or counsellor employs in the healing of the wounded.

Africans perceive the human soul as holistic, inseparable from the rest of the universe. Utilizing the understanding of the ancient Kamites, Baldwin defines African psychology as "a system of knowledge (philosophy, definitions, concepts, models, procedures, and practice) concerning the nature of the social universe from the perspective of African cosmology."[22] The author adds that African psychology is the "uncovering, articulation, operationalization, and application of the principles of the African reality structure relative to the psychological phenomena."[23] It is clear, therefore, that African psychology is the interweaving of all human processes, from the individual's spirit, mind, body, behaviour, and genetics; to socio-political issues; and to interaction with nature, God, and the whole universe. This perspective should not be confused with animism, in which people attribute soul to inanimate objects. *African psychology is not animism*. It is the belief that all nature is related.

Failure to care for the environment in my little corner of the world will contribute to my loss and the loss of many others in the long run. Nai'm Akbar, African American psychologist, orator, and scholar, notes that African psychology views the human personality as "purposeful in its emergence, harmonious with its ecology, and consistent with the laws of life."[24] He emphasizes that the human being is "neither a passive agent shaped by his environment totally, nor is he an exalted isolated God with goalless freedom."[25]

For example, the Meru people of Kenya believe that their lives are interwoven with the environment and with all of creation. The love of vegetation is ingrained in the very nature of Meru people. They do not cut down trees haphazardly. For every tree cut, several more are planted. The result of this commitment to environmental conservation is that the district is beautiful and green all year round. Between 2001 and 2003, the Meru District led Kenya in the number of trees planted on public land, in forests, on steep slopes, and in gullies.[26] The Meru did not build homes in swamplands or clear forests for agriculture. Indeed, to protect the forests, they were designated as the property of the tribal government, specifically for the benefit of the ecosystem. Swamps and lakes were given holy names, like *Iria ria Thai*, or "God's Lake." It was in these holy sites that sacrifices would be made to *Ngai* or "God" in seasons of drought and famine. This psychology of "interwovenness" protected society and preserved nature, forcing each individual to think beyond the self and remain accountable to the whole system: God, nature, and all of humanity. Professor Wangari Maathai, Nobel Prize laureate and founder of the Green Belt Movement of Kenya, spearheaded community education and empowerment that renewed and rebuilt this kind of environmental awareness in Africa.[27]

The African perceives life as continuous and harmonious, with the human being standing above nature in his or her capacity for will, choice, knowledge, and self-direction. This model is value-based and transcends shifting societal norms. In contrast, Western psychology has followed a pathology-driven model, defining a "normal person as someone who is not abnormal."[28] In this approach, what is *normal* becomes the individual's ability to conform to the dictates of society. Definitions are formulated – only to be dismantled a few years later. However, for the Christian counsellor in Africa, the understanding of who Africans are and what is expected of them emerges out of their biblical heritage, the history of the church in Africa, and the leading of the Spirit of God. Planted in holistic cultural motifs that give it expression in diversity, the Christian way of life enriches culture and discovers meaning in both individual and cultural traditions.

For a long time, Africans have been taught to believe that because it is white, and emanates from the West, it is therefore good. Many Africans have seen through this lie. Whatever factor it might be, white or black, West, East, or South, if it does not pass the divine test of goodness, then it is not good. Hence, Africans need not totally throw away something just because it is perceived as *white*. Various types of colonialism forced Africans to disregard their uniqueness's, making them ashamed of their songs, dances, poetry, music, and even their thought systems. Conversely, one should not assume that just because something is African, it is altogether good. Instead, it is important to utilize the same critique used in assessing Western theoretical approaches, in relation to African indigenous systems. The Christian counsellor should make this aspect of questioning and searching an integral part of preparedness for ministry.

Kato encourages the new African church community to continue to "express Christianity in a truly African context, allowing [the faith] to judge the African culture and never allowing the culture to take precedence over Christianity."[29] He adds that the new community will need to "express theological concepts in terms of the African situation," and then, scratch "where it itches"[30] by having African theologians provide guidance to tackle African problems of polygamy, family structure, and other issues so that biblical answers are found.

Throughout this book, readers will be encouraged to examine their own indigenous cultural understandings of human functioning, including coping and other mechanisms of survival, features of marriage and the family, and perceptions of child rearing and youth training. However, it is important that in adopting positive indigenous cultural practices that have been devalued by Western education for so long, Africans not be tempted to simply *add* Christian faith to the practice of African traditional rituals. It will be necessary to ascertain the deep human needs expressed in ancient African rituals, and then to see how our belief in God's faithfulness addresses those needs. We cannot worship God and serve our own gods. God judged the Israelites for this practice.[31] Israelites were to worship only Jehovah and not to adopt the gods of the people they lived among or of the nations they drove out of the lands they were to occupy.[32]

African Counselling

African counsellors within the church face many questions. Does Africa even need counsellors? If so, what kind of counsellors? Do Africans have a history of healing traditions and wisdom for living? If so, what were they, and where have they gone? What will it mean for Christian counsellors to provide help to African brothers and sisters?

Dr Mwiti: In the early 1980s, I attended a conference in the United States where I met with a group of women. When I told them that I had left my teaching profession to train as a counsellor, they were very surprised and asked, "Why? Does Africa need counsellors?" I answered by telling them that Africans needed counselling now more than ever because of enormous change and instability on our continent. I explained how Western education was slowly eroding the traditional structures that had held our people together but had failed to fill the void with African and Christian values. I told the women that Christian counsellors in Africa would play a vital role in filling the vacuum created by Western education and bringing life back to our people and families.

In African indigenous societies, counselling addressed all aspects of living, and those who could not heed a message presented through one medium found the truth presented through another. This practice took many forms and took place in many settings ranging from the training of children through folk tales to conflict resolution in high-level community meetings.

Counselling in Africa involved wisdom and the use of proverbs. Here are some examples from the Meru[33] of Kenya: *Uume bwa muntu umwe ni gacigo*, meaning "One man's wisdom is only a small part of the whole." Moral: Do not rely on your knowledge only; seek the validation of others in community. *Tonga mwanka ugaire ngaara* is a blessing: "May you be so rich as to have enough to share with the field mice." Moral: Riches are never worth having until the whole community benefits, and that community includes even the animals in the wild. *Ruri itara rutithekagira ruri mwikano* means "The firewood up in the drying rack should not laugh at the one by the fireside." Moral: Never laugh at anyone in any unfortunate situation, for you never know when you, too, will experience the same." Such foolish proud people are later chastised with another proverb: *Uranthekaira maigo-akwora*, translated "You laughed at me; now your white teeth have decayed!"[34]

Counselling can transform troubled persons through the use of folk stories. Imagine the wisdom gained by listening to this Meru folk tale:

One day, an old man saw a boy standing at the riverside. He asked, "What are you doing standing alone at the riverbank?" Answered the boy: "I am waiting for the river to pass by so that I can cross over to the other side." On hearing this, the old man was surprised and answered, "My son, if you will not put your feet into the water, you'll never be able to cross the river for the rest of your life."[35]

Moral: Those who are afraid of "getting their feet wet" in taking risks will never move ahead into unknown areas of their lives.

Counselling has an ecological dimension. African indigenous communities had their own understanding of illness and health and utilized both preventive and curative health measures. Malidoma P. Somé writes that Africans know that "human beings are vulnerable to physiological and biological breakdown, and that this general instability touches all aspects of their existence."[36] Therefore, Christian counsellors in Africa cannot divorce their care for people from their care for creation and the environment. Healthy farms, full crops, clean water, healthy bodies, clean homes, fresh air, and a balanced diet are all part of counselling and wholeness.

African Indigenous Christian Counselling

African counselling that is truly Christian emerges out of the life of a people, is consistent with the spirit of Christian teaching, and seeks healing where there is suffering. It does not deny culture but affirms what is good in it. It takes myths and stories (African and Western) and interprets them through both the Hebrew Scriptures and the practices of the New Testament community. Rituals are practiced in such a way that they reflect the culture of the reign of God. Healing takes place in the context of the community, with an eye on larger political realities.

Christian counsellors are God's representatives in the community, and issues of justice and peace are central concerns in God's care for his world. It follows that the Christian counsellor in Africa cannot divorce his or her work from the masses of people and their needs. Many people believe that the only stability in Africa lies in faith and the church. This is one of the reasons why the church is often trusted to mediate among political parties and factions. Many Africans listen to the voice of the church. Counselling that is biblical and truly African will safeguard this position of honour and influence, as counsellors model the justice and peace for which they stand.

Jesus as Model

Our approach to counselling seeks to be consistent with the example of Jesus, which is beautifully illustrated in the biblical story of Jesus and the Samaritan woman at the well.[37] Jesus begins where the woman is, moving from the known to the unknown. "Will you give me a drink?" he asks. Her response is to distance herself by bringing up an obvious social barrier: "You are a Jew and I am a

Samaritan woman. How can you ask me for a drink?" Many questions come to the mind of the counsellor. What do we know about the woman? The Bible does not tell us much, but we can speculate. First, she is a Samaritan, a member of a people group rejected by the Jews. Second, she is at the well alone at midday. This is not normal, because people usually drew water at the end of the day rather than in the heat of midday. Indeed, drawing water was the role of women and they went to the well together in the cool of the evening.[38] So, what is this woman trying to avoid? Why is she alone at the well and at midday? Realizing later that she has had five husbands and that she is currently living with a man to whom she is not married, the counsellor might wonder: Was she divorced five times? If so, then she may have carried the effects of broken relationships, possible rejection, and perhaps abuse. Was she ever widowed? How many times? If so, then she may have had to deal with loss and bereavement. Had she been healed of these past hurts? If she kept changing husbands, were there possibly some issues from childhood blocking her ability to develop stable male-female relationships? Does this woman have any children? Are there stepchildren, and the related strains of such relationships?

Then there are these men in her life. Were any of them married before? Has she wounded other women who may have been related to these men – mothers or wives? What of the man currently in her life? Why is she not married to him? Does this woman have issues of guilt and shame? Could there be a history of prostitution? Jesus pursues her by stating that he is able to give her that which physical water cannot give. He says, "I know what you're searching for. And I am able to satisfy the longing that you've nursed for so many years. I can also heal your wounds. I love you with a love that will not let you go. I give living water, and you need never thirst again."

Jesus and Discernment

When the Wonderful Counsellor intervenes, he reaches to the very core of the human being. He does not deal with superficial thirst or fix symptoms temporarily, only for them to spring up in another setting, another place. He uproots, transforms lives, changes, and fills up. He makes the promise, "Everyone who drinks this water will be thirsty again, but whoever drinks the water I give them will never thirst. Indeed, the water I give them will become in them a spring of water welling up to eternal life."[39] Jesus offers abundant life that deals with the deep longings of the heart, the source from which motivation for behaviour arises. He watches for the woman to open up and sense that her searching has come to an end. She begins to do that and asks him for help.

Jesus could have stopped there and offered something to soothe her emptiness and loneliness. However, with a heart of discernment, he sees deeper than she thought he would. He knows that she has a past and a story that should become part of the present counselling. The past has a great influence on the present. For many people, the past consists of broken pieces and painful memories, whose jagged edges hurt any present-day peace of mind. Holistic counselling brings up past hurts and relationships and re-members the broken parts, so that God can heal old wounds and restore wholeness. Jesus knows full well what this woman's life is like, yet he leads her to confess or tell him about it herself. All he does is to make leading statements that cause the woman to respond and tell of her past: "Go, call your husband and come back." "I have no husband," she says.

Jesus the Healer without Judgement

This response leads to Jesus's discernment of the problem. He can tell her about her past without a judgemental attitude. He simply states a fact, after he has commended her for telling the truth. A judgemental attitude causes people to hide in self-defence. Christian counselling does not accuse. It accepts people just as they are. Although the Lord does not confront or judge the woman, she is not ready to look inside to see herself as she is. She declares that Jesus is a prophet, since he knows so much about her, but she quickly changes the subject and begins to discuss the theology of the proper place of worship for Jews versus Samaritans. When people are forced to look into their lives and hearts, the whole prospect is so scary that often, subconsciously, they try to move to safer areas.

The Lord does not confront the woman, but he leads her to the point of acknowledging her need. Unable to evade the issue any longer, she is ready for change when the Lord declares that he is all that she and her people have been waiting for. The woman, who has always hidden away from the public in loneliness and possible guilt because of her lifestyle, is set free at last. Her freedom leads to the community's blessing. Indeed, she returns to the village calling, "Come, see."[40] As a result of Jesus's counsel, this woman's life changes; "because of the woman's testimony"[41] many are led to conversion and transformation.

Jesus the Village Elder

Jesus met the Samaritan woman very much like a village elder would a confused female. He sat at the well. He asked her to serve him with a drink. He talked as if he could see deep into her heart. His were words of wisdom that did not condemn her, as many others may have. She opened her heart to him, looking for a safe place much like the large-leafed village tree where everyone found shade. The tree was a safe, non-threatening place, and this was what Jesus became to the Samaritan woman. He took on the role of a wise village elder.

Surrounded with love, acceptance, knowledge, firmness, and wisdom, the woman's defences could no longer hold. Elder Jesus became a clear, loving mirror to her. She saw herself as she was and faced what she had become for the first time in her life. The well was no longer too deep, because his eldership and wisdom brought it close enough for her to drink and never be thirsty again. Jesus became for her an anchor, a safe place.

Jesus, the village elder, approached each person with openness and care. He possessed a repository of knowledge about the Samaritan woman's "tribe," as he did about other people he met along his way. He knew her needs and met them in such a way that he became a place of refuge for her and her tribe. The instability of her life was changed into stability. Jesus's methods of counselling were unique, in that he did not set up a dichotomy between the woman's individual needs and her relationships. He touched her, and then she in turn spread the healing to her entire community.

Besides his unique methods, Jesus had unique qualities as a counsellor. Just like a village elder, his track record was clear and authentic. Wherever he went, he spoke words of wisdom and teaching. He divined people's problems, understanding their deep struggles long before they opened their mouths. Yet, as with the Samaritan woman, he did not wave this knowledge over their heads to intimidate them. He gently and humbly enabled people to realize and describe their own conditions.

Jesus earned the rights of an elder, not because he was elected but because he was an *opinion leader*. Opinion leaders are respected elders who are listened to because they command respect by their very lifestyles and characters. Jesus was linked to the supernatural. What he said happened. And so, with deep spirituality, an authentic lifestyle, and a proven track record, this elder with a difference addressed the needs of the villagers wherever he went. Some were blind and needed to see. Others ran out of wine at a wedding and he met their need. Still others were children who needed his touch. Even a woman caught in sin, judged and sentenced as a sinner by fanatically religious men, found safety at his feet. Such was this village elder – a safe place for all.

Christian counselling is also a matter of prevention. Christian counselling does not wait for people to break down and then try to "fix" them. Instead, Christian counsellors are called to be the teachers and trainers of Christians living in the church. Many people fail in holistic living for lack of knowledge. African society has neglected important expectations for teaching and training about marriage, parenting, communication, relationships at work, self-care and conduct, integrity, etiquette and good manners, housekeeping, and general hygiene. Lack of knowledge in these areas has the capacity for causing much pain and conflict. Yet teaching and training on them is absent from many homes, schools, and even churches.

One of the main roles of the Christian counsellor is to teach and train others how to relate to themselves, to others, to God's creation, and to God himself. Jesus modelled this type of counselling. Indeed, Christians are told to "teach all that Christ commanded and taught . . . doctrines about God, authority, salvation, spiritual growth, prayer, the church, the future, angels, demons, human nature . . . marriage, parent-child interactions, obedience, race relations, freedom for both men and women, and personal issues such as sex, anxiety, fear, loneliness, doubt, pride, sin, and discouragement."[42] In addition, Christian counsellors, especially in Africa, have an imperative to sensitize the people about issues of justice and advocacy on behalf of the weak and downtrodden. African people also need urging to care for others and for the environment.

The Christian counsellor in Africa faces a unique responsibility to seek the peace of the city, or the wellness of the overall community wherein the counsellor works. Jeremiah counselled Israelites in exile to settle down in their foreign land: "Build houses and settle down; plant gardens and eat what they produce. Marry and have sons and daughters; find wives for your sons and give your daughters in marriage, so that they too may have sons and daughters. Increase in number there; do not decrease," and to seek the prosperity and peace of the city in which they found themselves.[43] Similarly, as strangers and pilgrims in the world, Africans, too, are called to seek the peace and prosperity of their cities and countries. This will involve caring for the environment, planting gardens, and keeping the soil fertile, cities clean, and institutions renovated and refurbished.

With so much conflict in Africa, peacemaking cannot be assumed – be it at the individual, community, or church level. Indeed, the church has often been blamed for preparing people for heaven but ignoring the truth that life on earth is supposed to be abundant and enriching. In discussing the relationship between the Bible, peace, and development, Nlenanya Onwu, New Testament Professor at the University of Nigeria in Nsukka,[44] writes that humanity needs three types of peace: individual peace, community peace, and peace in the midst of conflict. Such peace begins with Yahweh, the source of Shalom.[45] To communicate this peace, the Israelite prophets became God's voice in the community and aroused the conscience of the Hebrew nation. The author notes that these prophets were not professionals, but because of their relationship with God, they could call the nation to order, stressing that real covenant with Yahweh must find expression through moral action and upright living. Living at a time of rapid change and yet rooted in the here and now, the prophets became the voice of the voiceless and the advocates of the orphan, the widow, the refugee, the poor, and the disadvantaged. Thus "anchoring their proclamation firmly in social reality, shalom became the central prophetic message."[46] All this means that the Christian counsellor in Africa has the role of becoming God's voice for community wholeness, a voice springing from a heart committed to righteousness which seeks the wholeness of the city, not just the wholeness of individuals in the city. The strength of the cry for peace in Africa cannot be overstated. Archbishop Desmond Tutu, renowned African theologian and leader, has said on many occasions that peace is cheaper than repression.

We close this chapter with a statement by Jose Chipenda, former General Secretary of the All Africa Conference of Churches:

> God has given African people the wisdom and ability to launch new social and political structures [that] are just, appropriate, harmonious, participatory, egalitarian, ecologically sustainable. The new breed of African social scientists needs to inspire politicians to understand that freedom is cheaper than repression. The discussion of these possibilities must include new concepts of political theory, [the] meaning of law and order in an African setting, the scope and nature of authority, [and] the use of available resources to meet local, national, and continental needs.[47]

CHAPTER 2

Personality and Brokenness

African and Western cultures differ in their understanding of personhood and community. Similarities and differences between these two main cultures on these themes dramatically affect how people understand illness, create contexts for healing, involve a counselee's community, and provide counselling. In this chapter we will first explore an Afrocentric view of personhood that is both holistic and Christian, and then examine the myriad ways that Africans experience brokenness.

African and Western Cultures

What do we mean by "culture"? Human culture incorporates traditions and customs of given groups of people: the worldview that undergirds who they are as persons, how they perceive their humanity, how they regard other people who do not belong to their group, and how they pass on their customs as a legacy to future generations within their people group. Culture is a composite of values, morals, taboos, and rules, written and unwritten, that are embedded in language, practices, childrearing and training traditions, rituals, symbols, rites of passage, clichés, proverbs, songs, dances, and folk tales.[48] Culture shapes who people are, gives them personal identity, unites them, and provides them with a sense of meaning and direction.

Cultures can become *problematic*, however, when people in a particular culture group perceive themselves as *better* than those in other groups, when they force their cultural way of life on others, and when they fail to engage in self-examination. Western culture is aggressive and competitive. It is influenced greatly by a Euro-American worldview that holds such beliefs as "rugged individualism, competition, mastery and control over nature, a unitary and static conception of time, religion based on Christianity, and separation of science and religion."[49] With these values, it has built world economies, conquered and ruled, and succeeded in making the world more Western through media and communication.

However, just as all good things can be abused, Western culture has been used as a tool of colonialization in an ethos in which leading indigenous peoples to accept Western culture was seen as *developing* them. Local "lifestyles, customs, and practices were seen as uncivilized and attempts were made to make over the 'heathens.'"[50] This attitude has led to what Derald W. Sue (Professor of Psychology at the California School of Professional Psychology) and David Sue (Professor of Psychology at Western Washington University) label as a *monocultural ethnocentric bias*,[51] a status that robs other people of their culture, impoverishes their collective unconscious, negatively impacts their identity, and compromises their coping ability.

Today, post-colonial Africa is waking up. For decades, Africans have been memorizing Shakespeare, singing Celtic ballads, and learning the steps of Scottish dances. Africans have been baking French bread to perfection in villages, when there is nothing wrong with African yams and sweet potatoes. Dr Jan de Jongh van Arkel from the University of South Africa (UNISA), who is Secretary/Treasurer of the International Council for Pastoral Care and Counselling, notes that most of the counselling theories currently in use in Africa have been derived from the highly secularised culture of Europe and North America, and that thus, African Christian counsellors find themselves working in situations of *"anthropological impoverishment."* This is because "Africans have been robbed of their culture and identity by a history of colonialism and exploitation. Christian missions were part of a 'deculturizing' process forcing Africans to sever their roots and lose their authority if they wanted to take part in what was presented."[52]

Traditional, indigenous African cultures can be defined as "mythical . . . in which the human being participates in the ambient game of the forces of nature."[53] African cultures arise out of the belief in the interconnectedness of humanity with the environment and with past generations. African communities are undergirded by a worldview that is "eco-systemic at heart [with] no division between the animate and the inanimate, between spirit and matter, between living and non-living. Everything is in constant relationship with one another [as well as with] the invisible world."[54] Essentially, African cultures have a holistic perspective on life and community, with an interdependent, inseparable human-nature relationship.[55] Africans seek balance and harmony among the various aspects of the universe. The survival of the family and the community is more important than individual fulfilment. Spirituality, communal responsibility, and cooperation are some of the most basic African values.

Since this is our starting point for understanding Western and African cultures, what does it mean to be Christian within culture? Christian culture is neither Western, nor African, nor Eastern, and at the same time, it can be embodied in all cultures. Christian culture, as we see it, is shaped by Jesus's message of the reign of God. It transcends colour, race, and gender, and *celebrates* cultural heritage. The Christian message is cooked and presented within calabashes of culture. Kwame Bediako, Ghanaian theologian, founder/director of Akrofi-Christaller Memorial Centre for Mission Research and Applied Theology in Akropong Akuapem, Ghana, says it well. Christianity can be "one song sung in many tongues."[56] Because of this, Christian counsellors live with the imperative to be students of the culture within which they work.

Due to its individualistic nature, Western Christian culture may perceive the Christian faith as involving individuals in dialogue with a system of ideas and a vertical relationship with God that encourages neither dialogue with the people around them nor concern for nature and the environment. Such individualism negates holism.

Faith within African culture, however, is a transcendent primal expression connected with the community of both the present kin and the departed ancestors, a vertical and horizontal linkage that seeks to celebrate and ensure the continuity of that connectedness through ritual, myth, and folk tales. Suspended between impoverished indigenous means of communal expression and an individualized, dichotomised Western understanding of faith, the African church seeks authentic belief. This authenticity would shape Africa's cultural demonstration of faith that incorporates an expression of Jesus's love for people as well as Paul's conviction regarding the interrelatedness of the body of Christ.[57] It is gratifying to note that the church in the West is also waking up to the reality of community, with Christians seeking to live and express their faith both vertically and horizontally. Christian culture ought to be rich in individual and communal expressions of faith that are connected upwards to God, inwards in the transformation of individuals, and outwards, touching others and impacting God's world.[58]

Views of the Self: Western, African, and Christian

We shift now from culture to considering the individual person. To fully understand an indigenous, African Christian model of healing and wholeness, we need to see clearly the similarities and differences in the role played by the perception of the self as an entity in Western and African counselling practices. Self-psychology is a major anchor of Western psychology but does not reflect African nor, in our opinion, Christian worldviews that call for concern for others over and beyond the individual.

Western Psychology of the Self

Throughout the history of Western psychology, basic statements about human nature and human behaviour have been founded on assumptions about what it means to be human. The self has often been the major element of study, as evidenced in questions such as: What influences individual development most – nature or nurture, personal choices or heredity, the mind or body, universal issues or cultural factors?

The whole debate revolves around an understanding of self-psychology as "the creative, purposeful nature of individuals [with] internal controls rather than external forces as the major determiners of behaviour."[59] The "self" in Western psychology is an organism that interacts with its environment. It responds to both internal and external demands from other people and from nature. We will briefly describe the following views of the self in Western psychologies: the behavioural, the cognitive, the biological, the emotional, and the relational.

Behavioural Psychology

This approach seeks to understand the self in terms of behaviour and is based on the work of psychologist B. F. Skinner.[60] We can use the letters "A" and "C" to explain the process.

A=Activating event (stimulus)   ⟶   C=Consequences (outcomes)

Letter A stands for an activating event, or stimulus. This can be anything that motivates behaviour. Letter C stands for consequences, or outcomes. So how do A and C relate to each other? Behaviourists believe that A causes C. For example, let's say that an "activating event" such as being called names causes one to respond by hitting someone. Since hitting people isn't a particularly good idea, a behavioural therapist will teach new ways to respond to an activating event, or stimulus.

A=Activating event (name calling)   ⟶   C=Consequence (hitting) or
A=Activating event (name calling)   ⟶   C=Consequence (walking away)

Cognitive Psychology

The cognitive approach seeks to understand how the mind functions within its environment and uses the A-C behavioural format but adds the letter B in between. The letter B stands for belief system, which can include a person's attitudes, expectations, perceptions, and values. Cognitive psychologists believe that the human being thinks before responding to the environment and that this thought is based on his or her belief system.

A = Activating event ⟶ B = Belief system ⟶ C = Consequences

For example, before the angry person hits someone, he or she has already interpreted the stimulus and decided that hitting is the appropriate mode of behaviour, as maladaptive as it might be. Cognitive therapists work to change the client's belief system, in order to change behavioural outcomes.[61]

Biological Psychology

The biological viewpoint stresses that a person's genetic inheritance makes him or her a unique individual.[62] But while genetics provides the original factors that make up one's individuality, the environment shapes how this personhood is expressed. Since both genes and environment differ from person to person, no two people are exactly the same. This uniqueness leads to individual traits that form each person's character. However, there are also common traits that are shared by individuals who are members of the same culture and are linked by social values or mores. This biological approach emphasizes the individual within society, with personality developing from genetics as well as from environmental influences.

Emotional Psychology

The emotional approach in Western psychology refers to the self, both in diagnosis and in treatment of pathology, with terms like self-actualization, self-affirmation, self-awareness, self-concept, self-disclosure, self-efficacy, self-enhancement, self-esteem, and self-perception. These terms are mainly based on Carl Rogers's Self Theory which undergirds Western humanistic psychology and which gave birth to the Client-Centred therapeutic approach. Rogers viewed self-actualization as the basis of all human behaviour, defining it as an innate directional urge "evident in all organic and human life . . . to expand, extend, develop, mature – the tendency to express and activate all capacities of the organism."[63] Human personality is a result of how the individual fulfils his or her emotional potential. If the evaluations of others fit the category of *unconditional positive regard*, self-perception may then lead to *positive self-regard*. This unconditional regard from others does not impose any conditions and gives an individual freedom to express his or her desires without necessarily giving in to the requirements of others. Out of respect for the individual's self-direction, many Western mental health personnel in this orientation shy away from *teaching* people how they ought to live or what responsibility for the wider society looks like.

Relational Psychology

The relational view of the self is evident in family systems theory.[64] Increasingly popular in the West, this approach understands the self as part of a system that includes the family, the neighbourhood, and the larger society. It assumes that as one part changes, all parts are affected. In families, the symptoms a child may manifest are related to the structure of a family. For example, a rebellious adolescent may be unconsciously responding to the controlling nature of her parents. Change comes only when the family changes, not just the adolescent. It is possible to scapegoat the individual when one does not take the family dynamics into consideration. Western psychology assumes that the individual or family has the resources to change. Sometimes emphasis is placed on changing the larger political and cultural context.[65]

This is certainly not a thorough description of Western psychologies, but it does give us a flavour of the ideas, the concerns, and the language used in describing the person. Many African counsellors have now been trained in Western approaches and we think it is important for African counsellors to be conversant with these approaches, while remaining firmly grounded in their indigenous understanding of the person. We turn to that understanding next.

African Views of the Individual in Community

The African counsellor is concerned about the needs of the whole person, including spiritual, mental, biological, genetic, behavioural, and social elements.[66] In discussing African psychology, Dr Daudi Ajani ya Azibo, associate professor of psychology at Florida A&M University and specialist in African psychology, notes:

The original African psychology [the understanding of human behaviour and psyche] can be traced to the time when Blacks of Africa produced an organized system of knowledge (philosophy, definitions, concepts, models, procedures, and practice) concerning the nature of the social universe from the perspective of African cosmology."[67]

While we could describe how we view the self in general in Africa, the following is an indigenous Meru view of the self.[68]

The Other Gives Me Identity

First, the self that seeks to find meaning on its own does not exist among the Meru and, indeed, in most of Africa. Instead, it is others who give the self its identity and meaning. This does not mean that the self as an entity does not exist. It means that other people, and God, in particular, act as mirrors for the self in order to give the self its personality, credibility, and structure. For example, among the Meru, people did not name themselves. *Others* named them. Individuals did not applaud themselves. *Others* applauded them. People did not nominate themselves. *Others* nominated them.

Dr Mwiti: To explain just how the Meru view of self works, I will tell you what happened during the first year of my doctoral studies at Fuller Theological Seminary in California. I read an announcement that the Graduate School of Psychology was offering Merit Awards to deserving students. Merit Awards are given for accomplishment. In Africa, accomplishment is recognized and rewarded by others. As a good student, I was sure that someone would nominate me for the award. However, when the day came, my name was not there. I was eager to know why I did not merit the award. Then I realized that I had to nominate myself! Impossible! How does one describe one's good attributes in a bid to be recognized?

The next year, I gathered enough courage to nominate myself and I received the award. The following year, I decided not to nominate myself again because I thought one award was enough over the six-year duration of my doctoral programme. Then I noticed that people nominated themselves again and again. So I nominated myself again and I won for the second time. After this, I obeyed my indigenous warning: Don't be greedy and give others a chance.

The Other Gives Me Worth

Among the Meru, individuals described themselves through the "eyes" of others. The word *eye* is used here deliberately and incorporated looking and seeing, which literally meant observing and perceiving. For example, a saying that determined the self-worth of young women among the Meru people went like this: *Nkenye cia Njeru bukumagirua mbi? Tukumagirua kurimia na kwegera gaaru.* Translated, it states: "Young women of the Njeru clan, where does your worth come from?" "Our worth is known through our accomplishments as expected by our tribe: through our beauty and industry." This meant that the measure of their self-worth was not only prescribed but also was moderated by cultural tribal stipulations and expectations which rewarded beauty and productivity. The basis of worth was clearly laid down, communicated through strict training, then rewarded by others, and in the process, owned and celebrated by the young women. The recognition came from others and not from the self. This *external* recognition did not rule out individual responsibility, but instead it assured a sense of *internal* accountability that was beyond self-gratification and self-absorption.

It is no wonder that many songs and folk tales among the Meru centred on themes of heroes and heroines who served others, denying themselves pleasure so that others would survive. They practiced self-discipline while always aiming at rewards that were distant and obscure. On the other hand, the culture was also full of stories of those who could not wait, those who were selfish, seeking to eat alone. People in Africa would be shocked if they were to hear that someone took out a sandwich in full view of everyone else and proceeded to eat *alone*. How could one eat alone and not share?

My Whole Self

Among the Meru of Kenya, every human had three parts: *mwiri* or "body," *mathuganio* or "thoughts," and *nkoro* or "heart." The heart was closely linked to the *mwoyo* or "spirit." The *nkoro* was the seat of emotions. When a person was anxious, we would say, *Nkoro yawe ni ikuthagika*, meaning, "His heart is disturbed." When someone grieved for a long time, Meru said, *Nkoro yawe ikuthangika kagiita*, meaning "His heart has been disturbed for a long time." When a person died, it is the *mwoyo* that departed, leaving the body behind. However, death was referred to as the individual's departure to another land, for example, with the expression *naretirwe*, meaning "He was called."

The Kamba people of Kenya believed that emotions emanated from the heart, which was also "the screen on which one's personality is displayed. It can be 'big' (i.e., furious), or 'soft' (i.e., kind and generous), 'hot' (i.e., cheerful and sociable), or 'dead' (i.e., sorrowful and sad)."[69] This holistic understanding of human functioning among Africans means that an individual seeking help from a healer or elder will indicate symptoms from any of these aspects as well as any impacting self, family, friends, or community. Healing, then, should embrace more than the individual, because in the African understanding of life as an ecosystem, healing eventually reaches the whole environment.

My Spiritual Being

African people are notoriously religious and spiritually minded. Nthamburi observes: "It is almost natural for Africans to take for granted the presence of God in every situation."[70] Since the spirit of a human being emanates from God and lives on after the body dies, people consider it the dominant area of functioning. Indeed, for the African, the spirit of an individual is perceived as present at birth and continuing after death. Among the Meru of Kenya, when someone died, the saying was usually *Tugucoka naria twaumire*. Translated it means: "We have returned or gone back to where we came from" – meaning that we do not even belong here. Africans are people who spiritually come from some other place and go to some other place.

Due to the centrality of the spirit in the understanding of human functioning in Africa, "any science which precludes the spiritual is alien to the understanding of people of African descent and how they comprehend all forms of life."[71] Indeed, Africans believe that the human being is essentially spirit, and that continued existence of the spirit represents the ultimate survival of the person. This holistic belief in the survival of the spirit leads to a hunger for the transcendent, a reaching out to God, longing for that which only he can give – life. The African, therefore, is always searching for the spiritual meaning of life.

African Christian Views of the Self

To fully understand an indigenous African Christian model of healing and wholeness, we also need to comprehend the role of the self in the biblical context. It is interesting to note that the Bible does not encourage a preoccupation with the self, nor does it emphasize *self-regard*. Jesus taught *other-regard* and *God-regard*. He modelled the truth that whoever "loves their life will lose it,"[72] and "whoever finds their life will lose it, and whoever loses their life for my sake will find it."[73] To love one's life in the here and now means to concentrate on one's own success, desires, accomplishments, pleasures, and likes and dislikes, to the exclusion of others, and of the world around us. Ultimately, this self-absorption may result in failing to meet God's desire for what it means for us to be truly human. This, Jesus said, is to lose what really matters.

Instead of emphasizing self-actualization, the Bible teaches against self-indulgence, self-seeking, and selfishness. It calls for self-control and self-discipline, which curb the inclination to satisfy the cravings of the *self* and instead lead the individual to seek out what pleases God and blesses the rest of humanity. Instead of self-preoccupation, the Bible urges faith and love,[74] respect and hospitable behaviour,[75] uprightness, holiness, purity, and godliness,[76] preparedness for action, prayer, and alertness.[77] This list suggests that wholeness comes not from self-centeredness, but from centeredness on God and others.

Africans generally believe that at creation, "humanity was originally put in a state of happiness, childlike ignorance, [and] immortality, . . . [and that] God is the explanation of [humanity's] origin and sustenance."[78] The rest of creation is humanity's environment. Therefore, people ought to live with the view that their livelihood is intertwined with that of the rest of creation. Mbiti writes that African creation myths place the making of man and woman towards the end of God's first acts in forming the world. The two genders are clearly specified: male and female. God often visited with humanity and spent time with humans, acting very much like a parent among his children.

Mbiti points out that this bliss ended – in a way that various African people groups explain in different ways. For example, some say that people failed to obey God's rules (the Banyarwanda, Barotse, Chagga, and Elgeyo). Inhabitants of the Upper Nile region say that a hyena accidentally broke the rope connecting heaven and earth, and that when God could no longer visit his children, death and tribulations came into the world. African people generally believe that the original relationship between God and his children somehow broke, and that we live seeking ways and means of reconciliation.

Many African Christians believe that the human person was created in God's image as a tripartite being (body, mind, and spirit). The *spirit* is the dominant part of humanity, and it communes with God through a personal relationship with Jesus Christ. When this spiritual need for communion is fulfilled, the *body* and *mind* are in harmony with the *spirit*. With this assumption in mind, the counsellor can begin counselling fully aware that God who created humanity in his own image desires each person's restoration, and that humanity thirsts for this harmony. African indigenous Christian counsellors might view their work as similar to the African forest twine that links and holds up weak twigs, interlocking them with the everlasting forest oaks. In the same way, African counsellors seek to link a thirsting humanity with a loving Creator.

Brokenness and the African Self

> *Dr Mwiti:* When I was in California, I watched the movie "Hotel Rwanda" with a church group. For several hours, we stared in horror at this story of the 1994 genocide. At the end, I and many others were weeping. Finally, the audience asked me to help them understand the reason for this tragic genocide. I did not have any answers because I, too, still seek to understand.

Tutsis and Hutus had always lived side by side in Rwanda, danced together, intermarried, and loved each other. However, many years before the massacre, colonial administrators eager to divide and rule planted a seed of discord among them. Contrary to God's word, one brother started to nurse hatred for the other. Individuals in this largely Christian nation began to live with divided loyalties. People put their love for God in one compartment and their hatred for others in another. Those who desired to use the situation for personal gain fanned the flame. Fragmented spiritual practice is not alien in cultures where the gospel as the whole message of Christianity never took deep root, and where holistic cultural values have been eroded through lack of recognition and affirmation. Bishop Jonathan Ruhumuliza believes that part of the reason for the Rwandan genocide was shallowness of Christian faith among the believers in that nation. Christianity never went deep enough into the heart of Rwandans, he says.[79]

For many Africans, immersing oneself in the life of the church is a means of dealing with alienation from God and from other people. Indeed, Nthamburi notes that being a member of African Independent Churches means being part of a new family, the family of God, where members are concerned about one another's welfare.[80] Belonging, fellowship, individual discipline, and concern for each other in the body become elements that make the church a healing community. Breaking away from such nurturing networks engenders pathology, and enhancing such connectedness protects one from the alienation that might well lead to brokenness. However, Nthamburi notes that there is need for balance when people live in closed communities, because the desire for uniformity can lead to legalism and the stifling of individuality – aspects that can also breed pathology.[81]

For example, Musau[82] was a village money lender. He was mean and demanding, milking all the interest he could from his customers. Although the interest he charged was unreasonably high, he was also friendly anytime he lent money, so the poor of the village went to him. Slowly, he gained a reputation as a lender who extorted more than his share from his borrowers. Many times his collection agents – a band of ruthless school dropouts – would descend on a poor widow and take all her belongings, from chickens to firewood, selling them for a pittance supposedly to recover the widow's late fee. Women muttered behind Musau's back, but he did not care. He was too eager to make money. Then one day, he became sick and sought counselling. He told the counsellor that he was lonely and depressed and that nobody respected him anymore. The more his health failed the less money he had to lend. He complained to the counsellor that nobody came to his door. Nobody spoke to him. Nobody greeted him. He soon learned that community connectedness matters.

Broken Relationships

Brokenness began in the Garden of Eden due to people's disobedience and desire to break free from what they perceived as God's suffocating control. Communion between God and humanity was broken when Adam and Eve declared themselves independent from God. As a result, the two were banished from his presence and also from God's perfect Garden of Eden.[83] Instead of gaining *security*, they became *insecure*; instead of *significance* they suffered from *insignificance*; and instead of *worth*, they experienced feelings of *inferiority*. Wronging God meant estrangement from his sight, enmity with other created beings (wild animals), banishment from the garden, and broken relationships with the rest of humanity. This alienation led to selfishness and striving that must have caused the first callous retort to the Creator, when God asked Cain, "Where is your brother?" Although Cain knew that he had murdered his brother, his answer was, "I don't know. Am I my brother's keeper?"[84]

When individuals persist in their alienation from God and humanity, they are likely to set themselves on a path of worshiping what could be called the *unholy trinity*: me, myself, and I. This leads eventually to indifference to the plight of others. According to Genesis, after the first recorded murder, even the ground would not cooperate to yield a plentiful harvest. This interconnectedness indicates that within God's reign, humanity and nature are related subsystems, and that the vitality of one depends on the other. In Africa, droughts are considered a voice from God, as are plentiful rain and a good harvest. When people live in obedience to God, even their cattle, sheep, and goats are blessed, as is the fruit of the human womb from generation to generation.

Brokenness and Spiritual Thirst

The Garden of Eden pointed to God's presence and pleasure in human beings and in nature. Since their banishment from the garden, human beings thirst spiritually for the original fellowship that God intended.[85] However, instead of seeking God's guidance from the Bible and the Christian community, many people turn to broken cisterns, ideas and methods that do not satisfy. What are broken cisterns? These are any self-made strategies that negate the need for God or community.

Convinced that Western education devoid of any godliness is the answer, some African parents bring up their children with all the material possessions they may ever need but deny them church worship or community fellowship. Such young people grow up surrounded by *things* but lacking a value system that forms their identity. Eventually, the foundations built with money and titles crumble under stress. Consequently, many such parents end up in the counselling room with the child or adolescent in tow. Often, the child is the *identified patient* because the young one is failing in school; using drugs and alcohol; engaged in early sexual activity; or causing conflict in the school, home, or community. This type of parent-constructed cistern gives way under pressure. A feeling of worthlessness is a symptom of depression and leads to hopelessness and continuing separation from God and humanity.

In our yearning for the Spirit, we drink from self-made wells. Therefore, the best way to understand people is to find out *where their needs are being met*. Which self-made psychological strategy are they using to quench their thirst for the Spirit? And when they fail to get their thirst quenched, what happens to individuals in their relationships with God and others? Looking at the bigger picture how does individual brokenness impinge on community suffering and pathology? We describe next some of the many forms of psychological and spiritual brokenness.

Denying Accountability

What are some African "self-made wells"? One is the denial and disowning of our deepest longings. Individuals who are alienated from God express deep longing to get closer but use substitutes and refuse accountability. For example, Apostle Weru founded the African Church of Victorious Saints International. For four years he grew in power and wealth as he preached a gospel of prosperity among the poor. However, as he rose higher and higher in terms of human regard, he began to lose respect because of his tendency to womanise. Many beautiful young churchwomen were found with Apostle Weru in compromising situations, but he always explained that he was counselling them. He continued to live in denial of his need for accountability. His board of deacons was confused. They did not know what to do.

Seeking Achievement

In a society that rewards accomplishments, many people are tempted to satisfy their deep longings with hard work and the rewards that it brings in areas such as business, sports, politics, family investments, and even church ministry. However, anything other than God soon proves to be a broken cistern, leaving such people thirsty again.

Mateka, for example, was born in a poor family. He entered politics early and rose quickly to an important party position. He swindled many people in the name of his party, *The People's Patriotic Front*. He bought a fleet of buses that ran from the city to his hometown, owned the biggest commercial building in his neighbourhood, and ran a bar that supplied all of the alcohol in the area. Mateka did not have a good word for anybody and looked for every opportunity to enrich himself. People looked at this young man and wondered, "When will enough be enough?"

Manipulating Emotions

Some individuals enter relationships only to manipulate other people to meet their deepest longings for love and belonging. However, without give and take, a relationship soon becomes unhealthy and co-dependent. Such unhealthy interactions can occur in the context of Christian service, marriage, raising children, and even giving to the poor. If the focus of relating to others or helping them through service is oneself (i.e., looking for one's own emotional satisfaction), this, too, becomes a frustrating "broken cistern" – because the blessing in relationships lies in giving rather than receiving.[86]

Personal Defensiveness

When we have a need that we cannot meet, the human psyche often repackages the yearning into more manageable proportions. This attempt to minimize wants and desires is a form of defence mechanism. For example, some people will deliberately disown or suppress a problem. Suppression soon becomes a habitual way to repress anything they do not like. Others are quick to explain away their problem using persuasive language, while still others will blame someone else for their problem. Some will take out their frustration on weaker individuals, or even on animals around them.

Sixteen-year-old Mrembo is a housemaid, an orphan that Mama Betsy brought home from the village. Mama Betsy works as a secretary for a very demanding and cruel boss in the Meat Commission and Packaging Company. With three young children to look after, Mrembo dreads the time each day when Mama comes from work. The maid can tell what kind of day Mama Betsy has had soon after she walks in the door. On a good day, Mama is generous, with kind words and concern for all the work Mrembo does in taking care of the three children. However, a difficult workday will reveal a very different Mama Betsy. She enters the house shouting and criticizing everything Mrembo has done that day. Mrembo cannot disagree with her employer, and so she takes her frustration out on the children. In her anger, she pinches the baby and oversalts the food. All this is done quietly, but with the utmost resentment towards Mama Betsy. In this situation, the lowest person in the order of things suffers most.

Corrosive Idolatry

Some individuals will exchange allegiance to God for allegiance to their own gods by being totally devoted to a job, a sport, a person, money, cars, or other objects. Others join cults and sects that promise a quick cure for all ills. Whatever takes the place of God in our lives becomes an idol. Merle Jordan suggests that one form of depression occurs when the gods we worship let us down, which inevitably they will.[87]

Brokenness and Emotional Outcomes

Not only are many Africans broken in their communities, relationships and spirituality, but after years of deaths from AIDS and from genocide, their hearts are broken as well. They weep for the suffering of others; their thoughts, emotions, and decisions are affected by these national calamities. When human institutions let people down, and when they fail to get satisfaction from self-made strategies, they experience negative emotions including betrayal, sorrow, fear, jealousy, anger, pain, shame, emptiness, bitterness, frustration, confusion, sadness, and depression.

How do many African men and women handle unpleasant emotions? Men typically show stoic attitudes. Women will talk among themselves in private, where they freely express their feelings and cry on one another's shoulders. When working in Rwanda for many years after the genocide of 1994, it seemed to me (Gladys Mwiti) that men may cry but their tears "flow inwards", meaning that they do not feel free to express their feelings of sorrow openly. One can understand the desire of men to appear stoic and emotionally strong, but if men suppress their emotions, they may eventually feel angry and hurt inside. Men's emotional suppression and rejection of dealing with their feelings are at odds with the Bible. The shortest verse in the Bible reminds us poignantly that Jesus did not hesitate to be fully human. He wept after the death of his beloved friend Lazarus.[88] He also wept over the sins of Jerusalem.[89] Painful emotions are difficult to bear, and over time, each person develops his or her own strategy of dealing with them.

Denial is a deliberate attempt to push down certain emotions into the subconscious part of the mind and so avoid taking care of the matter at hand. Let's look in on Mbuta, who is a quiet, reserved man. Mbuta is married to a very beautiful woman, Koki, who is also very sociable and enjoys being admired. In social gatherings, other people seem to listen to Koki so intently that Mbuta feels left out and ignored. He has become increasingly angry about all the attention his wife gets. Instead of discussing his anger with her or with someone else, he keeps it all inside.

An individual can ignore an unpleasant emotion instead of facing it. When anger is hidden away in the heart, however, the feeling is not stored as anger for long. It soon changes to resentment, which in turn becomes bitterness. This malignancy spreads like a cancer, destroying an individual and negatively affecting that person's relationships with those around him or her. Anger that festers for many years is capable of locking an individual into a prison of fear, depression, and broken relationships. So, after ten years of marriage, Mbuta begins shouting at his wife. He accuses her of leading other men on. He declares that she dresses up only to show other people how beautiful she is. He has recently received an early retirement and so he sits at home in self-pity. In this situation, he anxiously waits to see his wife come home after work. Still, he does not talk to anyone about his fears. This is destroying his marriage. Suppressed emotions do not go away on their own accord, so for now, reconciliation for this couple seems impossible.

Instead of trying to manage negative emotions on one's own, an individual can acknowledge a problem and describe his or her feelings to God, a counsellor or prayer partner, or other caring individuals. Such transparency opens one's heart to healing, a mystery that is not easy to understand. After Christmas celebrations, Mbuta's brother came home, and was finally able to talk to him about the need to seek help. He also urged Mbuta to register for a small loan with the micro-enterprise company in their village, so as to begin a chicken-keeping business. With help, Mbuta began to gather the courage to express his anger to his wife, something that motivated Koki to monitor her behaviour, as well as her need to provoke reactions from other people. The couple's communication improved over time, and with the help of a pastoral counsellor, they were reconciled.

Brokenness and Physical Ailments

We turn now to our bodies. A holistic model of humanity examines and focuses on the needs of the body, in addition to the needs of the mind and spirit. When any part of the individual is injured, other parts hurt as well. The body, designed for its own survival, will move away from anything that causes it pain. Consequently, a malfunctioning body may contribute to psychological problems that also affect the spirit. Recurring sicknesses pose a threat to health and may point more deeply to psychological and spiritual problems. A Meru proverb says, *Murimo jwa mucoka niju jurijaga mwana*, meaning, "The sickness that [keeps returning] is fatal to the child." For Africans, physical illness is often considered as having a spiritual source, but this could be from the spirit world or from a displeased ancestor. Nonetheless, prayers for physical safety are addressed to God as Father who is all-knowing and who can protect us from evil and danger.

Since the body is considered the home of the spirit and soul in many African societies, care of the body is very important. From a holistic perspective, the health of the body impacts the whole system. Among the Meru, sickness of the body is taken as a normal thing, but health is also sought. *Mwiri juri tharike jutiagaga murimo* translated means, "Illness is normal as long as blood flows in the body." When a person dies, people are reminded that the body survives for a season, but that the spirit lives on. The moral here is that the spiritual aspect of existence should receive as much, if not greater, care and attention as the body.

The Body Affects the Spirit

How the body affects the rest of the system is evident when depression occurs as a side effect of a physical condition involving medication, diet, or illnesses like cancer and AIDS.[90] Similarly, many women experience depression that comes as part of the menstrual cycle. Others become depressed soon after childbirth (postpartum depression). After an abortion, the mother is often immersed in depression (post-abortion syndrome), with feelings of grief, guilt, detachment, and inner psychological pain. This response could result from hormonal changes and also from emotional reactions related to losing the baby.

After people experience an adrenaline high during an emergency, their bodies may become exhausted. This leaves them feeling not only physically tired, but also emotionally drained – a state that can easily lead to long periods of depression or burnout. People who have undergone situations of emotional crisis need to understand that rest, exercise, and a balanced diet can hasten recovery from such periods of emotional stress. Crisis counselling is necessary for individuals who have experienced traumatic incidents.

Western research indicates that some hyperactive children may be allergic to certain substances.[91] A child who was quite uncontrollable was found to be allergic to wheat protein. Eating bread would completely destabilize him. Other people are allergic to food additives.[92] Symptoms of food allergies may include migraine headaches, irritability, hyperactivity, chronic fatigue, eczema, and rheumatoid arthritis.[93] Some people with an imbalance in their level of blood sugar may appear sluggish. This may be the result of a slow metabolism rate, which is often linked with hypothyroidism, a condition in which the body lacks sufficient thyroid hormone.[94] Too easily we dismiss such a person as lazy for lack of a careful examination of the causes. This is not holistic counselling. People with hyperthyroidism may exhibit behaviours of anxiety, restlessness, or nervousness. They may also lose weight because of their overactivity.[95] Holistic counselling will refer such patients to medical doctors to help to stabilize their condition.

The Spirit Affects the Body

Whatever affects the mind and spirit may affect the whole body. Western research indicates that lonely people are more likely to suffer from physical problems such as heart disease or high blood pressure. There is convincing evidence that stress, including the stress of loneliness,[96] affects the immune system and reduces the body's ability to resist disease.[97] Children who experience extreme traumatic stress within family relationships, under severe discipline, or in cases of death or other traumas may regress into bed-wetting or suffer from stomach ulcers, skin eruptions, or headaches.[98] A counsellor must look beyond the physical symptoms for the cause of the problem.

Conclusion

Transformational counselling that meets the needs of African populations will require counsellors who understand the unique needs of the people across the life span. Counselling in Africa will need to be guided by approaches that are holistic in nature. These approaches will utilize a multiplicity of interventions and partnerships to achieve wellness among those served. The same methodologies must build on rich indigenous cultural practices that are consistent with a biblical value system. Africa's traditional oral psychology is rich in tools that have been used for healing over millennia.

For training, teaching, and counselling, African Christian counsellors can use folk tales, African proverbs, songs, dances, and musical instruments. Professional African Christian counsellors are called to a commitment to scholarship in Western psychological theory, so that they can both critique it and employ points of commonality with African understanding of health and wholeness. In the end, we hope that what is uniquely African may be enriched through cross-pollination with other systems of healing, be they Western or otherwise.

African indigenous Christian counsellors will also need to work against despondency and discouragement in the face of huge problems in African society. Many therapists suffer from depression and isolation when they work in remote *red zone* areas, often with little organizational support or understanding. Red zones have been defined as "those areas of the world where there is intense stress on a regular and sometimes daily basis, brought on by perceived or actual danger and threat to one's safety."[99] The ability to serve with commitment in such areas will be tested, especially if the community's needs seem so much greater than the possible impact of interventions. The challenge will be to remain focused on the call and on the joy of service, knowing that trails are being made, not necessarily for those who walk on them now, but for those who will come in the future.

CHAPTER 3

Objectives and Characteristics

Africa, we have suggested, is a land of values and vacuums, challenges and opportunities, wholeness and brokenness. African is not the "Dark Continent," as it has sometimes been known; God has been present all along. African stories, sages, communities, and traditions have often communicated God's presence in his world and served as a gift to humanity in preserving community welfare. In this chapter we will focus on the objectives and characteristics of Christian counselling in the African context. What will make counselling Christian? What will make it African?

We will begin by describing approaches to pastoral counselling by both Africans and African Americans. We will then outline the approach we recommend: African indigenous Christian counselling. Ruth and Maria will illustrate this approach with a counselling situation, and finally, we will discuss the character of the counsellor in our approach.

Three African Counselling Models

The African counsellor need not begin work without the assistance of various models and examples. Africans on both sides of the Atlantic have engaged in care that has emerged from their faith. We begin by reviewing three different counselling models: indigenous African, African pastoral, and African-American pastoral counselling.

Indigenous African Counselling

An excellent example of indigenous African counselling that makes no claim to be Christian is that of Malidoma Somé, from Burkina Faso, who writes from his West African Dagara culture. Somé maintains that the power of African ritual lies in its ability to manage the needs of the soul. Somé travels the world introducing African rituals and concepts of community as the gateway to spirituality and wholeness, as indicated by his own website and an organization called "Echoes of the Ancestors." Discussing the role of ritual in community, he states that community is a place of redefinition, where an individual draws on power to move on, so that alienation is reduced and wholeness is enhanced. Ritual ensures connectedness with another person and with the spirit world, which is made up of ancestors who have passed on. These ancestors serve as objective representations, keeping the collective unconscious spiritually alive among the people. The healer divines the problems of others, utilizing "reckless imagination, piercing intelligence and intuitive insights."[100] All rituals are interdependent, and healing is achieved through traditional forms that have been repeated generation after generation, ensuring continuity and health. Somé notes that in tune with the African sense of connectedness, whatever an individual "does alone, or in the presence of the village, is considered communal" since it ultimately impacts everyone.[101]

While we agree with Somé that African rituals must be recovered, as Christians we consider ritual important, but not sufficient alone for healing. Rituals take on meaning in the context of a larger web of beliefs, and in the life of a community. For us this means acknowledging God's presence in healing, with the Christian community providing a context for that healing.

African Pastoral Counselling

Many pastoral counsellors in Africa have shaped our thinking, including: Kasonga wa Kasonga, Emmanuel Lartey, and Daisy Nwachuku.[102] However, we will focus on Jean Masamba ma Mpolo, who teaches pastoral counselling at a theological institution in Kinshasa, Republic of Congo; and on Abraham Berinyuu, who is a member of the University for Development Studies in Tamale, Ghana.

Jean Masamba ma Mpolo states categorically that mental health services, psychotherapy, and pastoral counselling in Africa "have to take into account the African dynamic interpretations of illness and health."[103] We agree. He advises that diagnosis and treatment should incorporate the patient's worldview, including any mention of the influence of evil forces. Raised with belief in the connectedness of all of life, Africans will perceive mental illness as arising from spiritual or relational factors: bewitching, anger from neglected or offended spirits, possession, or broken relationships. In such instances, ma Mpolo recommends the use of insight-oriented therapy to explain the nature of emotional turmoil. This therapeutic approach has the following benefits: (a) it increases the patient's awareness of the presenting problems and offers an opportunity to express feelings and narrate experiences; (b) it strengthens the patient's ego boundaries in situations in which control has been compromised by fear; (c) it enhances the patient's self-sufficiency by negating feelings of dependence and helplessness; and (d) it helps the patient to become aware of repressed conflicts and memories that compromise healing and wholeness.[104]

Besides individual interventions, a form of group therapy is practiced among many African traditional societies. The Ewondo of Cameroon and the Ba-Kongo of Lower Zaire begin with the diagnosis of the patient by the healer or diviner. This expert brings the members of the patient's group together in a therapeutic palaver to diagnose the cause of the problem in terms of broken relationships, and to plan the goals of treatment.[105] The palaver is a tribal conference or council gathered to assist an individual member or to deal with a community or group need. After communicating hope, the healer plays the role of intermediary between the patient and the clan, utilizing directive therapy to help restore broken relationships.

The healer acts like a group therapist, encouraging new ways of perceiving and coping. His tools are analogies, words, symbolism, proverbs, and forms of expression known to the group. A redemptive resolution is explored. When the resolution is not favourable, the patient is held within a caring community, which will continue to provide a safe and tolerant place that might prevent further breakdown. Through such treatment, individual pain is held by the community, with the healer facilitating the healing process. The hoped-for result is individual self-awareness and growth, as well as enhancement of the community's education on mental illness. Where group therapy through discussion does not work, the healer utilizes insight-oriented approaches in work with the individual. For example, the healer might help the client to understand how his behaviour might have led to the problem. Resolution, then, would incorporate making right the wrong done, by community-specified means of resolution.

The second African pastoral counsellor we present is Abraham Berinyuu, from Ghana.[106] There is much about Berinyuu's work that we appreciate, including his African theological sensitivity in relating to such Western psychological theories as psychoanalysis. Berinyuu discusses the implications of ritual healing within the context of pastoral theology. For example, he uses the symbolism of the cross in the management of grief and death as a way to integrate original cultic meanings with Christian perspectives. Berinyuu bases his argument on Heinz Kohut's Object Relations Theory,[107] which states that within each person, there are different types of selves: unconscious, preconscious, and conscious. The nuclear self contains an "individual's most enduring values and ideals but also his most anchored goals, purposes, and ambitions,"[108] aspects that are formed through an individual's maturation and learning. If there is lack of cohesion over time, as is the case of African Christians dislocated from their cultural roots and not adequately planted in the Christian value system, there is a disintegration of the nuclear self and a disjunction between faith and practice.[109] A Christian with a dichotomized self will find himself or herself living at the mercy of divided selves. This is because on the one hand, the individual feels compelled to satisfy the demands of a faith that she has not quite clarified and owned. On the other hand, she may feel guilty when culturally indigenous means of healing and wholeness beckon and demand allegiance, and she feels helpless to comply. These demands are expressed from within the nuclear self, the unit that incorporates the collective conscious and unconscious, and serves as a reservoir that provides resources for coping when threatened.

We will focus on one dimension of Berinyuu's approach: his ability to interpret traditional African rituals and to theologically reconstruct them for the African church. We find particularly helpful his pastoral counselling approach to grief and to African funeral rituals. Regarding the application of ritual to pastoral counselling dealing with grief, Berinyuu states that according to the Nyaaba people of Ghana, ritual "connects, and identifies the individual within the community,"[110] and creates cognitive stability in the face of unforeseen destabilizing events such as death and loss. The traditional death ritual involves three stages: separation, transition, and incorporation.

Death is a physical separation. Berinyuu observes that at his death, Jesus was separated from the physical world, crying, *'Eli, Eli, lema sabachthani?'* (which means, 'My God, my God, why have you forsaken me?').[111] This act of separating from the world and yet remaining in it assures reconciliation between God and humanity, he says. This state of loss needs the careful observation of relevant rituals that help the individual deal with this separation.

During the transition stage in traditional death rituals, the dead person moves to the world of the ancestors, while the living relatives continue life without the loved one. Jesus joins the world of the departed, becoming an intercessor on behalf of humanity before God. Indeed, he told the disciples, "I am going there to prepare a place for you."[112] This means that Christians who have departed join the "communion of saints" composed of those who have gone before. Faith in Christ means there is a spiritual continuity with those from whom we have parted.

Finally, in the incorporation stage, the Christian is assured that, whether in life or death, the whole community of heaven is joined together as members of the household of God. There they will be "no longer foreigners and strangers, but fellow citizens ... built on the foundation of the apostles and prophets, with Christ Jesus himself as the chief cornerstone. In him the whole building is joined together and rises to become a holy temple in the Lord."[113] Berinyuu notes that the African church will need to go beyond the "dust-to-dust" one-hour funeral services imported from the West and could instead incorporate these three phases using a theology of the cross. We find this model of taking African rituals seriously and providing theological interpretations most important and helpful for the development of our own approach.

African-American Pastoral Counselling

It is not only native Africans who have been concerned about Christian counselling, but Africans in the United States as well. Their experiences and thinking are also part of our approach.[114] The process of reclaiming and recreating something to make it relevant to one's culture is an experience that Africans and African Americans share, as cultural kin and as brothers and sisters in Christ. Consider the words of a well-known African-American spiritual:

> Were you there when they crucified My Lord?
> Were you there when they crucified My Lord?
> Oh, sometimes it causes me to tremble, tremble, tremble,
> Were you there when they crucified My Lord?[115]

This hymn captures the theology of the cross that is so centrally important to many African Americans. The cross of Jesus represents the transformative experience from pain to empowerment, from victim to victor, from injustice to justice. The unique experience of African Americans began with slavery and continues today with the subtle impact of racism on the individual, families, and the community. So it is perhaps not surprising that many African Americans are distrustful of seeking therapy. They ask traditional psychologists and counsellors, "Were you there when ... ?" And they avoid the vulnerability of being caused to "tremble, tremble, tremble" and so re-experiencing pain without the guarantee of some form of healing.

Edward Wimberly, a prominent African-American pastoral counsellor, believes that healing or "being there and holding a trembling person" is guided by both wisdom and the acknowledgement of God's presence in this change process.[116] The counsellor joins with the counselee, not as an instructor or police, but as a channel of God's healing and wisdom. The use of prayer in the therapeutic process depends on the counsellor's sensitivity and expertise. Wimberly also stresses the need for the counsellor to "be there" and to be aware of the need to protect the unique "trembling" of the egos of African-American men, and to examine issues of "trembling" of self-hatred among African-American women.

Nancy Boyd-Franklin, an African-American family therapist, reminds us of the uniqueness of each family.[117] Overlooking the uniqueness of families and individuals implies that people seeking counselling can be lumped together on the basis of racial and ethnic factors – possibly leading to anger and resentment on the part of the counselee(s). Even within a family, the counsellor needs to acknowledge each member's unique experiences.[118]

An African Indigenous Christian Counselling Model

Building on the work of the models we have discussed, we propose a model that we call African indigenous Christian counselling. This is an eclectic model of counselling and psychotherapy that integrates indigenous cultural sensitivity,[119] biblical grounding,[120] and carefully selected non-African biological, social, and psychological insights. These three aspects are basic to our understanding of human nature, behaviour, and interrelationships with the world. The situation is similar to the three-legged stool on which the wise village elder sits. The entire stool is carved from one piece of wood, with the three legs held together by the seat. And so we believe that each aspect (culture, Scripture, and wisdom) needs to support the others.

Indigenous Cultural Sensitivity

Although most of African psychology is unwritten, having been handed down orally, many African communities continue to use indigenous approaches on a daily basis in training children, communicating marital expectations, disciplining wayward youth, and managing dissonance. In their own way, African communities also address the mental illnesses of schizophrenia, depression, phobias, and compulsions.

In these cultures, although the means of communication may vary in different contexts, such wisdom remains embedded in proverbs, folk stories, songs, and dance. Africans are now taking up the challenge to document this richness in writing and other forms. We assume that indigenous culture will influence the way we theologize and provide therapy in the future.

Biblical Grounding

In Christian counselling, we begin with the confession of the Christian community that God is our Creator, Sustainer, and Redeemer. This belief emerges from Scripture, which is foundational for understanding truth. It is in the life of Christ that we Christians find the standards for behaviour in culture. The Spirit of God guides us in wisdom and truth as we seek to act as a healing presence to the emotionally troubled persons we see in counselling. Our Christian confession also serves as the basis of interpreting and assessing indigenous cultures.

Non-African Psychology

In our model of African indigenous Christian counselling, we seek also to use those non-African psychological theories that may be useful. It is possible that more relational models, such as contemporary relational psychoanalysis or family systems approaches, could be helpful. Seeking to understand the biological basis of mental illness should not be forgotten. However, we are not at all interested in replacing local African traditions of healing with Western practices, because each culture tends to have its own indigenous systems of healing;[121] nor do we recommend approaches that run counter to our Christian convictions.

In addition to her training as clinical psychologist and her faith as a committed Christian, the first author (Gladys Mwiti) has indigenous roots arising out of the Meru tribe of Kenya. The Meru share a common heritage with other Bantu people, who cover most of sub-Saharan Africa. Although the languages of these peoples may be different, they have many common customs. This model seeks to encourage African Christian counsellors from varying backgrounds to examine their own cultural roots: modes of teaching and training, measures of worth, factors of community resiliency, proverbs, folk tales, songs, and other elements that can be utilized within a Christian framework to enhance community mental health and wholeness.

The second author (Al Dueck) is a Christian psychologist who teaches and conducts research in the School of Psychology at Fuller Theological Seminary in Pasadena, California. He has been actively engaged in cross-cultural programmes in Latin America and China. His roots lie in the communal Mennonite tradition that emerged out of the radical response to the

16th-century Reformation in Europe. He points to the reign of God to guide dialogue between culture, religion, and psychotherapy.[122] The basic premise is that the reign of God affirms that which is good in a given culture, and that it is the standard for righteousness in a culture. Based on the biblical account of Pentecost, all people present hear the Good News in their own language.[123] The result of Pentecost is the creation of a new community, the church, which seeks to reflect the ethic of the reign of God.

Objectives of African Indigenous Christian Counselling

Next, we will look at several objectives that shape healing in our African indigenous Christian counselling model. These objectives include re-establishing community connectedness, restoring the image of God, seeking wholeness, recognizing human brokenness, facilitating reconciliation, and enhancing community resiliency.

Re-establish Community Connectedness

In many parts of Africa, wise people, bishops, doctors, and healers do not work alone; nor does an ailing person seek help alone. The village healer has a bevy of helpers, and the ailing individual is brought to the healer in the company of many other people. The report is: "We are sick." The healer's rejoinder is: "Which one is the patient?" Healing is a group process, complete with supervised ministrations of the healer's prescriptions, prayers from the believers, and the administration of soups and herbal concoctions, until the declaration: "We are healed."

The foremost objective of the Christian counsellor is to re-establish community connectedness. The essence of community is captured in *umuntu*: "I am because we are." My humanity is caught up in your humanity, with my personhood realized through other persons and through God, who is the source of life and wellness and who holds everything together. God is the one who is calling forth and empowering a new community of wholeness and justice. Community connectedness is implicit in the word *harambee*, which refers to building houses together and working the land in teams, in addition to feasting, celebrating, and mourning together.[124]

Restore Creation

Humanity was created in God's image, but that image was tarnished. The Christian counsellor seeks with the Spirit's guidance to restore the original lustre. God has placed in every person a desire for physical, psychological, spiritual, behavioural, and relational wholeness. This makes the practice of counselling a partnership among God, the counsellor, and the counselee – all drawing on this desire for wellness. When creation is restored in the image of Jesus, the individual will in turn live in harmony with his or her environment.

Seek Wholeness

Our God who is whole desires the same wholeness for his people, in whatever condition they might be.[125] Indeed, through the sacrificial death of Christ on the cross, he has already provided *abundant life* to all who would receive it. Fragmented selves are brought together as we learn to follow our Lord Jesus.

Recognize Brokenness

The previous chapter described the ways in which Africa is broken. The Christian counsellor is able to recognize the cultural context of the brokenness of those who come for counselling. Recently in Kenya, a ten-year old child gave birth to a baby following her rape by an older man. In the past, such incidents would be punishable by the community, and a curse would be expected to befall the perpetrator. This kind of accountability ensured the protection of children. However, when adults grow up without fear of humanity or of God, brokenness in community kinship and irresponsible living follows – often evidenced in increasing cases of child neglect, abuse, domestic violence, drunkenness, youth rebellion, and other forms of problems. A disoriented society will have much pathology. In such a context, instead of labelling the broken as patients relegated to a life of continual pain, *umuntu* perceives them compassionately as having a capacity for change and also becomes involved in the change process.

Facilitate Reconciliation

We perceive healing as a process emanating from God, and passing through the counsellor, who serves as a channel for reconciliation between the counselee and his or her inner enemies, family, friends and God. Reconciliation makes community life possible.[126] A reconciled community creates a ripple effect to sustain wellness, wholeness, and resiliency.

Here is a story of reconciliation. Many churches in Africa have a revival fellowship or charismatic group of Christians who evangelise, leading others to a personal faith in Jesus Christ. Sometimes such groups set themselves apart from the rest of the membership, including the clergy. When a charismatic

Christian – a prominent church leader – died, some of his followers who were more nominal Christians planned the funeral for a date that coincided with a retreat already scheduled by the larger charismatic group. The leadership team of the charismatic group sat down to dialogue about the implications of this funeral in relationship to their programme. Many of the most vocal leaders felt that nothing, not even the funeral, should interfere with their meeting. After all, what did they, the true charismatics, have to do with the nominal Christians, anyway? One key leader seemed to sum up the group's feelings with the words, "We shall not go to the funeral. 'Let the *dead* bury their own *dead*.'"[127] Silence fell on the group.

Although the speaker cited Jesus's words, the passage was used out of context. The speaker had suddenly created a deep divide between the nominal and charismatic Christians, labelling the nominal group as "the dead ones." The charismatic boycott of the funeral would cause a deep wound that might not be healed and would certainly not encourage reconciliation. After some time, a wise leader among the charismatic Christians provided a bridge, declaring: "You know what? We all shall go to the funeral. Why? The dead man is our brother. The nominals may be dead, but he is our brother. And after all, how shall we witness to them unless we go to them and show them the love of Christ?" Many people present had been quietly hoping for a peaceful resolution. "Yes. Let us go," they responded with relief.

And with that, the peacemaker led the team to the funeral ceremonies. A wise man had spoken the wisdom of the gospel in a way that would provide the means of bridging the division between the two groups, saving the church from a split and a scandal. This response provided an opportunity for reconciliation, joining the whole community in the mourning ceremony. This is an excellent example of African indigenous Christian counselling.

Enhance Community Resiliency

Finally, broken relationships compromise community resiliency. Every individual is responsible for his or her own well-being, and for that of others. This approach is not only biblical, but also African. Healed, reconciled people make for resilient communities, and an awareness of the resources of the Christian faith enriches this resiliency. Such consciousness protects society from the erosion of understanding what it means to be human and provides an inheritance that can be passed on from generation to generation. By this practice, Africans assure survival.

Case Study: Ruth and Maria

We have suggested that African indigenous counselling is like a three-legged stool, built on culture, faith, and wisdom. Such an approach is deeply relational, holistic, and communal. To illustrate our model, we turn now to a conversation between an exemplary African counsellor, Ruth, and a woman needing assistance, Maria.[128]

Maria

My name is Maria. My younger sister, Lulu, died of AIDS soon after giving birth to a beautiful baby girl. The child was angelic, with long black hair and definite Caucasian features. Lulu had lived away from home, with many male friends in her life. Lulu broke all the rules of our clan by living as she did. She flirted around with men who were the age of our father, even selling her body for money. Older women clucked their tongues whenever they met my sister. "Who has bewitched her?" they wondered. I, too, speculated, although I kept my fears to myself. I also had my own problems.

I got married to Jonah, but our relationship did not produce any children. Jonah waited for two years, and when no pregnancy was forthcoming, he asked his mother to bring a diviner. She was an old woman who came by night and led me through various ceremonies in the presence of my mother-in-law and other women. Nothing worked. No one suggested that my husband might be the problem. In my community, failure to conceive and bear children is *always* the woman's fault. Finally, my husband sent me away and remarried. This rejection because of my supposed infertility left me angry and bitter, but I kept all my feelings to myself. As a result, I often had migraine headaches. Eventually, my sister Lulu got pregnant, and soon after, fell sick with the "thinning disease." Alone, she finally came home, had her baby, and died. I cared for Lulu till the end. After Lulu's funeral, I became the baby's mother, named her Kadogo, and proceeded to care for her.

Throughout the problems with my husband, Lulu's long illness, the eventual birth of the baby, and the funeral rites that followed my sister's death, I remained strong, showing no emotions. Other women marvelled at how tough I was to bear so much so quietly. However, the older women in the community saw through my mask, saying: *Maria akwaira mpaka mugongo juti nguu* ("Maria carries a wild cat on her bare back!"). They could see that although I appeared strong, I was carrying more trouble than I acknowledged, and that obviously, I was not asking for help.

As baby Kadogo blossomed into a cheerful, beautiful toddler, I decided to attend the local church, and eventually became a Christian. However, I remained emotionally and socially aloof from other members, and my headaches continued to disturb me. Doctors could find no physical basis for the migraine headaches but constantly prescribed painkillers anyway. Eventually, the pastor suggested that I seek the help of a Christian counsellor, and when asked to choose a trained counsellor, I picked Ruth.

Ruth

I became a committed Christian at an early age and have developed a deep love for my people. I have thought about the nature of the gospel for Africa and feel deeply God's desire to be involved totally in the healing of our continent. I believe that God has always been present in African history, culture, and the church. I would like to think that my belief in God has helped me to develop the ability to understand emotional problems in both an African and Christian light. I hope I can develop theological and biblical perspectives on the healing and transformation of people like Maria.

Dr Mwiti: This insight is Ruth's foundation, namely, a deep theological desire to see Christian responses to the issues that African culture creates. She is committed to the reign of God on African soil. Because of her spiritual gifts of discernment, wisdom, mercy, and godliness, it is no wonder Ruth has become a beloved counsellor, discerned as a healer by her whole community. Ruth is aware that she is growing as a professional counsellor. On a regular basis, Ruth joins the counselling team at her church to meet for supervision with Dr Mang'ati, a Christian clinical psychologist, or with Dr Papiwa, a Christian psychiatrist. Both are contracted by the church to act as supervisors for the counselling department. Ruth is recognized by all as a Christian counsellor who is sensitive to the fundamentals of the African indigenous Christian counselling model.

In addition to this foundation for Christian counselling, Ruth has particular qualities that make her stand out as a Christian counsellor. She embodies experience and wisdom in dealing with Africa's unique challenges, and possesses basic Christian qualities such as humility, gentleness, love, patience, and unity with the community. She is also committed to ethical practices.

Ruth

As I work with counselees like Maria, I pray privately for them, and when appropriate, with them. I also develop creative rituals and assignments to address the psychological, social, biological, and spiritual issues of my clients. For example, with Maria, I helped her to normalize her concerns about Lulu's funeral rites. Since her sister had died of AIDS, or the "thinning disease," many people in the community did not attend the funeral, and the local congregation did not even participate in the burial. Maria was heartbroken, but never shared her disappointment with her family or with the village elders. However, as she became emotionally stronger, we discussed how she could share her pain with her family, church, and community leadership, so that together, they could all revisit the mourning rituals for Lulu. Eventually, she was able to do this, and this brought peace to Maria. It also helped the community to take better care of other people dying of AIDS.

> *Dr Mwiti*: Serving so many people can be exhausting and physically draining. For this reason, Ruth has tried to discipline herself to develop a self-care regimen. She has also disciplined herself to obtain necessary training in her line of work. She enrolled in the nearby Bible school and completed her diploma in Christian Counselling. She has also completed a master's degree in Counselling Psychology. Her yearning for further learning and training will continue to raise her level of performance. Ruth was able to study examples of Western theories of psychology and to develop a Christian response to them, and also to explore some examples of an African indigenous understanding of emotional problems, reinforcing them with sound biblical teaching. Ruth's growth in all these aspects showed clearly in her work with clients like Maria.

Maria

Ruth amazed me with the deep love, respect, insight, and interest she expressed toward me and my condition. I felt very reassured when Ruth told me that I could trust her, and that she would keep everything I told her absolutely confidential unless she knew that I was going to hurt myself or someone else. I can describe Ruth as a humble counsellor who is a committed Christian, with a track record of a consistent walk with God since her youth. She knows and uses the Bible so well that all who know her respect her for her wisdom and humility. This woman listens respectfully to the older women in the village. Instead of looking down at our culture, she values the strengths of our indigenous community. For example, I have learnt that she consults with the wise village women for assistance in her work with church members who come to her with marriage problems. I wish I had done this when my own marriage became a nightmare. Other counsellors who have gone to college like Ruth assume that all wisdom comes from their many books written in America and England. But I still believe that in spite of our problems, there is wisdom among our African people.

I've always known that women in my community care for me, but I was too full of pain to socialize with them. Ruth showed me how I can begin to live again as a true member of my clan and my church. She explored the deep wounds in my life, including the way I lost my marriage, my sister, and my pride. The other day, Ruth reminded me that although I did not have a child of my own, I have Kadogo. I will never forget that. The child gives me hope for the future.

Ruth

In our church, our pastor has set up a little room where we counsellors meet with people needing prayer and encouragement, usually on Sunday after church and sometimes during the week. It took several meetings for Maria to tell her whole story, but as her story unfolded, so did her trust in me. I prayed in my heart that Maria would find in our counselling relationship a safe place to express her needs. So, I slowly built a relationship of empathy between us. I knew the village that Maria had come from, so we talked about village life, the people we both knew, and the annual festivals. I also acknowledged her losses and helped Maria to gain a holistic understanding of events in her life while providing her with biblical and psychological insights, and emotional support, in a spirit of faithfulness to her. Maria knew that she could trust me to walk this difficult road with her, and I often prayed that I would remain a safe place of refuge for her. I kept in the forefront of my mind the need to help Maria reconnect with her community – which I found necessary to sustain any progress achieved in our meetings.

One of the things I struggle with is the desire to make the counselee's problems disappear overnight. I want to rescue these people from pain and to hasten the formation of character. My supervisor tells me that it is best to allow people to grow slowly, and that since their problems and brokenness have persisted for so long, solutions will come slowly, too. This is my lesson in patience and trust in God. As I see people change with my help and with that of the wider community, I know for sure that it takes a *village* to bring about and sustain change.

The Character of an African Indigenous Christian Counsellor

What can we learn about the character of the Christian counsellor in an African context from this case? Ruth is a counsellor who protects her reputation, seeks wisdom and knowledge, displays empathy, understands narrative, recognizes physical symptoms, identifies problematic thinking, can hold the counselee's unpleasant feelings, uses Scripture wisely, adapts her counselling approach to non-Christians if any come to her for help, affirms spiritual needs, and builds community connectedness.

Protects her Reputation

The African Christian counsellor is one who is legitimated by the community. The pastor knew that Maria had picked Ruth precisely for this reason. Ruth was aware that the counselling relationship is a privilege that must be earned. She realized that the mirror she constantly turns on others must first be turned towards her. In Africa, counsellors' lifestyles can never be divorced from their practice. "You are a counsellor? Show us how you live out what you teach."

Seeks Wisdom and Knowledge

Ruth was the kind of person who was constantly in touch with her community, seeking help from wise elders in order to understand the dynamics that contributed to personal problems like Maria's. Ruth did not rely only on the knowledge she gathered from Western counselling books. She read and diligently researched African history, cultures, and traditions. She spent time reflecting on their nature, their role in the community, and their compatibility to her own Christian convictions.

Displays Empathy

Ruth had excellent counselling skills. Consistent with the biblical teaching to "rejoice with those who rejoice; mourn with those who mourn,"[129] she first built rapport with Maria by asking her to tell her story. Then she inquired about her family, her local geography, how her daughter was developing, and whether she had used any local remedies or consulted her tribal leader. In addition, Ruth created hope and gave comfort to Maria. She asked about persons in her extended family, people who exemplified hope in time of trouble. In particular, Maria's aunt introduced her to the women's fellowship group that met in the village. Maria found care and support among these women. Her days of loneliness began to become a far-off memory.

Understands the Story

Ruth listened carefully, without interruption, while Maria told her story with its sadness and disappointments. Ruth later acknowledged Maria's losses, grief, anger, and other negative feelings. As Maria told her story, Ruth sought to understand the problem from an African, Christian, and psychological perspective. From an indigenous African viewpoint, Maria was alienated from her people because of the way Lulu was treated during her illness and burial. In addition, her childlessness had become a stigma that was difficult to bear. Spiritually, Maria questioned God's love. How could he love her and not make her a full woman? Psychologically, Maria suffered from self-loathing after her husband rejected her barely two years into their marriage due to "her failure" to conceive. Maria withdrew into emotional and psychological isolation.

Recognizes Physical Symptoms

As Ruth listened to the history of the presenting problem, she also took care to ask the following: Is Maria physically sick? Does she sleep well? How is her appetite? Is there another member of the family who has a similar complaint? Does Maria need to see a doctor? At the end of the first meeting, to rule out physical causes, Ruth referred Maria to a medical doctor. The doctor reported that Maria was not physically sick, but that her blood pressure was slightly elevated, probably due to the stresses in her life. In addition, the doctor cautioned her to eat and sleep well, because she was underweight and appeared overwrought.

Identifies Problematic Thinking

Ruth listened to Maria's thoughts and to conclusions that she had made about life in general. For example, after her husband had sent her away and remarried, Maria had decided that all men were selfish and self-centred. These perceptions affected her relationship with her pastor, her relatives, and her friends. Ruth identified this as problematic thinking, and together, they listed Maria's destructive patterns of thought. The two used Scripture to come up with biblical thought patterns to replace the negative thoughts.[130] Maria recognized that she was generalizing and that some men had been kind to her. Ruth emphasized that Maria's growth would be dependent on commitment to Christian practices that would bring the new thought patterns into alignment with changed behaviour.

Holds Counselee's Unpleasant Feelings

Ruth explored unpleasant feelings such as Maria's anger against her husband and his betrayal of their marriage vows, her sadness over the loss of her marriage and Lulu's death, and the loneliness that Maria often experienced. Ruth was able to hold Maria's rage and sadness without avoiding it. In each discussion, she would encourage Maria to explore these feelings further, to talk about them and confess the state of her heart. Confession before Ruth and before God freed Maria to tell her story first to the women's fellowship group, and later to her family. News of changes in her spread through the village, and gradually people began warming up to Maria.

Ruth was concerned that for so long, Maria had remained self-centred in an attempt to protect herself from further hurt and pain. Ruth encouraged Maria to work at forgiveness and reconciliation, so as to rebuild relationships with those who had hurt her. For example, Maria eventually met with her mother-in-law, the woman who had maligned Maria because of her failure to "give her son" children.

Uses Scripture Wisely

Since Maria was a committed Christian, Ruth could freely but carefully use God's Word as a way to work through the deep needs of the spirit: thoughts, emotions, goals, behaviour, relationships, and physical care. Even so, Ruth was careful not to preach, but to allow the Word to speak to Maria's situation. She would ask Maria what Scripture she had found most helpful, and asked Maria's permission to share biblical insights. One day Maria discussed how she had linked Jesus's acceptance of the woman caught in adultery[131] with Paul's teaching on freedom from condemnation for those in Christ.[132] Maria shared that in the past, she had cowered in shame as people called her the "barren one." Now, as she responded more and more to God's love and acceptance, her dark thoughts were being transformed into self-confidence and love for others.

Adapts in Counselling Non-Christians

If Maria were not a Christian, Ruth would still have seen her in counselling, but her approach would have been different with respect to the use of the Bible in counselling. Ruth would have handled the client with deep respect, allowing God to quietly plant a seed of thirst for his Word through the counselling relationship. For example, even for those who do not know him, Jesus can still be an example. Christ died to redeem them, too, from fear and reproach. God loves everyone, making rain to fall upon the fields of everybody without partiality. Similarly, his sun shines on us all. However, he leaves to us the decision to avail ourselves of his love and care. Planting such seeds of God's abiding love and his desire for our best could open an unbeliever's heart to a God who loves us unconditionally and desires a relationship with us so that he can transform us into his image and so fulfil his plans for our lives.

Affirms Spiritual Needs

Ruth looked at Maria's spiritual needs for security, significance, and self-worth. How was Maria having these needs met? Beginning with a focus on God's love and faithfulness, Ruth helped Maria to peel away labels she had pasted on herself or labels she had accepted from others. Maria began to *put on* labels found in Scripture. Ruth would never forget the day they read Isaiah 43:4: "You are precious and honoured in my sight, and ... I love you." Maria wept for a long time as she heard God speak these powerful words to her. At the end of the session, she had a smile on her face, one that radiated a joy that no one could ever take away.

Builds Community Connectedness

Ruth examined Maria's community connectedness. The women in the village felt that Maria was a loner, since she did not even attend the normal women's gatherings at such events as weddings, the "Merry-Go-Round," or church women's groups.[133] The excuse Maria gave was that baby Kadogo needed her all of the time. However, as counselling proceeded, Maria gathered courage to connect with others. Women in her community opened their hearts and embraced the lonely woman. Slowly, with love and care, Maria's anger began to leave, and laughter could be heard in her home. The village women invited her once again to join in wedding planning, and in the church women's group. Eventually, Maria even joined the Merry-Go-Round and found much to share with other women in social settings. Some of them shared their money with Maria for her various needs.

As the women witnessed her change and transformation, they were happy to note: *Mpanuri ithiragia mweere murune small small* ("A small lid empties millet from the granary bit by bit"). They meant that big problems are resolved by small steps, with listening, obedience, and application, leading to wisdom. This is the essence of counselling.

Conclusion

This chapter may possibly surprise counsellors in Africa who have been trained in the West, or been exposed only to Western psychological theory, methodology, and practice. It should *not* come as a surprise that some African clients in need also seek the help of the wise village elder and sometimes the medicine men – even when Western psychological and medical help is available. How many physically sick people run to the diviner when Western medicine seems to fail? How many believers hop between two worlds, with one leg in the Christian faith while the other leg is set in superstitions in an attempt to explain strange happenings in their lives? How many people with troubled marriages leave behind the city's Western-trained counsellors and travel to villages to find comfort from their mothers and to seek the wisdom of elders in order to settle a marital dispute?

This does not mean that the practice of Western psychology is irrelevant. It may serve as a reminder, though, that perhaps something is missing, and that African people may feel disconnected from the Western therapist. Appreciating people's indigenous cultural value systems, speaking in a language they can understand, discovering and using their metaphors, and planting seeds of change by using biblical practices that build on people's traditions – all these will build up a practice of psychology and counselling in Africa that resonates with people's identity. This way, healing will be sustainable over time and will become a ripple of positive change over generations.

CHAPTER 4

Stress Management

Counsellors do burn out. After years of listening to the stories of their troubled counselees, they can experience chronic fatigue and become depressed or persistently ill. In this chapter, we will focus on stress management for Christian lay and professional counsellors, pastors, and leaders in Africa.

> *Dr Mwiti*: Early one morning, I stood waiting for someone at the gate of a hospital in Africa. A well-known psychiatrist came walking through the gate. He looked thin, tired, and dazed. He passed by without even looking at anyone. In my culture, failure to greet people is an indication of either pride or disconnection from reality. The watchman at the gate looked at the retreating figure and remarked quietly to his friend, "Look at that doctor. I hear that he swallows more pills than he prescribes for his patients!" His companion answered, "The poor doctor should treat himself first. Some of his patients are *saner* than he is." Later on, I learnt that the doctor was a Valium addict and that he used alcohol on the side. There is no telling the level of stress he may have been under.

How can we recognize the symptoms of stress, and what can we do about them? Here are two cases that illustrate burnout in a pastoral leader and in a therapist.

Samuel, the Bishop who Never Said "No"[134]

Samuel was the youngest bishop in his denomination. Long before he was nominated as bishop, Samuel was known as the hardest worker in his whole church. He was always there. He did not know how to say "no" to anyone. He served the national council, sitting on many committees. He was also determined to make his diocese the best in the nation. As a charismatic speaker and avid worker, he attracted many donors. A few years after his election as bishop, he had already repaired the old mission hospital, started several health centres, encouraged women's projects, and increased the diocese's contributions to the national theological seminary. In his diocese, all young couples chose him to officiate at their weddings. He was asked to be present at almost every funeral service. People requested that the bishop pray for them at difficult times, since they believed that no one else's prayers were as effective.

The bishop's wife patiently supported her husband, but she wished that he could be home more with their growing children. Samuel understood her feelings and tried as much as possible to play with the children, and to attend parent-teacher meetings at school as well as the children's many school activities. When he could not be there because of other commitments, he felt guilty and ineffective as a parent. As he became busier and busier, he did not even find time to pray. When could he pray if even early in the morning, there were people waiting to talk to their bishop?

At 45 years of age, Samuel already appeared to be an old man. He looked haggard, slept badly, and did not have enough time to eat. Samuel began to suffer from headaches and stomach pain that would not go away. He also had regular colds and bouts of flu that did not respond to medication. People suggested that the bishop delegate some responsibilities, but he did not. He believed that in time, all of these symptoms would go away.

One day, Samuel woke up and found he could not breathe. In a panic, he called his wife, and was rushed to hospital. As he lay in bed with all kinds of lab tests being administered, he prayed: "Lord, why? I have served you faithfully. I built the diocese from nothing. I did not even have a secretary when I started. Look, Jesus, at all I have done for you! Why, God?"

Rachel, a Burned-out Therapist

Rachel grew up in a Christian home, where she was taught to serve others. However, the Christianity she followed was so Westernized that its worship and practice left out any local cultural expression. Similarly, Rachel was never taught to speak her mother tongue, because her parents and teachers felt that Western expression was the mark of a truly educated African. After college, Rachel trained as a psychologist and later received her graduate specialization degree at a university abroad. Studying in a secular university, however, she had no idea of how to integrate her faith and her professional practice. She was taught all through university that psychology should be practiced independently from spirituality, and that the sacred and the secular should be kept separate.

Trained in client-centred therapy, Rachel was coached not to tell clients what to do about their problematic situations. Answers were to come from within the clients themselves. On the other hand, her tribal culture affirmed that young people should be taught the expectations for adulthood. In that culture, indigenous counselling for young people would assess where they were failing in respect to responsibilities to the self, peers, family, and society. Tribal elders would then exercise directive approaches in coaching and mentoring the youth.

Trained in the client-centred therapeutic approach, however, based on a belief that the client was intrinsically good, the counsellor would affirm or clarify values that young people brought to a counselling session, listen to their emotional presentation, and then guide them towards change along their chosen path. Slowly, Rachel began to feel that she was not making any impact. This values-clarification approach did not seem to work for her. How do people clarify what they do not possess in the first place?

Besides working with young people, Rachel had several severely mentally ill patients, referred to her by a medical doctor in town. She knew that she should refer them to the psychiatrist at the national hospital, but she had not found time to write referral letters – and more sick people just kept coming to her. Not only did she take on too many clients, but she also obtained supervision only occasionally, even though her mentor was willing to see her once a week. When she did make an appointment to see her supervisor, Rachel was often late for the session.

Rachel, a single, attractive woman, at one point felt very attracted to a client who showed more than usual interest in her. She found herself thinking of the young man during the week and began looking forward to her sessions with him. When he suggested that they meet after therapy for tea, she agreed. They discontinued treatment, became good friends, and eventually got romantically involved. Rachel did not share these developments with her supervisor.

During the past three months Rachel has felt emotionally drained, and on several occasions has actually forgotten that she had a session with a client. Rachel is aware that she needs to take good care of her health as well as her spiritual condition. She is so tired on weekends, though, that she does not exercise, watch her diet, or participate in the life of the Christian community. She has not taken a vacation for two years and has only two close friends. Rachel is burned out and disillusioned with the profession of counselling, but she is also frustrated because she feels that she has few other career options now.

Indigenous Culture and Stress

Among the Meru people of Kenya, there was no word for "stress." There are words such as *kumaka* for "worry" or "panic," *ngiitu* for "depression," and *ngutugunya* for "overworking," but "stress" can only be described in other words to the Meru, because the concept of stress did not exist in tribal understanding. This may be because African communities in general are people-oriented rather than task-oriented.

Dr Mwiti: Our village church is also a community meeting point. People long to connect, to talk, to fellowship, to share with one another. The stress level is low because individuals do not "do" church. Instead, they celebrate fellowship and build community among themselves. We also belong to a church in Kenya's capital, Nairobi. Here, the pace is faster. Some are angry when the pastor preaches *forever*, and the service lasts more than 90 minutes. However, the same people will hang around talking to friends for an hour after the end of the service. In their heads, they want to focus on the *task*, but their hearts long for community connections. A few may leave, only to join another group elsewhere building community – at a birthday party, a goat-roasting and family reunion, or a women's Merry-Go-Round. These people live between the old and the new. Balancing this tension can contribute to stress.

Although my Meru people are industrious agriculturists who make sure that the land is ready for planting and that crops are harvested in time, the indigenous culture encourages a *people orientation*. My mother-in-law was a living example of such stress-free existence. She had several friends who were also close confidants. Before land demarcation, many families lived on one plot of land and farmed other parcels scattered here and there. Therefore, walking miles to another small farm was common. My mother-in-law would leave home to go to her farm, but then en route meet one of her confidants. They would stop on the path to talk and talk for hours on end. They would decide to eat whatever food they had packed for the journey, talk some more, and then part to go home. The next day was there for farm work!

How, then, can someone be productive with such a relational orientation? The women often worked in groups. They might decide that since the rains were coming soon, they would work together to get the farms ready for planting. My mother-in-law might talk to a neighbour in the evening: *Mbikia ngugi ruuju*, "Join me tomorrow to work on my land." Sharing their energy, a small group would move from farm to farm, "One day in mine, tomorrow in yours." This way, they would build community, get their emotional needs met, and complete their tasks. I'll never forget hearing women sing away as they worked together on each other's farms.

Culturally, then, indigenous Meru encouraged balance and a people orientation as a means of doing work and surviving emotionally. People like the bishop, who ran too fast or were full of stress and anxiety, would be cautioned: *Cokera akui*, "Watch before you go too far." Such hurried people find it difficult to make friends, for the simple reason that relationships take time to build. Not all of us are person-oriented, but to value people is already in itself a stress management strategy. With more and more emphasis on work and organizational competition in a new Africa, people need to learn to "work smart." We need to use things and value people, not to use people and value things.

Dr Mwiti: My friend Rose is a pastor's wife. She and her husband once pastored our Nairobi congregation, a united place of worship under the patronage of three mainline churches: Methodist, Anglican, and Presbyterian. Once a year, the church hosted the heads of these three churches for a special Confirmation service. Rose and I juggled ministry and bringing up young families. After the service, the three bishops and their spouses would be hosted for a luncheon in the manse, and our two families would cook and wait on the guests. On one such occasion, we welcomed the distinguished older couples into the manse and while our husbands entertained them, Rose and I set about getting ready to serve lunch. Our three sons, then active young children, were running in and out of the house chasing each other. Hoping to create a peaceful environment for the bishops, we decided to ask the noisy children to stop and to settle down in another room. As we called the active boys and tried to control them (obviously stressed that they were a disturbance), one of the bishops gently and quietly called us and said, "Gladys, Rose, what have the children done? Leave them alone." Among the Meru and in many parts of Africa, children are allowed to be children, and they are not perceived as stressors. Limits are set, but within those boundaries, the little ones have the freedom to be themselves. The bishop's admonition to us was that we were allowing our task-orientation to stress us so much that we were forgetting to let the children be children.

Symptoms of Stress

The symptoms of stress may vary some from culture to culture. Usually there are physical, mental, emotional, relational, and spiritual symptoms. Seeing the toll of uncontrolled stress in the lives of Christian workers and their families, Archibald Hart,[135] a specialist in stress management and professor emeritus at Fuller Theological Seminary's Graduate School of Psychology, emphasizes prevention. He urges that caregivers learn to identify stress symptoms in both themselves and others. Stress can become extremely damaging, affecting the whole person: body, mind, spirit, and relationships. We will look at each of these areas in more detail.

Physical Symptoms

Physical symptoms of stress can include bleeding ulcers, indigestion, and coronary problems. Note how tired Rachel, the burned-out therapist, was. Common physical symptoms of stress may include general fatigue; nail biting or picking the skin around the fingernails; disturbed sleep; low appetite, lack of appetite, or overeating; constant headaches, stomach aches, or diarrhoea; wringing of hands; drumming fingers on a surface; heart palpitations; and shallow, fast breathing. For some people, symptoms may include tense muscles, trembling, sweaty hands or brow, and carelessness in grooming and in other self-care. Substance abuse of drugs, alcohol, or tranquilizers may occur. Extreme and continued high levels of stress can lead to stomach pain, skin rashes, insomnia or sleeplessness, asthma attacks, migraines, high blood pressure, and coronary heart disease. Doctors caution that even some types of cancer may be related to debilitating levels of stress.

Emotional Symptoms

A combination of the following emotional symptoms may be indicative of stress: emotional outbursts; low self-concept; a desire to prove oneself; unrealistic self-expectations; finding no time for rest or feeling guilty about rest; inability to concentrate or make decisions; forgetfulness or memory lapses; a critical attitude; increased irritability, hostility, and anger; impatience; loss of humour; anxiety; and fear of specific events, people, or things related to the cause of stress. Some of these symptoms were evident in the stories of both the bishop and Rachel.

Relational Symptoms

If the history of the individual includes social withdrawal or isolation from others, this may indicate stress reactions. Social withdrawal slowly becomes detachment and isolation, which can lead to depersonalization (i.e., distancing from people), looking down on people, reacting negatively to them, and developing an attitude of "I wish people would go away and leave me alone." Sometimes the opposite occurs. In her stress and loneliness, Rachel, the therapist, became sexually attracted to her client. Unfortunately, she failed to make use of regular supervision, where such feelings could have been addressed.

Spiritual Symptoms

From a holistic perspective, physical, emotional, and relational difficulties affect spiritual functioning. Occasionally, workers will tell us that they are spiritually depressed. When we explore other areas of functioning, we discover that they display symptoms there as well. One affects the others. Spiritually, as stressful conditions persist, individuals may begin to believe that God is powerless in their situations and that salvation will come from their efforts alone. However, their personal resources are so depleted that as they try to pull themselves up by their bootstraps, they fail to change their situations. They may even begin to doubt God's very existence – resulting in a deeper sense of hopelessness.

Stress on the spirit often begins to show as:

❖ **Spiritual dryness**. Reading the Word of God, prayer, and fellowship – all previously loved and enjoyed – become drab and unappealing. Thus, the individual may abandon these activities.

❖ **Pessimism**. God's love and care become distant and unreal. Some people describe feeling as if their prayers hit the ceiling and bounce right back. Some feel that God is no longer able to help them. Their attitude is one of pessimism, but if confronted about that, they declare that one must be realistic about things. They feel that they must take matters into their own hands instead of relying on God.

❖ **A critical, judgemental attitude, or for some, indifference**. As one's Christian walk loses meaning, the individual becomes legalistic toward both self and others. Without experiencing the love of God, one cannot pass it on. The result is legalism and harshness. This storm of self-hatred and self-dissatisfaction may harden into a critical, cynical attitude. The individual may increasingly view others merely in terms of their failings, rather than as whole persons.

❖ **Murmuring and grumbling**. Since God is viewed as powerless, a critical attitude leads to constant complaints about negative situations and finding fault with anything that does not meet one's expectations. Thanksgiving and rejoicing have become a thing of the past.

❖ **Bitterness**. Murmuring gives birth to bitterness. The person is filled with resentment, which leads to unbelief and lack of forgiveness.

❖ **Despair and hopelessness**. If no help is forthcoming, the result is a downward spiral into despair, helplessness, and desperation.

Burnout

Prolonged stress of any kind can lead to burnout. What is burnout? It is a pattern of emotional exhaustion, depersonalization, and reduced personal accomplishment.[136] Burnout is "the gradual process by which a person; in response to prolonged stress and physical, mental, and emotional strain; [begins to detach] from work and other meaningful relationships. The result is lowered productivity, cynicism, confusion . . . and a feeling of being drained, having nothing more to give."[137] Many professionals are vulnerable to burnout, including bishops, pastors, counsellors, psychologists, psychiatrists, hospice caregivers, lawyers, policemen, and prison wardens. What do these people have in common? They are all "people helpers." They are supposed to be there for others, to meet people with a smile, to deliver to others, and not to expect support from their clients or from those who depend on their services. These people are supposed to be warm and loving, never rude or emotionally cold, always giving. Should they fail to deliver as expected, they are likely to receive harsh criticism.

Pastors and other "people helpers" who live with continual stress are vulnerable to burnout. Burnout doesn't happen overnight, but over time, it causes people to lose their enthusiasm, joy, energy, vision, perspective, and purpose. In Rachel's case, her inability to appreciate her African heritage and adapt her counselling style to her native culture seemed to result in a loss of impact. That, in turn, created more stress.

A person coping with massive stress begins to move on a downward spiral, which may eventually lead to clinical depression or physical collapse. Nurses who work day and night to make more money on overtime have fallen asleep while driving home. Some individuals have been known to ask for prayers of protection from demonic attacks when they begin to experience blackouts and epilepsy-like seizures. However, rather than victims of demonic attacks, these may be individuals whose bodies and minds are beginning to shut down due to too much stress. They may also fail to realize that physical exhaustion can sometimes become a doorway for spiritual oppression. Other people experiencing extreme stress reactions may suffer spiritual collapse in the midst of organizational conflict, family stress, infidelity, and marriage break-ups. Prayer alone does not solve these problems, just as "faith without works is dead." Such persons also need to act by seeking help to recover from burnout.

Processes of Stress Reactions

When a person feels stress, what is going on? What spiritual, psychological, and biological reactions occur?

Psychological Reactions

Both internal and external factors affect how people react psychologically to stress. We will look at some internal factors first.

Internal Factors: Personality and Perception

An individual's personal history, personality, and perception are internal factors that may affect reaction to a stressful situation. For example, a woman who worked in an earlier placement with an abusive employer may find herself more prone to damaging stress if a new employer is also abusive. If she had a difficult, abusive childhood, her coping abilities may be further compromised – and burnout may be imminent. In Rachel's case, she became romantically involved with the counselee when she was burned out. Just as in the past, when she was frustrated, she turned to others for comfort. In this case, since she had no friends, she turned to a client for nurture. Another internal psychological issue was her need to be effective. She tended to use culturally inappropriate approaches to therapy, and so became discouraged. When Rachel truly sees herself as African and sees God at work in her life, she may become less stressed.

In discussing personal motivation for overcommitment, Lingenfelter and Mayers observe that task-oriented people focus solely on their professional projects as a means of obtaining contentment. On the other hand, person-oriented individuals relish interaction with other people more than completing tasks. What are the outcomes of these opposite orientations?

Task-oriented people are likely to experience higher levels of stress than person-oriented people. This, they say, is because the former frequently:

Aspire to complete a greater number of tasks than is humanly possible in the time they allocate; as a result, their lives take on a frenetic pace filled with activities. Many become workaholics, allowing tasks to so dominate their lives that other people are viewed as merely part of their schedule. Person-oriented people find their satisfaction in interaction with others. Their highest priority is to establish and maintain personal relationships. They enjoy the social interaction required to sustain these relationships.[138]

Internal Factors: Duration of Stress

Besides personality and perception, another internal factor is the duration of stress. People like the bishop and Rachel, who are exposed to damaging stress for a long time, are susceptible to burnout. Studies also indicate that the more people believe that they have less social support and God-support, the higher their level of perceived damaging stress.[139] Religious participation, through which we sense God's support, creates an avenue for cognitive processing of stressful situations as well as enhancing social support to help us to deal with demanding circumstances.[140] Other stressors, of course, compromise one's ability to manage new pressures, leading to vulnerability and burnout. For example, an individual whose close relatives have died of AIDS and who is nursing many AIDS patients in a hospital is likely to find him or herself under a lot of pressure, which may lead to stress and burnout if help is not sought.

External Factors

Just as internal factors can affect a person's response to stress, so can external factors, such as those related to one's work environment. One well-known American psychologist, Christina Maslach, notes that because role ambiguity is not uncommon in the workplace, employees often do not know what is expected of them.[141] This ambiguity affects productivity, lowers self-worth, and increases hopelessness. Other external factors include the fact that some organizations do not have a regular plan that encourages rest and recreation for employees. Others do not have specific means of managing conflict or caring for a counsellor after crisis situations.

The strain of caring for people with problems may also lead to periods of extreme physical fatigue, with disturbances in appetite and sleep. This kind of exhaustion has been called *compassion fatigue*. Such a disturbance will often vary with the nature of the counselee's problems. For example, counselling clients who have experienced extreme horror and death may well affect the Christian counsellor more than counselling a more basic case of family relational problems.

To evaluate the counsellor's optimal ability to function, it will be necessary to evaluate the nature and location of work, the number of helpers in the field, and the amount of the individual's work to be done.

Biological Reactions

What are the biological reactions to stress? Canadian researcher Dr Hans Selye was probably one of the most recognized authorities on how an individual responds physically to demands (positive or negative) made upon him or her.[142] Selye thought that the body passes through three universal stages of coping with stress. First there is an *alarm reaction*. The body prepares itself for responding to or avoiding a stressor: the "fight or flight" response. Remember the last time you almost had a car accident or found yourself in a dangerous situation. What did you experience? Your heart began beating faster so as to get blood to the muscles. Without your knowing it, more acid was pumped into your stomach, to get emergency nutrition from food that might be there. However, a body cannot sustain this condition of excitement for long. In a second stage of *adaptation*, we develop resistance to the stress. If the duration of the stress is sufficiently long, the body eventually enters a stage of *exhaustion*.

Not all stress is negative, and indeed, a certain level of stress is necessary for normal functioning. Healthy levels of stress can trigger creativity or keep a person committed to a course of action until success is realized. For example, during a period of examinations, students are under considerable pressure as they study. This urgency keeps their minds focused on one goal, and the stressful interval soon passes as they finish writing their papers and complete exams. However, when stress levels become unmanageable and uncontrollable, the body experiences wear and tear that sometimes leads to mental fatigue.

Spiritual Reactions

In Africa, the most important part of self-care involves the spirit. The spirit is really the essence of the person, the core of functioning, and the location of the human conscience, discernment, sensitivity, vision, and ambition. When the spirit fails, however physically fit we might be, the whole system suffers; and our individual suffering impacts others around us. Spiritual well-being comes through maintaining contact with God through a lifestyle of holiness and obedience to the teaching of Jesus. Daily activities may include prayer, Bible reading, meditating on God's Word, fellowship with other believers, worship, and service. Spiritual self-care may also include practicing the spiritual disciplines of solitude and silence, listening for guidance, prayer for oneself and intercession, study and meditation, repentance and confession, yielding and submission, fasting, worship, fellowship, simplicity, service, and witness.

Spiritual Disciplines for Managing Stress

Are there ways to manage stress? We suggest the following practices in which Christian counsellors can engage for spiritual self-care: remembering one's call, focusing on what is important, building and maintaining healthy relationships within our faith communities, practicing accountability and transparency, delegating, discovering and using one's gifts in ministry, and getting adequate rest.

Remembering One's Call

The discipline of remembering one's call means that we understand our work as God's invitation to a task. This sense of call answers the question, "Whose work is it, anyway?" Jesus's testimony, time after time, was that he was on his Father's mission – meaning that his ego was not tied up with his mission. Hear Jesus's words as he talked to his Father just before he faced the cross: "I have brought you glory on earth by finishing the work you gave me to do."[143] Remembering one's call to be a healer can renew and strengthen a sense of direction.

Focusing on What Is Important

Rachel, the therapist in our story, took on too much. She could not distinguish between what was simply a good opportunity and what was the most important thing for her to do. The curse of many efficient people is taking on too much, and lacking the discipline to say "No." Huggett and Huggett write that Jesus has set for us an example of *refusing the tyranny of the urgent*: "The example Jesus sets presents a challenge to those of us who find ourselves overwhelmed by work, [and] over-stimulated by people and ideas."[144] We are told that very early in the morning, Jesus went up to the hills to pray, after a hectic day of healing many and driving out demons.[145] He sought solitude and focus. The disciples came to him with the news, "Everyone is looking for you!" Instead of going back to the place of ministry where he had astounded many with his teaching and his demonstrations of power over evil, his answer was, "Let us go somewhere else." Jesus had the inner freedom to say "No." Because he was not in bondage to the need to achieve, he was both free and focused.

Relating to our Faith Communities

Therapists often "graduate" from church life when they complete their training as counsellors and become busy meeting people's needs. However, relationships with Christian brothers and sisters can motivate the individual towards purposeful living as well as create community where accomplishments can be celebrated. Africans believe that shared successes become more meaningful. Indeed, a Ugandan proverb states: "People are like cloths. Wrap yourself with them."[146] Jesus modelled the need to build a team, calling and training his disciples to co-own his vision. Jesus loved his disciples,[147] called them friends,[148] ate with them,[149] prayed for them,[150] walked with them,[151] and visited with them.[152] He took time to build and maintain relationships.

Accountability and Transparency

It is extremely important for the Christian counsellor to be accountable for how he or she lives. Just as traditional village elders were to live lives above reproach, Christian counsellors, too, are called to display character that is above reproach. They are like letters that are to be openly known and read by everybody.[153] People-helpers in Africa cannot escape the public eye, which demands that they live holistic lives to earn the privilege of helping others with their own lives. Christian counsellors struggle with brokenness just as other people do. However, the way they manage their own problems will model to clients and counselees how to face up to periods of testing.

The Christian counsellor adheres to a biblical value system. This means acting as a follower of Jesus, who illustrates for us God's standards of love, holiness, faithfulness, care for others, self-sacrifice, accountability, genuine commitment, and integrity. How therapists live may provide a model of accountability for those who are counselled. The Christian counsellor remembers that his or her ultimate accountability is not to an employer or counselees, but to God.

Dr Musau, a local psychiatrist, illustrated this sense of accountability. She was beloved by her patients, friends, colleagues, and members of her church. It was obvious that she and her husband cared deeply for their three children. Both spoke regularly at couples' seminars, often reminding people of the cultural riches of practices and rituals that could be utilized within the church to enrich marriages and strengthen parenting skills. The couple had kind words for people of every age group and social status, offering their expertise where needed. Whereas other doctors at her level kept away from the general population, Dr Musau mixed freely with everybody, an attitude that endeared her to the community.

The Discipline of Delegating

Like Jesus, the African Christian counsellor can train others and delegate to them tasks such as mentoring young people, visiting and comforting the bereaved, or spending time with lonely children. Over a period of three years, Jesus recruited, trained, mentored, stretched, empowered, deployed, and evaluated a team that would carry on his work after he was gone. Collins, a proponent of Christian coaching, notes that Jesus prepared his disciples for delegation through coaching: "He held out a vision. He talked in stories. He was a superb listener. He believed in people and gave them opportunities to stretch. He had a band of twelve people who made up his team, and he coached them to try things they'd never tried before."[154] Delegation depends on taking time, investing oneself in others, letting go of control, encouraging beginners, giving honest feedback, and helping people grow.

Knowing One's Spiritual Gift

The Christian counsellor does not possess all the gifts listed in the New Testament. Counselling for emotional healing is only one part of the life of the Christian community. We know that nature involves networks, in which the health of one system impacts the others, and, likewise, illness in one affects the rest. The apostle Paul spoke of networks in his teaching on the body of Christ. To the church in Corinth, he wrote: "You are the body of Christ, and each one of you is a part of it."[155] Each service component is part of the body of Christ, just as the universal church is part of Christ's body. Each component has a specific gift and cooperating with other units does not weaken any organ but rather multiplies its usefulness. When any one person decides to carry the whole burden alone, the result is that the meagre resources available are spread thinly, exhausting the giver and denying others an opportunity to serve.

The Discipline of Spiritual Rest

God rested from his work of creation, and Jesus modelled the importance of rest. O'Donnell and O'Donnell note that the two metaphors of running well[156] and resting well[157] "are the intertwining, balancing concepts . . . foundational for our health throughout the various phases of [the Christian worker's] life cycle."[158] They add that running to win is intertwined with resting to win, and that this must be a discipline, "a personal, community, and specialized practice – an *intentional* practice – to help renew us and to help us remain resilient."[159] The result of following this practice will be that the Christian counsellor is renewed in energy and vision. A tired therapist is not a good healer.

Psychological Disciplines for Managing Stress

To combat stress, we must take care of ourselves physiologically and psychologically as well. The counsellor must understand that the demands of caring for others may often lead to periods of extreme stress, both physical and emotional. Self-care involves the ability to recognize the causes of stress and make necessary changes, both internal and external. Those changes may involve deliberately slowing down, setting and observing priorities, maintaining awareness of one's limits, and developing a sense of worth that is based on who one is, and not what one does.

Stay Physically Fit

First, let us look at the physical self-care of the Christian counsellor. Counsellors who are physically fit are more able to carry the stress of their work. The apostle Paul says: "Do you not know that your bodies are temples of the Holy Spirit, who is in you, whom you have received from God? You are not your own; you were bought at a price. Therefore honour God with your bodies."[160] The teaching here is that our bodies are sacred, and therefore, to be handled with care and respect. This is an aspect of stewardship.

The Christian counsellor must remember that his or her health is an asset to be cared for with absolute commitment. How can we care for the body? Holistic self-care might include aspects such as interspersing activity with rest, eating nutritious food, controlling the intake of caffeine or tea, and getting adequate sleep and exercise.

Mentally Care for Oneself

Next, we need to look at our mental self-care. The Bible admonishes us to care for our minds. "Finally, brothers and sisters, whatever is true, whatever is noble, whatever is right, whatever is pure, whatever is lovely, whatever is admirable – if anything is excellent or praiseworthy – think about such things."[161] Our thoughts have the power to shape us because we slowly adapt ourselves to become what we think.[162] Do not give power to negative thoughts. Negative thoughts can be banished when we replace them with a focus on positive thoughts and, thereby, renew our minds.[163] Regardless of the actual working conditions, the individual's perception of events taking place determines that counsellor's effectiveness. In the community, there may be cruelty, abuse, criticism, unrealistic expectations, favouritism, unbending bureaucracy, and organizational or interpersonal conflicts. The obvious natural reaction is often cynicism, grumbling, murmuring, helplessness, and complaining that drain the mind and cause mental fatigue.

Staying mentally fit means not only monitoring our thought life, but also enriching it. Some healers stop reading in the field of counselling once they have completed graduate training. The competent Christian counsellor, however, will continue to be enriched by reading about new research and therapeutic approaches, as well as biographies, novels, and devotional literature. Our counselees deserve counsellors who are mentally alert.

Care for Oneself Emotionally

Emotional self-care is possible if the counsellor learns to deal appropriately with problematic emotions. Instead of keeping negative affect in our hearts, Peter reminds us to cast "the whole of your care – [all your anxieties, all your worries, all your concerns, once and for all] – on Him; for He cares for you affectionately *and* cares about you watchfully" (AMP).[164] God is always aware of our emotional states, but he needs us to regularly acknowledge and surrender to him all our burdensome emotions, in exchange for peace and joy.

Nurture Relationships

In addition to self-care of the body, mind, and spirit, there are many other things a counsellor can do to manage stress and prevent burnout. A therapist colleague once mentioned that when taking a break with a friend over tea, if the conversation turned out to be entirely about her friend's personal needs, the therapist felt that she had not really had a break. This same therapist returned radiant from another time of tea with an older person. Their conversation had been mutually nourishing, and she was refreshed by it.

The relational style that prepares the Christian counsellor to be a channel of God's healing involves moving towards others with warmth and learning to receive the love of others. If we have learned to receive God's love, it is easier to thank others for the blessing they have been in our lives. Christian counsellors who have been loved will be ready to sacrifice on behalf of those in need and to look for positive aspects of those around them.

Develop a Realistic Workload

Counsellors like Rachel will find themselves with too much to do. Unless they learn the skill of setting limits and maintains a balanced lifestyle, they will easily get frustrated and burned out. Christian counsellors will need to discipline themselves to handle a realistic workload, proportional to their strength and ability. Especially in a period of crisis or in the case of a chronic shortage of staff, one must be careful not give in to peer pressure or idealistic organizational expectations. If in doubt, the counsellor can listen to advice from family, close friends, and the community. For example, if elders among the Meru people of Kenya say in your hearing: *Ai! Ukwina wabucha* ("You've danced yourself to the extreme"), they mean that whatever you are doing, you've done it to excess. The word *Ai* has no translation in English; it simply means, "Stop and listen!"

Set Priorities

Developing the kind of discipline that enables you to commit yourself to the right priorities is important. For example, we can adhere to priorities of obedience and commitment to God, commitment to spouse (if married), to family, friends, work and ministry, in that order. Proper ordering of priorities will reduce the stress that can result from feeling that one should do everything. One cannot do everything. Juggling too much is like trying to eat in two places at once. Once again, a caring community may speak in proverbs in this type of difficulty. Among the Meru, the elders may caution: *Ati, ukaurira magati ta Kiundu*, meaning, "If you do not concentrate on one thing and try to do everything, you will get lost in the middle like Kiundu." Kiundu, the tale goes, tried to eat in two villages at the same time! Doing the best in the areas of life to which one has committed oneself will reduce stress.

Select a Mentor

We cannot emphasize strongly enough the importance of having a mentor. Here is a suggested list of qualities for a counsellor's counsellor: The mentor is a mature, committed Christian – a person of the Word, of prayer, a burden bearer, and Spirit-filled. As far as possible, the mentor is of the same sex as the counsellor, unless the relationship involves couples. He or she could be around the counsellor's age, and not more than 10 years older. This puts the mentor and counsellor in the same range of experiences and development, which is especially important in cultures where young people cannot easily correct an older person. The mentor should be someone who is willing to take time to be a good listener, affirmer, and encourager. The responsibility here is mutual. Finally, we encourage counsellors to safeguard such relationships with much care. They are rare, very precious, and take a long time to develop and flourish.

Seek Supervision

We strongly recommend supervision for the counsellor by another qualified counsellor, either individually or in groups. The time spent with a supervisor per counselee should be at least one to two hours for every ten client hours. When beginning one's work as a counsellor, the more time spent with a supervisor, the better. The Christian counsellor must be accountable to a professional who adheres to the practices and ethics of Christian counselling. This requirement can be explained through the Ki-Meru African proverb: *Guti njau iicunaga mugongo*, meaning, "No calf can lick its own back. It must depend on its mother."

Seek Spiritual Direction or Personal Counselling

Counsellors provide counselling, but does the counsellor ever see another counsellor? This is an important question. Counsellors bring to the consulting room all of their own personal problems. Sometimes, those problems get in the way of good care for the counselees. Take Rachel, for instance. Therapists are sexual beings and may become attracted to a client. Rachel's feelings for her client could well have been discussed in personal therapy. The therapist is not a perfect person but one who is in process, aware of his or her own weaknesses and, most important of all, hopefully, addressing these weaknesses. For this reason, professional counsellor training programmes often require that the trainee go through personal therapy before graduation.

Care from the Organization

While it is important that counsellors take care of themselves, it is equally crucial that organizations take care of their counsellors. Organizations ought to make sure that staff members take annual leave, that the work schedule and job expectations are manageable, that resources are available as needed, that conflict is resolved, and that channels for expressing grievances are in place. It is important that programmes for staff motivation are included in organizational management, that salaries are paid on time, that resources are available to meet basic staff needs, and that workers are trained in recognizing and avoiding stress and burnout. The organization should also examine its communication patterns with staff to avoid ambiguity, show appreciation and encouragement to staff, and provide crisis debriefing teams to provide aid to workers after any critical incident. Regular individual and organizational evaluation will ensure healthy growth, promote positive changes, and increase awareness of factors that might cause stress and destabilize the organization.

Sadly, the focus for many Christians in ministry, as well as for the organizations that employ them, is on productivity, performance, evaluations, timelines, numbers of people served, reports, and more reports. While we work closely with many community-based organizations, relief and development agencies, churches, NGOs, and corporate groups, we are surprised at how many such organizations do not provide holistic care for staff. Such negligence negatively impacts staff so much that personnel turnover is common. When one staff member *burns out*, another is recruited, and the former employee leaves the organization – often with much bitterness.

As professionals and staff in the field advocate for better organizational staff care, individuals – including counsellors in professional practice – do well to make sure that they are proactive in self-care, so that they can continue to work without stress or burnout.

Conclusion

In this chapter, we have discussed three types of care to avoid burnout and ward off damaging stress. First, in self-care, we remind the Christian counsellor that closeness to one's indigenous culture, as well as personal commitment to biblical disciplines of service and regular professional supervision, will offer continued inner support. Secondly, we have emphasized that beyond individual care, we should care for each other through accountability and bearing each other's burdens. Finally, in organizational care, the church as well as service institutions should have inbuilt systems of caring for staff so that people do not burn out in ministry.

We have emphasized that in the ministry of caring for other people, we can easily burn out from too much stress – especially when we neglect our own needs and those of our close support systems in favour of the people we serve. We have noted that African indigenous cultures cautioned against excesses of any kind, and that biblically, we have a mandate to care for our bodies, minds, spirits, and relationships so that we can be fit enough for God to continue to use. Ministry is not about excesses, nor is it about showing off how much one can handle. Such tendencies are often self-focused versus other- and God-oriented. God calls us to serve humanity from a commitment to him rather than to the task at hand.

CHAPTER 5

God's Benevolence and Mass Suffering

Our counselees often ask us, "Why has this bad thing happened?" or "Why must we suffer?" In this chapter, we will seek a deeper understanding of God's benevolence as it relates to mass suffering. To help to answer these questions, we will review some African indigenous views of suffering, explore Christian responses to suffering in Africa, and discuss ways we can address the needs of a person in pain.

Dr Mwiti: Let me tell you what happened to me as I experienced first-hand the suffering of our people. It was 1995. I was on a plane flying into Rwanda. A year before, Rwanda did not exist in my worldview. Yes, I knew that it was a small nation in central Africa with political struggles between the nation's two main tribes, the Tutsi and Hutu.

One year before, the world had watched while these people killed one another in bloodshed that brought back memories of Nazi Germany. As the killings went on, hordes of refugees fled to neighbouring Congo and other nations of Africa. The United Nations and other international groups evacuated their staff from Rwanda, leaving the nation to its own fate. Suddenly, the cameras of the world focused on Rwanda. Television news carried pictures of horror: bodies littering the streets, corpses floating down rivers, heaps of human remains, mass graves, weeping mothers, orphaned children, and raped women.

These images raced through my mind as I looked through the window of my plane that morning in February. It was a clear day. The beauty of Africa spoke to me from below. There was Mount Kilimanjaro to my left, snow-capped and majestic, rising into the African sky. The Rift Valley was spread out like a green sheet to meet the volcanic ranges of western Kenya. Lake Victoria lay like a huge sheet of clear glass, littered here and there with small, beautiful islands. Fishermen's boats sailed below taking in Nile perch and other delicacies from the world's second largest freshwater lake. In southern Uganda, the fertile plateau of eastern Africa reminded me of the *matoke*, the Ugandan banana staple, and the sweet potatoes that had sustained this nation through the evil days of Idi Amin Dada. Then came the long meandering rivers, the edge of central Africa, and the first glimpses of Rwanda, "the land of a thousand hills." Such breathtaking beauty was taking shape below me that I was unprepared for the emotions that overtook me. I could not fathom that in this land of utmost grandeur, of beautiful trees, mountains, rivers, and sunshine, death had come in a season, like a wave that caused brother to turn against brother, to kill, to destroy. I wept over Rwanda. Through my sobs and tears, feelings of absolute helplessness swept over me. Why, God? Why all these deaths? Why Africa? Why me? What could I hope to offer in this place? I felt small, overwhelmed by discouragement and helplessness.

The year before, the United Nations had asked me to work with the expatriate staff they had evacuated from Rwanda five days after the onset of the genocide. For three months, with a team of four other professionals, we completed the job, and then presented our final report. However, while I worked with U.N. staff, my heart broke for the Rwandan people. I kept asking everyone, "What about the horror and trauma of the Rwandan people themselves? Who is helping them to deal with their loss and grief?" I was referred to many groups: The United Nations High Commissioner for Refugees, relief agencies, and church groups. No one seemed to have a mental health intervention plan in place. All they were doing was what they knew best: providing food, shelter, and medicine.

Finally, my husband said to me, "You keep asking others what they are doing about Rwanda. What are you doing yourself?" "Me!" I responded, "I have nothing. Oasis Africa Counselling Centre is a small indigenous organization. I am also an African woman. What can I do?" He looked at me and responded, "I thought that you were a Christian before all those other things." It was then that I took the challenge. Getting on my knees with my faithful, prayerful staff, I began preparing myself, believing that soon God would open the door into Rwanda. And he did. I had already researched and written a crisis counselling training manual for lay counsellors, so I translated it into Kinyarwanda and printed it. Then I sat back and waited.

The Episcopal Anglican Bishop of Kigali Diocese, a man with a heart for his people, had heard about my work. He invited me to co-lead the first Rwandan national pastor's retreat after the genocide for the Episcopal Church. I was to speak on inner healing. On the team was Bishop Kolini, later archbishop of the Episcopal Church of Rwanda. This retreat was to commence our ongoing programme in Rwanda. As we visited memorial sites displaying preserved human remains of men, women, and children with visible machete cuts, nails from the huge clubs still detectable on shrunken skulls, as we equipped trauma counsellors in that nation, and as we helped many to deal with their grief, one of our deepest questions was always, "Why, God?"[165]

Where Is God? An African Question

In every part of Africa, many quietly wonder: Where is God in the midst of pain? Why does God allow death and destruction? Can God see the genocide, AIDS, hunger and famine, immoral governments, and raping of Africa's resources by more powerful nations? These questions ring out from Rwanda to South Africa, from the Sudan to Sierra Leone, from Mozambique to northern Uganda.

So Africa continues to lament. Why is there suffering and evil in the universe of a good God? The actual inquiry is: Why do we suffer? Why does suffering seem to single out black people? God, on whose side are you? Are you black or white, anyway? Set against the context of neocolonialism and North versus South oppression, unequal North/South trade, connived political upheavals, and many deaths from preventable illnesses, African questions about theodicy need urgent consideration because they touch the lives in many tangible ways.

Some of the poorest nations in the world are located in Africa. Many Africans suffer from poverty.[166] Indeed deaths from starvation as well as from lack of medication for the sick have become common, especially with millions dying from malnutrition related to HIV and AIDS. Africa has hordes of refugees: for example, the Dinka of the Sudan have lived in Uganda for many years, and the refugee camp of Kakuma in Kenya contains people of many African nationalities. In northern Uganda, visiting a Dinka refugee camp some years ago, I (Gladys Mwiti) was overcome with sadness at the loss experienced by these tall, proud, nomadic people. Driven from their country by the civil war in southern Sudan, these roamers of grazing lands and proud owners of long-horned cattle were confined to a refugee camp with little to do all day. Their loss included not just family, cattle, property, and a nation, but also a way of life.

African Indigenous Cultural Perceptions of Mass Suffering

Africans believe that in this world evil will always be a reality. People can be possessed to do evil or can displease God, and suffering follows. Rituals restore balance and help to reclaim wellness, whether by cleansing the evil from people or by seeking forgiveness from a wronged God. This approach is essential to the African belief in the presence of God, while acknowledging the presence of good and evil in human history.

We will explore specifically the cultural perceptions of the Meru, with the hope that readers will examine their own indigenous cultures for insights on mass suffering. Among indigenous Meru, the *Mugwe* or "holy man" was akin to a prophet, and thus, was the centre of all Meru social life.[167] The Mugwe's office, a hereditary position, was religious as well as secular. His presence provided structure for work and blessing, a place of refuge where people would be assured of their connection with God. People worked for the Mugwe and protected him. In return, his presence provided a guarantee for the continuity of the community, even in a time of calamity.

Although the Meru people had priests and other leaders, the Mugwe was most significant in the overall relationship of the tribe with God. He spoke the mind of God and reprimanded those who brought calamity on the tribe through their disobedience. The tribe visited the Mugwe as a group to seek blessing, as well as for instruction about what to do in times of crisis. Blessing was the assurance of God's happiness, and disaster would sometimes be seen as a sign of his displeasure. Communal accountability was a means of preventing disaster, while collective penitence was a way of managing calamity.

Prayer became a shared activity when the tribe visited the Mugwe. Together, they owned their traumas, and together they sought God's blessing and intervention. Such communal activity was one of the most poignant sources of social support in times of trauma or blessing for African indigenous societies. The Mugwe blessed the country and prayed:

Kirinyaga, mwene into bionthe,
"Kirinyaga, owner of all things,
ndakuthaitha umpe mabatara jakwa
I pray Thee, give me what I need,
ni untu ndina thina,
because I am suffering,
na antu bakwa,
and also my children [are suffering]
na into bionthe biria biri
and all the things that are ...

nthiguru iji yakwa.
in this country of mine.
Ndakuromba utuuro,
I ask for a good life,
 buria bwega buri na into,
a good blessed life,
antu babega bati murim[o],
healthy people with no disease,
ba[gu]ciara [a]ana [babe]ga.
may they bear healthy children.
Na kinya aka baria barikitie
And also women who suffer
kuthata, uingure njira . . .
because they are barren, open the way
bone twana.
by which they may [have] children.
Mburi, ng'ombe, irio, mauuki.
[Give] goats, cattle, food, honey.
Na kinya mathina ja ntere ingi
And also the troubles of other lands
iria ntikumenya, urite.
That I do not know, remove."[168]

In his prayer, the Mugwe asked God to ease the suffering of people in other lands and asked that the poor would prosper. He prayed to ward off natural disasters, famine, invasions, and epidemics that threatened human survival.[169] The Mugwe advised people to labour, to practice thrift, to be generous both to each other and to the animals (even those in the wild), to avoid laziness, and to practice industry.

In times of calamity, it was the responsibility of the Mugwe, diviners, and community leaders to ask God where society had gone wrong, and why people were suffering. To seek answers to these questions, it was common practice for the tribal elders to go up a mountain for days of prayer and sacrifice.[170] Women would sing *Thathaiya Ngai, Thai* ("Let us pray [to] God, pray") as they poured out oil made from the castor plant along the path that the elders were walking. The elders moved silently up the mountain, carrying a lamb. The lamb would be sacrificed to God to restore harmony between him and humanity. The group stayed on the mountain for several days. Finally, a horn and a drumbeat signalled their descent. If the prayers were called during a period of drought, for example, the group thanked God when a heavy downpour finally swallowed up the dust and brought the promise of a new harvest. The Meru believed that sacrifice provided a way out of both disharmony and natural calamity.

In the Meru culture, the Mugwe was the father of fathers. These "fathers" included medicine men or tribal doctors who met the needs of the people at the local level by treating illnesses. These fathers also included the *Njuri Nceke* or "council of elders," who provided the social and political organization of the Meru people. Below them were clan elders, who provided grassroots leadership. This intimate connection of the political, social, and spiritual leadership of the people meant that the question of calamity was handled by all of these leaders, asking, "Where have we failed?" Political and social leaders guided the community to explore leadership and social factors. If the problem was a natural calamity, the *Mugwe* offered sacrifices for God's intervention. In other words, people were careful to live as prescribed by the Mugwe and other religious and cultural leaders, interweaving every activity with an awareness of God's presence.

The Story of Faustina

Where is God when we suffer? Does God hear the cries of lament rising from African villages and cities? Just as Jews wondered where God was during the Holocaust, so Africans have wondered about God's presence during the Rwandan genocide. Here is the story of Faustina.

> I remember when life was happy in my village in Cyangugu, in southwest Rwanda. When the harvest was good, there was always plenty to share with everyone, and the village lay in peace and harmony. At 18, I was the favourite of my father, a Tutsi. My mother was Hutu, but this difference did not matter to anyone. There were many other such marriages all over Rwanda. People spoke the same language, ate the same food, and married each other. However, by the beginning of 1994, there was tension in the air, and some families started leaving to live with relatives in areas reputed to be safer.
>
> My father decided to stay. He argued that the south was safer and that little would happen there. However, this was not to be. A week later, killers came by night and the village was surrounded. My family was under attack. The killers seemed to have a list of who would be eliminated. I remember fleeing through the cornfield and coming to a stop only after miles and miles of running and stumbling in the darkness. I dared not call out for fear of getting caught, because I was sure I heard footsteps behind me in the darkness.

Finally, I was too tired to run anymore. I stumbled into a hole in the bushes, and lay there, panting. Tired and spent, I drifted off to sleep.

When I awoke the next morning, I was hungry and thirsty, so I decided to sneak back to my house. What I saw turned my stomach. Our home was a total mess. Blood was all over the place. One by one, I discovered the bodies. My father lay spread-eagled, with a huge gash over his head. My big brother, with a slit throat, lay in his own pool of blood. My two female cousins who had come to visit were in the bedroom. The way their bodies were spread showed that they had been raped, then cut up with machetes. I ran out again, and kept running and running, with inner screams of horror. I thought I was in a dream.

Later, as Faustina sat among eight others in the Oasis Africa trauma counselling healing group, she relived that hellish night. She spoke with sighs and groans, and then would stop and weep awhile. Oasis Africa had trained the counsellors not to interrupt such a narrative. All they did was hand Faustina tissues, hold her while she wept, ask her if she needed some rest, or tell her that she could continue her story when she was ready. She chose to go on each time, feeling the support and empathy of the group.

As Faustina completed her account, surrounded by a group with similar stories of hopelessness and death, she stopped mid-sentence and remarked, "All this time, I kept asking myself, 'God, are you really there? Then why do you not deliver me?' Where was he? Where was God?" An older man who had lost 45 family members said, "I agree with you, Faustina. Where was God when my whole family and village died?"

The training team was silent, waiting. Finally, another older man, Bizimungu from Ruhengeri Prefecture, stood up. His name, Bizimungu, means "He sees me." The old man was tall and gaunt, with a lined face, and grey hair. One fateful night in his city of Butare, a mob set his home on fire, stole all his vehicles, and killed his entire family. Only two teenage sons escaped, and even now Bizimungu did not know of their whereabouts. Maybe they were dead, or in some refugee camp in a foreign nation, or even in prison. He did not know. Yet in his confusion, Bizimungu hung onto his faith: "Where was God, we ask. I believe that God was always there in each of our villages, situations, and conditions. He was weeping with us and holding us to himself." His words echoed African perspectives on theodicy, a subject we turn to next.

An African Theodicy

Old Bizimungu's words echo those from another genocide, on another continent, almost half a century earlier. In his book *Night*, Elie Wiesel, a survivor of the Holocaust, narrates an account of a hanging in a German concentration camp:

> The SS hung two Jewish men and a boy before the assembled inhabitants of the camp. The men died quickly but the death struggle of the boy lasted half an hour. "Where is God? Where is he?" a man behind me asked. As the boy after a long time was still in agony on the rope, I heard the man cry again, "Where is God now?" And I heard a voice within me answer, "Here he is – hanging here on [these] gallows."[171]

Lord, where are you when bad things happen? Questions regarding God's goodness in the presence of evil can be classified within the branch of theology called *theodicy*. Theodicy is defined as "the attempt to affirm divine justice despite the suffering in the world, suffering which so often seems arbitrary and gratuitous."[172] The word *theodicy* was coined by the German philosopher Gottfried Wilhelm Leibniz and is based on two Greek words, *theos* or "God" and *dike* meaning "justice."

In a culture where God is perceived of as all good, mass suffering causes disorientation. For those involved in such suffering, the world becomes disordered. Things become unpredictable. Evil seems to take over, displacing goodness. Confusion reigns where once order triumphed. At such times, what do we do? How shall we understand?

God Is Present

According to African theologian John Mbiti, many African creation myths explained that God created human beings and put them in Paradise.[173] From this view, suffering and pain cannot be attributed to God's presence. Therefore, calamity must be caused by something else outside the scope of God's love and benevolence. Indeed, Mbiti notes that Africans perceive God as kind, loving, comforting, faithful, good, holy, and full of justice. However, he adds: "Among some societies, the experiences of sorrow, misfortune, and calamities are interpreted or explained as signs of the anger of God."[174] Africans are always trying to restore the bliss that was there at Creation. In this context, Muzorewa notes that in trying to establish the origin of good and evil, "Africa[n] traditional religion spends much time dealing with causes and effects of evil."[175] In much African thought, evil is a reality that is present in society, and yet, even in evil times, the God of comfort is near. Indeed, the Akamba of Kenya describe God as *Ngai* or *Mulungu ula ukiakiasya*, meaning "The God who comforts."

A Place for Lament

American theologian Walter Brueggeman[176] notes that the ability of the human heart to cry out unreservedly to God creates the opportunity for a healing relationship between wounded humanity and a caring God. The book of Psalms contains accounts of such deep cries in times of despair. Known as laments, these writings present prayers by both individuals and a whole community. The raw, unrefined cries found in the Psalms remind us that we do not have to package our pain into tidy bundles before we ask God to make sense of disaster. There are many examples of laments in the Psalms:

- ❖ People call for help, crying out: "O Lord!" "My God," "My Deliverer."
- ❖ They cry for his immediate response: "Arise," "Help!" "Save me!"
- ❖ They complain when it feels as if God is too far away and unresponsive: "Why have you forsaken me?" "How long will you hide your face from me?"
- ❖ They ask for, and expect, his intervention: "Be not far from me," "Vindicate me."
- ❖ Sometimes, they rave about those who oppress them: "There is no truth in their mouths."
- ❖ They openly demand that God should punish oppressors: "Let them be put to shame."
- ❖ They declare that they have been faithful and have not gone against God to merit their suffering: "I have walked in my integrity," "They hate me without cause."
- ❖ They confess their sin: "I have sinned against you," "I confess my iniquity."
- ❖ They voice their trust in God's protection: "You are a shield to me."
- ❖ They promise to serve God when trouble is over: "My lips will praise you."

Laments are not a mere mouthing of platitudes or an expression of surface emotions. When people lament, they speak from their hearts, baring their hurt before God, naked and unashamed, transparent before a father who understands and feels deeply for them.

On the Importance of Waiting

The prophet Habakkuk was extremely troubled when God allowed Babylon, a heathen nation, to invade Judah and finally destroy it and take its people captive. Habakkuk had lived in a period when Judah's last four kings had rejected God's law and oppressed their people. He wondered: How can a just God use a wicked nation like Babylon to punish[177] his people? Why is God not answering, even though we keep calling for help?

At times like these, the temptation to give up is intense and can easily lead to despair. However, Habakkuk was not afraid to come to God with his doubts and questions. He found that God did not turn him away. God spoke to him in the midst of pain and confusion. Habakkuk[178] realized that:

- ❖ God is still in control of his world in spite of the apparent triumph of evil.
- ❖ God's timing is not our own. He may seem to disregard sin and sinners, but he is the God of holiness and justice and will surely punish sin one day.
- ❖ He is a powerful God with plans that we cannot see. One day, everything will work together to fulfil his plans.
- ❖ Knowing this, we can run to him as our place of safety. We should not be afraid. God will guard us and protect us for all time.

At the end of his search, Habakkuk affirmed his continued trust in God, even in the middle of calamity:

> Though the fig tree does not bud and there are no grapes on the vines, though the olive crop fails and the fields produce no food, though there are no sheep in the sheepfold and no cattle in the stalls, yet I will rejoice in the Lord, I will be joyful in God my Saviour. The Sovereign Lord is my strength; he makes my feet like the feet of a deer, he enables me to tread on the heights.[179]

For the Glory of God

John tells the story of a man born blind. The Jewish rabbis had developed the principle that "there is no death without sin, and there is no suffering without iniquity." Based on this principle, Jesus's disciples asked: "Rabbi, who sinned, this man or his parents, that he was born blind?" Jesus's answer was, "Neither this man nor his parents sinned,… but this happened so that the work of God might be displayed in him."[180] In this fallen world, innocent people will sometimes suffer. Our focus as Christian counsellors must be less on the reasons for the suffering and more on supporting people as they go through pain.

The African Christian Counsellor and Suffering

We may not have answers to suffering, but we can help to alleviate it through service and presence. In one of the Oasis Africa training seminars in Rwanda, Mujawimana, a man serving on the staff of a Rwandan orphanage, stood up and asked, "Did I do enough?" He explained that while conducting devotions for the children during the previous week, an eight-year-old boy stood up in the middle of the service and asked him, "Mujawimana, tell me, where was God when they cut up my whole family? My Dad is dead, my Mom, too, and my little brother and sister. I ran away and hid in the sorghum plantation. I could hear them searching but they never got me. The night was too dark. Where was God, Mujawimana?"

With bated breath, other seminar participants waited for Mujawimana's answer. Finally, Mujawimana spoke: "I did not say anything to the boy. Instead, I found myself opening my arms, and the child flew into them. As I hugged him, my tears mingled with his. After some time of weeping with him, he left my embrace and sat down again, at peace. I continued with the devotions. Did I do enough?" It seemed that the child was not really looking for a philosophical response. With that embrace and those tears, Mujawimana became a safe place for the young boy. That was all that the little one needed.

So what can Christian counsellors do or say when people ask, "Where is God when we are hurting?" First and foremost, we must be careful not to resort to quick, easy answers in a bid to describe God's role in their suffering. This is because there are no easy answers, and often, the more we struggle with a question, the deeper it becomes. Second, there are many practical things a Christian counsellor can do to help alleviate the suffering experienced by Africa's people and communities. To be most effective, the African Christian counsellor should have specific goals in mind when he or she sets out to help those who suffer.[181] During a disaster, the Christian counsellor can assist with coping, help to rebuild broken trust, affirm indigenous efforts in dealing with loss, provide social support, focus on community practices, and remember special needs. Holism means that the Christian counsellor will keep in mind the need to care for all the areas of the client's functioning and provide referrals for other services as necessary.

Assist with Coping

The counsellor may be able to help a person to cope with a disturbing situation so that as far as possible, the individual can return to an original level of functioning. Counsellors may help counselees to focus on tasks immediately at hand that need to be completed: achieving safety, finding food and shelter, locating missing family members, and obtaining any necessary medical treatment. They may support people as they tell and retell their stories. However, care must be taken that this help does not interfere with the counselees' natural recovery process. Assistance must never be forced on anyone. Let people know the nature of services that are available, so that they can utilize them when needed.[182]

Deal with Negative Affect

To decrease anxiety, pain, and confusion, provide a message of hope. The very presence of the Christian counsellor should communicate encouragement. Note that God's healing flows like a river, and wherever the river goes, everything begins to live.[183] The counsellor will respond to negative affect such as fear, sorrow, grief, discouragement, shame, guilt, hopelessness, and depression.

Process Denial

The counsellor can help the counselee avoid denial. Although many cultures do not know how to deal with pain, the counsellor can encourage people to admit that they are in pain. We can encourage them to lament, as described in the book of Psalms, and remind them that Christian counselling is not a "quick fix" that rushes people through their grief. Staying with the emotionally wounded in their deepest pain and grief is a central part of counselling. The process of healing is as important as the goal of healing.

Help Manage the Crisis

Christian counselling does not end with the healing of wounded hearts. We can teach counselees crisis management and disaster prevention skills. Preventative measures ensure that individuals and communities are not caught unprepared. Counselling is an ongoing ministry that may leave individuals and the community even richer than they were before a crisis. People who have lived through famine in areas prone to drought have learnt how to find water and build irrigation schemes.

Motivate Transformation

We can use biblical teaching as well as appropriate indigenous cultural values to motivate the counselees towards change and transformation. If a disaster has impacted the community, the Christian counsellor's role extends to teaching the community disaster prevention through opening their eyes to factors that have contributed to crises. Transformational healing after tribal animosity includes reconciliation and peace building so as to avoid a repetition of the cycles of civil war.

Rebuild Broken Trust

Our presence in a wounded family or community can act as a catalyst for the rebuilding of broken trust, where there has been betrayal. In Rwanda after the 1994 genocide, one of the greatest causes of pains among counselees and trainers was broken trust. Trust is a gift that enhances community and individual connectedness. When people are wounded, trust is broken. Such people walk around with a huge open wound in their hearts. No one with a physical wound on his chest can freely hug someone else. His desire is to protect the wound. In a similar way, wounds of the heart break trust. It follows that the greatest ministry to those who have suffered loss, including bereavement, is offering to them the comfort of Christ. Comfort enhances healing. Such ministry begins with listening and learning. It's important to begin by identifying a safe, quiet place where counsellors can meet with the wounded and bereaved. Listening to people who have had similar experiences in a group format also provides social support. Groups should be small enough (no more than eight people) for people to build trust and closeness. Group members develop ground rules regarding confidentiality and equal treatment of one another. Counsellors working with traumatized people should obtain specific training in this area, so that they can ably facilitate the group process.

Affirm Indigenous Efforts in Dealing with Loss

To build a resilient community after a disaster, it is important for the Christian counsellor to understand indigenous cultural factors related to the disaster, to know his or her own indigenous culture well, and to be able to utilize community resources that will enhance resiliency and recovery. This also creates an awareness of what elements are biblical and which are strictly cultural. The counsellor can learn about the people before commencing work among them by reading about their culture and asking questions of those who have worked within this context. We must fit our ministry into the already-existing fabric and especially into structures that enhance community resiliency. What rituals do a specific indigenous community utilize after loss and bereavement? How much can these practices be used by the church working within this community? Listening to local people on the part of Christian counsellors will increase the people's sense of support by the church during times of trauma.

Provide Social Support

Research indicates that the traumatic grief experienced by a bereaved person is often moderated by social support.[184] Indeed, the more social support systems that an individual has after a traumatic event, the less damaging the stress and the faster the person's recovery. It is necessary, therefore, to set up social support structures as soon as possible after a disaster, through establishing community support. For example, a counsellor can join others in keeping vigil in the home of the bereaved, create means of meeting the basic needs of the affected person (people), and create community support groups.

Examine Community Practices

Holistic care will also involve the examination of community practices that compromise the emotional health and physical well-being of the bereaved. For example, with so many people dying of AIDS, war, and other diseases in Africa, Christian counselling will have to reach beyond caring for one individual at a time, to focus on the survival and resiliency of the whole community. The African church needs to be challenged to care for those infected by HIV and those affected by and living with AIDS.[185] We can invest effort and resources in teaching fidelity in marriage and chastity in singleness. Caring for the affected will bring up the huge question of what to do with AIDS orphans in a community whose resources are depleted, and whose age-old community structures are broken. Yet, even then, God can use whatever exists to begin rebuilding through us.

Remember Special Needs

The Christian counsellor remembers that wherever displaced people live in crowded refugee camps away from home, work, and property, one will find problems such as idleness, alcoholism and drug abuse, stress, anxiety, depression, conflict in families, antisocial behaviour, attempted suicides, child abuse and abandonment, and poverty. In some countries, refugees may not be welcome, may be rejected outright, and may suffer harassment. This leads to hopelessness and helplessness. Special needs exist among the most vulnerable groups, who form the majority of the population in most refugee camps: young children, often unaccompanied or orphaned, and women. Children are sometimes born out of rapes in refugee camps, as the most vulnerable are taken advantage of in their defencelessness. Other special populations in such camps include child-headed families, where parents are dead or missing; traumatized elders who can no longer give hope to their broken communities; people with disabilities; and idle young people who see no hope in their futures. Trauma counselling programmes should therefore be planned with these needs and populations in mind, with the realization that almost every uprooted person will be grieving some loss or other.

Be Holistic!

In ministering to the uprooted, once again, interventions must be holistic. This approach calls for the church to network with other Christian organizations in refugee camps, so that the needs of the counselees are met in a sustainable fashion. Working teams should be selected to initiate listening meetings with the displaced people for needs assessment. Such interaction creates a partnership, in which the community can nominate individuals from that community to be trained as trauma counsellors and helpers to enhance their own recovery.

Bernadette

We believe that Bernadette's[186] experiences will facilitate your understanding of just how important Christian counsellors can be in helping people who have been traumatized by horrible events. As you will see, counselling helped to ease Bernadette's suffering to such an extent that she was able to go out and help others.

> When the war broke out, I was in Kidaho commune. We heard that the presidential plane had crashed, that the president had died, and that after his death, the killings had immediately started. Because we lived far from the place where killings began, it took two months before our place was affected. When the war finally reached our area, my parents, brothers, and sisters were scattered. Amidst many problems, I joined the crowds walking miles and miles to Zaire as we ran away from the war. I thank God that by God's grace I was eventually reunited with my family in the refugee camps.
>
> After three weeks in Zaire, seeing many die from cholera and exhaustion, a missionary with whom we worked told us that he was going back to Rwanda, and that whoever wanted to could go with him. Although I was very afraid to go back home, I welcomed the opportunity to leave the misery of the camp,

where people were dying in great numbers because of hunger and illness. After crossing the Zaire border, I made my way to Kigali. I was a troubled person with all the memory of suffering that I had experienced and witnessed. There were so many sad people around me.

Finally, I got work with a Christian organization, trying to help people. However, as I shared God's Word, I was always afraid because of the insecurity around us. Fear was all over because we thought that people would be arrested or killed. I could not sleep well and was always anxious with all sorts of physical problems. Most of my colleagues at work were also in the same state. We had no peace of mind. I kept seeing images of dead or dying people all around me. Then I was appointed by my organization to attend the Oasis Africa trauma counsellors training in 1996.

During the first seminar, I was helped by what Dr Mwiti taught us. As I listened to her, I realized that I was emotionally traumatized. Later on, in the debriefing groups, I was able to tell my story for the first time since the onset of the genocide. Among a caring group of other traumatized people, I related what had happened to me. I emptied my heart of all the many months of pain. It was as if a heavy burden was lifted off my heart. God healed me and my heart was free. My fear was gone, my illnesses taken away, and horror was replaced with hope and a quiet assurance of his presence in me. What God has done for me has stimulated me to seek to help others in my community. Before I attended the first Oasis Africa seminar, some of us in our church had set up a reconciliation programme because we were concerned about the anger and bitterness in our community. However, all of us were sick people, the blind trying to lead the blind. Fortunately, three of us from my community came to the Oasis Africa training seminar, and God touched all of us. We sat together during that week and made a plan about how to take the message of change and hope back to our church and community. Our goal was inner healing and reconciliation. With the help of some Christian organizations, we began a series of similar seminars in all areas where our church operates. Using the Oasis Africa manual, we trained more people to help us. After taking them through the healing process, they, too, joined us in our work. Together, we reached more than 1,500 persons through seminars and church groups and those people, also, are helping others, beginning with members of their own families. We have also set up a permanent committee, which has responsibility for coordinating both training and follow-up in our church. The committee members travel from region to region, overseeing the effectiveness of this work of healing and transformation, as well as training more trainers and counsellors. We thank God for the power of healing that he has released among us, and for the gift of Oasis Africa, which has provided regular supervision and training materials.

Conclusion

Bishop Desmond Tutu believes that African traumas are a liberation theology issue. More than from any other type of theology, Tutu says the understanding of God's love for Africa must emerge from a "crucible of human suffering and anguish."[187] In Africa, he notes, people cry out: "Oh, God, how long?" "Oh God, but why?" He continues:

And so, liberation theology is really a theodicy. It seeks to justify God and the ways of God to a downtrodden and perplexed people so that they can be inspired to do something about their lot. Those who suffer so grievously have not usually doubted that there is a God. They have not even doubted that such a God is a living God, a powerful God, and a God of righteousness and goodness. It is precisely because they have believed that their perplexity has arisen: if they had not believed, there would be no need of a theodicy. If they believed that God was neither good, nor loving, nor powerful, then there would be no problem. There would just be the brute fact of their suffering forming part of the givenness of a truly harsh reality.[188]

Africa continues to lament.

CHAPTER 6

Building Resilient Communities

Wars, disasters, famines, and epidemics destroy communities. What was patiently created over centuries can be destroyed in days and weeks. In the past, African rural communities stored grain in barns after the harvest in case of drought and famine, but resiliency is compromised when the land is not even tended. When there is famine and reserves are used up, the balance and stability of the community is shaken. When leaders are absent or unfaithful, the community is weakened and becomes fragile. As resiliency is compromised, recovery becomes more difficult because vulnerabilities increase, and remedies decrease.

In this chapter, we focus on building resilient communities. How do Africans reconstruct broken communities? How can existing communities develop the resiliency to rebound from the effects of war and disease, and even from the social threats posed by Western consumer culture? First, what do we mean by *resilience*? This term refers to a community's ability to swing back towards health and wholeness after a period of destabilization.[189] Resilient communities have resources that help them to readjust. Indeed, resilience, a factor as old as humankind, has helped many communities to survive in spite of calamities.[190]

The "Crunch" model suggests that a disaster may occur when a hazard meets a vulnerable situation, since "people are vulnerable when they are unable to adequately anticipate, withstand, and recover from hazards."[191] In this model, various factors influence vulnerability: fragile economies where people have no credit or savings; dependence on a few natural resources; lack of skills; physical illness; living with the AIDS pandemic; disorganized, fragmented communities; or poor leadership.

We begin this chapter with a story of a pastor in a community with little resilience, and one of his parishioners, Monica. Mariko was the pastor of the church in Maitoni village. One morning, he sat in his small office deep in thought, reflecting on the happenings of the day before. Monica, a deeply devoted church member, had come to see him with a sad story that was similar to many that he had heard recently. Monica was a widow. Her husband had lived away from home, working on a tea plantation, for many years, returning home only once a month. The tea plantation did not have any accommodations for families, and so administrators discouraged the workers from bringing their families to live with them. Most of the men who left home to seek work in such places left their wives behind to keep their families going as well as they could.

Things were never this way in the past. Then, families worked on the farms together, the men with their chores and the women with their responsibilities. Children were raised communally, with the whole village teaming up to ensure their upbringing. This is the origin of the African saying, "It takes a village to raise a child."

When Westernization came, things changed. Those who went to school received minimal training and hence, money became crucial for survival. Traditional foods were devalued. Women sold eggs in the market and bought doughnuts for their children. People ate bread instead of yams and sweet potatoes. Many of these new foods cost money, and there was never enough money. For this reason, many men left the village to look for wealth on the plantations or in the cities.

Like other women whose husbands worked away from the village, Monica toiled from sunrise to sunset. She bore eight children – all conceived during her husband's brief visits to the family. She was a hardworking, faithful woman, who laboured without grumbling. She tilled the land, harvested the crops, and made sure the children were fed and that they attended school. She milked the cow and participated in village activities including church life and community groups. Her energy was unending.

Eventually, Monica began to worry about her husband. He came home rarely, and, in the end, she learnt that he had a concubine at the tea plantation. After two years of brief communication, he came home ailing, and finally passed away. Over the years, four of Monica's sons left home soon after high school to look for work in the city. They hardly came home, since with their meagre income, they could not afford regular transportation to the village. One son became a headmaster in a distant primary school and was busy raising his own family. Monica's eldest daughter married, but two daughters became pregnant in their teenage years and were raising their fatherless children in their mother's home. From time to time, those daughters left to look for work, and Monica was left to care for her three grandchildren. Monica's youngest daughter was still in primary school.

At last, Monica came in tears to see Pastor Mariko. She had been ailing for a long time, and finally, the doctors told her that she had a fatal disease. What was she to do? Where was the fruit of her many years of labour? Pastor Mariko knew a number of families like Monica's in the village. The women could hardly hold things together anymore. In the past three years, the AIDS epidemic had finally arrived in the village. The young men who had lived in the city had started coming home to die, as well as some of their fathers, who had taken concubines in the city or on the plantations.

For the first time Pastor Mariko realized that local children were beginning to lose both parents, and that the children's relatives were either dead or unable to help. What was going to happen to the village? In the past, funerals were community affairs, but there were too many these days, and people were too sick to be able to tend the ailing, much less to attend their funerals. Many farms were turning into bush, because there were no longer enough people to work the land. Pastor Mariko suddenly felt all alone. He had talked to the local government councillor representing the village, and also to their Member of Parliament. But these politicians had disappeared from the village as soon as they were voted into office and had come back several years later only to ask for re-election – based on what would turn out to be more empty promises.

The village pastor suddenly felt that the burden of caring for this flock was too heavy for him to bear. Pastor Mariko had his own family to think of. Thankfully, his devout wife was supportive of him and the children were doing alright. A peaceful marriage and stable children were the pastor's sources of strength. His abiding faith was that God was fully aware of these struggles in Maitoni village.

Community Resiliency in African Indigenous Cultures

The Christian counsellor can take encouragement from the fact that African communities have been relatively resilient; otherwise, they would have vanished long ago. There are a number of reasons why African communities have maintained resiliency. For communal survival, leaders have protected village unity, utilized collective wisdom, encouraged industry, protected the environment, and taken care of the less fortunate. Society has mandated that leadership be accountable to God, and that they institute actions to prevent disaster, as well as develop long-term programmes for the training of children and young people.

Protection of Village Unity
Tribal organization among the Meru created a cohesive, united society, which was one of the elements that provided resources that protected them from extinction.

The Meru people did not have a king. Instead, each clan was led by a council of elders. They controlled all of the corporate activity of the clan, both within the clan and in relation to other clans.[192] What assured the tribe of survival and enhanced community resiliency? There was unified action – be it for law reinforcement, protection of the tribe from marauding forces, or the passing of knowledge from one generation to the next. In addition, society ensured mutual adherence to a set of common rules for moral conduct regarding marriages and family relationships. There was common observance of rituals related to the beginning and end of life, as well as prayer for God's benevolence. The tribal judiciary, or *kiama*, was empowered to pass judgement after a crime, and the community adhered to the decisions of this legal body. In other words, chaos was discouraged and set patterns of counsel were honoured. Freedom was allowed, as long as respect for the well-being of the whole body was maintained.

Communal Wisdom

Among the Meru, the *agambi* were the "elders," the actual leaders of the tribe.[193] They possessed the wisdom that was able to influence the decision-making of the rest of the eldership. These individuals were not elected, but emerged because of their giftedness right from childhood, demonstrating above average skills, intelligence, and integrity. The Meru loved and endorsed wisdom. Those who listened to the wise were known to thrive, and those who ignored them usually failed. Ability to seek and adhere to the *kwathwa* ("counsel") of the elders was considered a measure of maturity. The richness of this counsel provided for community resiliency.

Encouragement of Industry

The Meru valued industry and hard work. From childhood on, children were trained to work rather than sit around.

> *Dr Mwiti*: My mother, for example, was an illiterate woman, but she had a work schedule with clear duties for each of her eight children with chores appropriate to their ages. The night before would be the time to communicate duties for the following day. My mother gave assignments, and she supervised. We had plenty of time to play – but when it was time to work, it was time to work.
>
> Among the Meru, people were not supposed to sit around telling stories during the day. Instead, folk tales were told around the fire in the evening, as children waited for food to cook. While we waited with rumbling tummies,

stories would start, as mother roasted potatoes or bananas for the very hungry young ones. We were warned that we would grow a monkey tail if we listened to folk tales during the day. Enterprise and industry were taught and rewarded, and this healthy attitude fed into community resiliency.

Environmental Protection

The Meru people protected wetlands, forests, lakes, rivers, the soil, and the whole environment. No one was allowed to cultivate near particular swamps, since these were viewed as containing holy water. In a similar fashion, trees were handled with respect; for any one tree cut down, ten or more would be planted. The soil was kept fertile by letting it lie fallow, as well as by using compost and animal manure. This practice abides to this day, and as a result, the Meru District looks like a forest from the air. Cultivation close to riverbeds was outlawed and only certain crops (like tubers) could be grown there. The burning of bush land was prohibited. People believed that whatever you take from the land must be put right back. Environmental protection ensured community resiliency.

Care for the Less Fortunate

We have already seen that people in traditional African societies shared liberally with the less fortunate. There was always something for someone who had less. Even to this day, neighbouring tribes, especially the Kikuyu of Kenya, have a saying about the plentiful food served by the Meru. Whenever anyone serves masses of food, the Kikuyu say, *No Meru inginiina ici*, meaning "It's only the Meru who can eat up this much food." This is not because the Meru people eat so much, but because they prepare food for all those present at a meal and also for all who might walk in. Such has been the wealth of community sharing and caring for the less fortunate. Resilient communities have resources and are willing to share them.

Dr Mwiti: My mother modelled this for us. We would prepare a meal for twice the size of our family, and, because our home was just behind a shopping centre, people coming to the market would drop in throughout the day. There would always be something for them. My mother practiced both biblical hospitality and traditional care for the less fortunate. Stragglers who inhabited any market location, the mentally ill, the developmentally challenged, the old and lame, all found a place at my mother's table. She also gave and gave from her pantry. I recall many times when a child would come with an empty calabash: "My mother says, 'Please give us some cooking oil.'"

> My mother would always oblige. She was so loved by the less fortunate, and we never lacked. We would give away the last grain of sugar, and a few minutes later, an old man my mother had fed yesterday would arrive with a load of yams to say thank you.

Accountability to God

The Meru of Kenya felt a sense of accountability to God because he created them, delivered them from slavery in a place called *Mbwaa*, and guided them from a place far away to their present land. This sense of indebtedness made them accountable to the Creator. A sense of accountability to God meant that the people were careful to follow whatever God laid down for them as standards of behaviour. Since God was represented among the Meru by the Mugwe,[194] the Mugwe provided standards for land care, agricultural activity, and other skills. For example, he taught the Meru the value of honey and care for bees, as well as harvesting techniques. Each age group received appropriate training in work, such as soil care and bee keeping, and learned about medicines for the healing of various ailments. In this way, God was understood to be present to bless, teach, guide, reprimand, and preserve society through the Mugwe and other leaders who were subservient to him. Everything was founded on a sense of accountability – not to humans, but to the divine. Such accountability to God created community resiliency.

Accountable Leadership

Within the Meru culture, there was a system which "produced judges, teachers, politicians, philosophers, technicians, medicine men, and religious leaders like prophets who led and maintained the society together against many odds like diseases, epidemics, inclement weather, attacks by enemies, and other calamities."[195] A traditional legal system emphasized the quality of leadership and maintained justice among the Meru. Legal matters were to be mastered by each age group, so that all levels of leadership would observe justice. For example, there were laws regarding the protection of land and other property, marriage, and debt repayment. Leadership selection among the Meru was not by appointment or electioneering. Instead, people grew into leadership through a consistent demonstration of gifts and abilities. Recognition of natural gifting reduced conflict, and created respect for and sustainability in leadership positions, protecting the community. Strong leadership created resilient communities.

Prevention of Disaster

Prevention of disaster involved a range of issues from simpler ones like childcare to major matters such as war and community survival. For example, boys in particular loved tree climbing and exploration, but some trees, like the castor oil plant, were not strong enough to support a child's weight. To make sure that the boys kept away from this tree, they were told that this plant was out of bounds – and if anyone broke this rule, he would be fed with soup made out of *kiumbu* or chameleon. No one could imagine something that horrible!

A more serious matter was food security. Besides storing grain for hard times, the Meru were known for growing *nkwa* or "yams." This ensured that there was a supply of yams during times of famine. Breaking any of the tribal rules regarding food was so serious that folklore abounds with examples of those who behaved in ways that jeopardized survival.

The Imenti, a sub-tribe of the Meru, have a story of a clan that was given a derogatory name because of their greed and self-centeredness.[196] It is said that during a time of drought and famine, people used up all the food, including grain reserves. Afraid for the future, the *kiama* or council of elders decided that each family would set aside some seed grain, so that this could be planted when the rains came. The seed was collected and hidden high up in a holy tree, which no one was even supposed to approach. However, late one night, a family afraid of starvation and death cut down the tree, stole the seed, and used it for food. From then on, they were cursed, and called *Mbura ya Kaau – Kaau* being the family name, and *Mbura* referring to a curse of annihilation for abhorrent behaviour. Such observances involved united action, which ensured the society's survival and strengthened community resiliency.

Training of Children and Young People

Passing on the tribal heritage from generation to generation was a major concern among the Meru. Along with informal instruction through tales and proverbs, there was also institutionalized training. Both Mwiti[197] and Bernardi[198] write of an educational system that originated from childhood and was managed in stages until old age. Underlying this formal training was the concept of the age group. Mwiti writes: "People of the same age group refer to themselves as *aba* or 'comrade,' *mutanocia* or 'brother,' and *mwarocia* or 'sister.' They begin life together and they grow up together. The Ki-Meru saying 'grow with your age group' is a force that pulls one age group together because they are trained together, circumcised together, and bring up children together."[199]

This system of training younger generations created a positive peer group that assured each individual of not only accountability, but also of mutual affirmation, identity, and group support at each stage. In the next chapter, we shall discuss more on child training and age groups among the Meru of Kenya. This passing on of traditions from generation to generation preserved positive elements that provided for societal bonding, conservation of tribal value systems, and community resilience.

> *Dr Mwiti*: It is true that much change has come to Africa. We Meru are a poor representation of the once-gallant tribe of the Mountain. However, we still bear the name, Meru, and can bear no other. Within us is a collective sense that maintains some of the precious values that God stamps in each of our hearts such that wherever we are, whatever we become, we long for the authenticity of our roots. This is why our children, although living in faraway nations, will at some time return to ask, "Mama, tell me about our people." As the winds of poor identity blow the family and individuals hither and thither, people long for the values that helped their ancestors to survive, although they had not as much as entered the door of a modern classroom. This is our indigenous psychology of survival.

Biblical Perspectives on Community Resiliency

There are many biblical perspectives on how communities can become resilient. One way of viewing God's work in the world is the creation of a people, not simply of individuals. For example, the Hebrew people were foretold to Abraham, delivered from Egypt, and given a land. They appointed kings and were alternately faithful and unfaithful to God. They were almost extinguished when taken into captivity. But thanks to leaders such as Nehemiah, the community was restored. The African indigenous Christian counsellor is one who can recognize what contributes to community degeneration and to community regeneration.

Watching for Degeneration

Like the elders of the past, counsellors are called to be watchmen for African society. This means that advocacy for the weak and care for the environment is not an option, but a requirement for those who speak God's voice in the world. God told Ezekiel, "Son of man, I have made you a watchman for the people of Israel; so hear the word I speak and give them warning from me."[200]

Prophets were spiritual watchmen, not just warning people, but also gauging the climate of the community, noting what was going wrong and what was missing, and helping people to see dangers before they arrived. It follows that if Christian counsellors are placed in the category of watchers, they must work to remain in "high places," i.e., lifted above the crowds spiritually, so that they can be prophetic. They must have the boldness to call leaders to accountability whenever community resilience is threatened. To be discerning, watchmen need to know what they are looking for, to interpret what they see once they find it, and then to formulate a strong response.

Watching for degeneration means being aware of the negative effects of the "powers of this dark world and . . . the spiritual forces of evil in the heavenly realms."[201] In his book *Unmasking the Powers*, Walter Wink[202] describes *powers* as systems that maintain evil and brokenness in any community. He advises that unless they are unmasked and named, the powers that destroy community wellness will remain unconscious, with the capacity to destroy quietly and surely. Wink suggests that these powers include political policies that encourage repression, economies that impoverish and imprison, financial systems that encourage laziness and corruption, educational institutions that do not equip people for life, ideologies that do not set people free, and theologies that do not bring salvation and healing. Wink believes that those powers have the capacity to constrain us and lead to massive damage that can destroy our very foundations, and in turn, compromise community resilience.[203]

Christian counsellors in Rwanda, for example, must first have an understanding of the roots of the country's ethnic conflict, if they are to help rebuild and restore community wellness. The initiation of the 1994 genocide was not in the killing that started that gloomy April night. The foundations of society began to crack there almost sixty years earlier, when the Belgian reforms of 1926-1931 were put in place, beginning the creation of modern Rwanda. This kind of colonial meddling is the basis of many of the problems that we see across Africa today. In Rwanda, the Belgian reforms created a centralized, efficient, neo-traditionalist, and brutal system. There was forced labour, excessive taxation, unpaid mass mobilization for public works – and beatings for those who did not comply with orders. Deprived of all political power and exploited by the Tutsis, the Hutus began to believe that they were inferior. Fuelled by bitterness and anger, the stage was set for years of revenge, an unending feud that has pitted Tutsis and Hutus against each other, brother fighting brother. In situations like these, seeds of discord grow deep roots and to terrible heights.[204] Watchers for degeneration might have noticed this situation before it was too late.

What powers are at play when communities are threatened and devastated? Wink is convinced that "these Powers are heavenly and earthly, divine and human, spiritual and political, invisible and structural, and [they] are both good and evil."[205] The author continues to argue that any inner and outer manifestation of power, especially oppressive domination such as what Rwanda has known through her history, eventually becomes demonic "principalities and powers" affecting political systems, spiritual institutions, and individual lives through philosophy, tradition, rituals, and religion.[206] This kind of truth may begin to dawn upon Christian counsellors in any African church that finds herself immersed within a repressive, authoritarian system.

The Christian counsellor is one who can recognize the destructive influence of "masked" powers in a community. When the negative effects of the powers are subconsciously repressed, chaos reigns in the community, because people's motives are hidden, and they appear to wear masks. No one seems to know where the problems are coming from. Darkness settles in and people begin to lose a sense of direction. In this type of confusion, people desire to make some order out of the chaos, so that they can tell themselves that they really know what is wrong. In a bid to explain the source of the evil that is threatening their very foundations, they create a scapegoat in an attempt to recover their communal unity.

What is a scapegoat? This is "a person bearing the blame for the sins, shortcomings, etc., of others, especially as an expedient."[207] Let us take the story of the Gerasene demoniac healed by Jesus as a possible story of scapegoating.[208] Wink traces the history of the Gerasene community, which was first colonized by the Greeks, then by the Romans, and finally placed under Syrian control by Emperor Pompey in 63 BC.[209] There was much cruelty as Rome sought to subjugate the people. The locals watched their "freedoms stifled, first by the Ptolemies, then by the Seleucids, then by the Jews, finally, by Herod."[210] Any dissension was silenced. In one incident, 1,000 young people were killed and villages burnt to restore control. Such domination was followed by mass repression and, to manage the conflict of loyalties, scapegoats were needed to cope with the repressed hurts and traumas. In Gerasa, the demoniac became the scapegoat that people could use, projecting on him their own fears. The "possession" of the demoniac represents the communal pathology. The "demon" goes public in "collective possession." Wink argues that a repressive nation cannot face its own illness.[211] Instead, it makes scapegoats of any who have been marginalized, and these people are driven out, excommunicated, or stoned to death. Such a nation seeks to purge itself through scapegoats. These are difficult issues, all which church leadership across Africa needs to begin to address. Christian counsellors, or "watchmen in high places," are one of the groups that God can use across struggling communities in Africa. Wink believes that the only way to engage the powers is to first take time to rigorously examine ourselves.[212] Without this self-examination, Christians can behave exactly like the powers they are supposed to engage, thus becoming agents of those same powers.

> *Dr Mwiti*: Soon after the Rwanda genocide, and during Oasis Africa's trauma counsellors' training programme there, I began to notice that in their fervent song and dance (Rwandans are graceful, spontaneous, and passionate in worship), most songs were about going to heaven, because many people found it difficult to face their pain and hopelessness. Understandably, in those early days, so close to the horrible memories of blood and death, many found it easier to engage in denial. It is easier to think of a safe haven in heaven than to ask difficult questions such as "Why the genocide? What factors eroded community resilience until massive annihilation was the only solution? Where did we fail in creating a cohesive Rwanda? What pain am I carrying myself, and how can I be healed so that I can become an open channel of healing for my people?"

Wink warns us that the destructive powers we see in the community were once good, but now are fallen, and so must be redeemed. He cautions, however, that unmasking a dominating system includes the uprooting of propaganda. For example, Prunier[213] writes that the killings in Rwanda were referred to as *umuganda* or "collective work," the chopping up of people as "bush clearing," and the slaughtering of women and children as "pulling out the roots of bad weeds." This propaganda effectively used peasant language as a means of sowing delusions in the minds of each ethnic group.

Facilitating Regeneration

Emotionally wounded people who have lived through the mass disasters in Rwanda, southern Sudan, Sierra Leone, and many nations devastated by AIDS, do not have the energy to rebuild broken communities. Christian counsellors can be agents that God can rely on to facilitate the regeneration of struggling communities in Africa. Sometimes, counsellors may feel that they have so little to give. However, "it is in the very act of giving, often from our own poverty, that we begin to catch a glimpse of a whole new dimension of life. As we are rubbed raw by the pain of others, we become aware of our own healing gifts – gifts we never dreamed we possessed."[214]

From the Garden of Eden, we see that God created the world with all we need for people, animals, and communities to survive as long as we do not destabilize its balance through sin, neglect of our duties, hatred for our neighbour, and disregard of the environment. In other words, creation provided the resources necessary for holistic survival. Similarly, God provided the means of assuring and restoring community wholeness from one generation to another. Where people broke his law, communities disintegrated and died out.

God restores balance by supporting and advocating for the dispossessed, the orphaned, the widowed, the poor, and those not receiving justice. In the Old Testament, God's first requirement of kings and judges was that they protect the powerless against all who would exploit them; "Defend the weak and the fatherless; uphold the cause of the poor and the oppressed. Rescue the weak and the needy."[215] God literally throws in his lot with the powerless.

Counselling for Peace

One major calling for the African Christian counsellor is to counsel for peace. How can Christian counsellors help the church to become the conscience of each nation to prevent future disasters involving scapegoating and abuse of power? The silent war in southern Sudan, one example of such a disaster, caused massive problems with dislocated communities, abused women, orphaned children, and a complete breakdown of infrastructure.[216] Counselling for peace means liberation from delusional assumptions that have chained Africa for generations.

If healing for the nations is to begin in the household of faith, the church must be actively involved in the process of engaging the powers so as to transform them into divine instruments. The first step in this task is to refrain from repaying evil for evil, regardless of what people have done to hurt us.[217] Second, Wink advocates Jesus's powerful model of non-violence, reiterating that Christ does not speak of inaction or overreaction, capitulation or murderous counter-violence. Jesus goes beyond that to a new response, fired in the crucible of love, which aims to liberate the oppressed from evil and the oppressor from sin. Are Christian counsellors prepared to be obedient to our Lord's call to love our enemies, and to make that a part of our counselling?

After discerning the powers that are holding the community captive, the Christian counsellor needs to become an agent of breaking the chains of inheritance that continue to link each new age group with the traumas and wounds of past generations. In Rwanda, for example, fallen powers were passed on subconsciously from generation to generation. In situations like these, hatred is perpetuated as children are taught to study war and to distrust the other side. The Christian counsellor begins counselling for peace by teaching people to put off hatred, laziness, ignorance, corruption, and self-centeredness, and instead to embrace love, enterprise, industry, integrity, and other-centeredness. The cross of Jesus breaks barriers. After naming or identifying the powers that have undermined the life of the community, the Christian counsellor serves as a catalyst in the process of engaging the spiritual Powers of Peace.

Advocating for the Poor

Christian counsellors must become advocates for the weak and helpless. Jesus spoke as a prophet, castigating the corrupt systems of the day, and also as a voice for the weak and the poor. This kind of advocacy not only raises awareness of the weak and marginalized but also empowers the voice of Christians, inspiring them to speak against exploitative practices. Such commitment becomes a major contribution towards community resiliency, empowering the weak and calling the strong to account. In his book *Rich Christians in an Age of Hunger*, Ronald Sider[218] criticizes rich Christians, especially those in powerful nations, who may be tempted to live as though in a bubble, totally disconnected from the realities of the larger world. Oblivious to the suffering masses, they pursue pleasure and leisure, while the rest of the world struggles to survive. Sider addresses his book to such Christians, arguing that Christians are called not only to a new life of simplicity, but also to one of stewardship and caring. With so much that God has given materially to Western nations, leaders of Bread for the World note that the United States spends less than 1 per cent of its budget on foreign aid and loans.[219]

Sider examines world hunger, pointing out an uneven distribution of resources resulting in poverty and food scarcity in developing nations. He links poverty to other evils such as illiteracy, poor healthcare, and disease. He challenges affluence, advertising that closes people's eyes to the needs of others, and the rationalization that justifies selfishness. Sider argues that the Bible does not let us off easily. No Christian can negate the fact that God deals directly with issues of injustice to the poor because God himself, in his compassion, identifies with the have-nots, and desires the church to do the same. In his book *Integrated African Liturgy*, Lukwata makes a case for a

Christian mission that is involved in alleviating poverty, disease, and hunger.[220] Nwaka states:

> If an African liturgy is conceived as one in which the people, after leaving their leaking roofs, gather with empty stomachs for a period of two hours, clap, sing and dance, and then return to their previous situations of want and abject poverty, those in charge of such a liturgy must be ready in the long run to do without the people. A hungry stomach does not listen to the Word of God although a full stomach may not be more disposed.[221]

Lukwata suggests that a time of receiving offertory can also be a time of receiving food items and other goods that the church can distribute to the needy in its community.

Remembering the Year of Jubilee

Mugambi emphasizes that the mandate of the church does not stop at saving souls. After all, this would leave Christians with a passive piety that does not take seriously Christ's mandate for his followers to live righteous lives, and to uphold justice in the process.[222] Mugambi points to Jesus's words:

> The Spirit of the Lord is on me, because he has anointed me to proclaim good news to the poor. He has sent me to proclaim freedom for the prisoners and recovery of sight for the blind, to set the oppressed free, to proclaim the year of the Lord's favour.[223]

Jesus considered it his mission to reach out to the poor, seek justice for those in captivity, open the eyes of those who had eyes and could not see, seek the end of oppression for the downtrodden, and proclaim Jubilee, the year of the Lord's favour.

In this passage, the "year of the Lord's favour" does not represent a calendar year but the coming of the Messianic age. It refers to the Jewish Jubilee,[224] when "once every 50 years, slaves were freed, debts were cancelled, and ancestral property was returned to the original family. Isaiah predicted primarily the liberation of Israel from the future Babylonian captivity, but Jesus proclaimed liberation from sin and its consequences."[225] Africa needs a year of Jubilee. Although many of our traumas are linked to our sins of commission and omission, Africans have also been sinned against through massive exploitation by multinational corporations and also by the propagation of neocolonialism, which seemed to benefit everybody but Africans.

Steps for Community Mobilization

Now we move to practical steps that the Christian counsellor can use for community mobilization. The field of community development has emerged both in the West and in Africa.

Problem Identification

The Christian counsellor must first assess the community's interpersonal, religious, and political climate. Where problems like hunger, famine, crime, and unrest are observed, what is the real issue that is not being addressed? Prevention calls for intervention at the root of problems. Treating symptoms alone not only postpones a solution, but also slowly weakens community resilience. One can ask the following questions: What problems are discussed in the newspapers, magazines, and other periodicals? What subjects are preachers addressing? What stories do people tell, even in casual conversation? What is the subject of dramas and current songs? What is the content of testimonies and prayer requests in fellowship groups, prayer meetings, and church gatherings? What is left unsaid, and why? What effect does this silence have on people? What methods are people using to solve problems, at home, at work, or in the community?

Identification of Resources

The counsellor will identify the resources available to begin community-based interventions. These resources start with God, who as the Creator asks us to work with him as agents of change. In addition, God has given us the resources we need, from the grassroots level, so that we can complete his assignment. We suggest counsellors invite other leaders in the community to brainstorm with them to come up with a list of some of these resources – God's Word, friends, time, money, and buildings, including homes, churches, and schools.

The recycling of resources refers to the fact that a loss in one area can be used as a gain in another. In this way, community resources are not wasted, but instead, are utilized to restore community resiliency. For example, young men who graduate from school can be encouraged to stay in their village and use fallow land to grow vegetables to sell, instead of leaving the village to search for poorly paid jobs in the city. Teachers in the community might take the lead in this project by beginning agricultural clubs to train these young men while still in school. This way, resources can be recycled back into the village. Some of the young men can also be hired by women to do work that they have no time to handle. Increased agricultural output can help pay the youth to remain in their village – and perhaps change their attitudes about blue-collar jobs as they literally see the fruit of their labour. Recycling of resources can increase community resiliency.

Beginning Community Based Interventions

Once the counsellor has proved himself as a respected community leader and earned the right to lead, he can share a vision for change with the pastor, the church community, and other Christian leaders, to obtain grassroots support. It is best to adopt an approach that empowers the people by teaching them what they need to know. The counsellor can train leaders and counsellors, giving them basic skills in Christian counselling and mentoring.

In Maitoni village, we learned that people are leaving. What can be done to change their minds? First, students need to be trained so that they can have a successful adult life in the village. This will mean an overhaul of the educational curriculum or, if an extreme change is not immediately possible, an enriched educational system. For example, community leaders, acting through the Parent Teacher Association, could request for the inclusion of classes that would train the young people, both male and female, for life in the village. One can create projects to benefit the young people, attract income-generating projects, and make small loans available. Counsellors can encourage the planting of crops that can be communally marketed, or they can encourage villagers who are doing well elsewhere to return home to inject life into the village.

Maitoni village surely must have political and civic representation. Monica's son, a headmaster in a distant school, could return to the village as a change agent. Enriching the community will increase its power of attraction, as well as multiplying alternatives for the youth. Community enrichment also includes teaching social values that will change destructive behaviours in the village, especially those that lead to HIV infections and also to deaths from AIDS.

Limitations

Counsellors refer out counselling that demands professional intervention. They are aware of their limitations, especially in working with psychotic individuals, severely depressed persons, or suicidal cases. In work with families, the counsellor may become aware of limitations regarding problems that are entrenched in a family's history, deep personality brokenness, or negative cultural practices. In community work with issues such as political strife, drug trafficking, alcohol abuse, and child abuse and neglect, the counsellor would need to know the key leaders in the community, and in local and national governments, who can help with the community's problem. It is best to seek out those who are supportive of counselling as a tool for community transformation. To navigate these challenges, each Christian counsellor needs to have a database of names of professional individuals to whom complicated cases in the community can be referred: psychologists, psychiatrists, medical doctors, clinical social workers, lawyers, legislators, and pastors.

The administration and interpretation of psychological tests without proper training or supervision is also a limitation. Clinical psychologists are trained to administer psychological tests which, if misused, could considerably harm the client. Any organization that desires to train or use Christian counsellors should also ensure that adequate training, supervision, and continued training are all incorporated into its programme.

Evaluation

Every programme needs to have regular appraisal to assess its merit, progress, and effectiveness. Since community projects are co-owned, the communal group should be involved in their evaluation. The outcome provides the stakeholders (all those involved in, and benefiting from, the project) with information on the programme's goals, whether or not expectations have been met, what the outcomes have been, the programme's impact on the community, and the resources that have been utilized. From these findings, an action plan can be drawn up and a new phase of the programme started. Strict accountability for all resources, large or small, must be maintained. This is important, because lack of integrity in Africa has eroded confidence in some project leaders. In turn, the health of many communities has suffered, the innocent along with the guilty. Many Western donors have withdrawn critical aid to Africa because of poor accountability. When the continent is littered with incomplete hospitals, failed water systems, and broken-down medical equipment, the vulnerable suffer for lack of leadership accountability.

Forward Planning – Responsible Use of Resources

The goal of any sustainable community project is self-sufficiency. This can be reached only if local resources are utilized and their use intensified. If there is a need to solicit external funds, these should be aimed at empowering people at the grassroots level and reaching those who can reach others through training and modelling. Many community-based projects can be initiated to manage resources that currently go to waste, increasing community resiliency. The

Christian counsellor can sensitize the community to the need for such projects. For example, in season, every mango tree is aflame with ripe mangoes. Children's faces are plastered with fresh mango nectar. Many women carry mangoes to the market, using special baskets woven to hold the fruit. Mangoes sit in bags by the roadside, waiting for a *matatu* or "transport wagon" to take them to the next town. Then, mango season comes to an end. Children roam from mango tree to mango tree looking for the last fruit, and fighting over the few they find, ripe or raw. The tragedy is that no one in the community realizes that mangoes can be tinned, dried, pickled, or made into mango juice to make the supply last until the next season. In such communities, so blessed during harvest seasons, drought and famine can also strike at any time. A crisis comes that could have been managed.

Conclusion

Our hope for Africa is not for an overnight transformation of political systems, but for the church to become a caring community, as well as a voice for the voiceless. Christian counsellors are called to encourage the church's involvement in societal transformation through analysing the specific needs of the community, identifying structures that threaten communal wellness, and suggesting and applying systems that promise restoration, as well as caring for the most vulnerable in society. Africa needs a multiplication of well-trained, biblically grounded, and professionally trained counsellors who work through the local church, Bible schools, theological seminaries, government institutions, the business world, and general society; all the while living lives that model transforming love. Their message of hope and new creation will bring comfort to those who suffer, as well as bringing transformation to entrenched systems that support exploitation of the poor by the rich.

In the next chapter, we move from community resiliency to a smaller unit, the family. We focus on preparing young people for marriage. We think that such preparation will help to build healthy marriages. However, healthy marriages also depend on resilient communities.

CHAPTER 7

Premarital Counselling

The joining of a man and a woman in marriage is a matter of great importance. Unfortunately, many couples seek marriage counselling too late. Couples in trouble have wept in therapy, wishing they had known before they got married the things they have learned in counselling sessions. With premarital counselling, they could have started their unions on a more solid foundation and saved themselves much pain. To their regret, they have learned that it is much easier to keep a fragile clay pot from breaking than to piece together the shards once the pot is broken. Given the state of some African marriages today, it is strongly recommended that premarital counselling occur for at least six months before the wedding. This means that hasty marriages must be discouraged as much as possible. The Ki-Swahili saying *Haraka haraka haina baraka* warns us, "No blessing ever comes with hurry-hurry." Taking time to fall in love, taking time to get to know the beloved, taking time to inform the family about wedding plans, taking time to receive counsel, both formal and informal, taking time to prepare, taking time . . . taking time . . . is the African way.

In this chapter, we will focus on our role as Christian counsellors in supporting Christian couples from an African indigenous perspective. We will look at ways we can help to build solid foundations on which future African families can form healthy relationships, raise their children, and serve God in church and society. We will begin by discussing reasons for premarital counselling and topics to be covered in counselling,[226] and then we will tell the story of Maritha and Sulaiman, whose engagement needed help. We will review courting patterns in African cultures that provide insights for healthy marriages. We will end the chapter by considering ways to respond to the needs of single individuals in African communities.

What can we learn from courtship patterns in African indigenous cultures? Ngugi wa Thiong'o reminds us that culture is to society what a flower is to a plant. The flower carries the seed for a new plant and is "the bearer of the future of that species of plants."[227] Building marriages on biblical and positive indigenous cultural value systems will provide the roots that we need for marital and also communal resiliency. Nyomi believes that the church has a major role in preparing young people for marriage through seminars, and specifically in preparing engaged couples for matrimony.[228]

Many couples with whom counsellors work are suspended between the old and the new. They have divided allegiance, on the one hand to traditional culture, and on the other to the modern world. No one has helped them to sort out and own the positive aspects of their cultural identity, or to stop to listen to and learn the language of a new Africa. Because people carry their stresses wherever they go, unresolved marriage and family problems may also affect relationships in offices, farms, businesses, and marketplaces. All of these factors underscore the need for premarital and marriage counselling.

African indigenous Christian counsellors begin their premarital counselling fully aware that most people want to get married to live *happily ever after*. On this positive note, the Christian counsellor can attempt to help individuals to realize their highest dreams. The counsellor can use the following practical suggestions as a guide in counselling couples prior to marriage.

First, help the couple to understand some advantages of premarital counselling. They can be told, for example, that counselling may help them to understand more clearly what being married involves. Counselling may help them learn how to interact, by understanding each other's likes and dislikes. It can help them to learn the basic principles of communication. It may help them to discover each other's goals in life and learn how to support each other's dreams. Counselling will perhaps help the couple to discover what each person is bringing to the marriage in terms of past experiences, behaviour patterns, religious beliefs, personality strengths and weaknesses, or even quirky habits. Premarital counselling will point to the need to grow together, both mentally and spiritually. It may help the couple to recognize the role of the covenant as the foundation of the Christian marriage and family. Hopefully, Christian counselling will help them to understand the role of a commitment to prayer and faithfulness in building stable marriages and families. The Christian counsellor will cover a broad range of topics with the couple planning to be married. A thorough discussion can prevent a host of problems later on.

Wedding Plans

What kind of wedding is the couple planning? In spite of so much poverty in Africa today, and with competition to make one's wedding better than others, many are tempted to overspend on expensive weddings. Couples might even be compelled to raise funds from strangers to be able to afford wedding expenses. Another matter of concern is the dowry, by which unscrupulous parents might try to enrich themselves overnight by asking for colossal amounts of money as a bride price, sums that may have no relationship to the cultural norms for a dowry. Because of this situation, some couples have begun their marriages in debt, and some brides have been taken "on loan," meaning that since the bride price set is far beyond what the bridegroom and his family can afford, the bride is given away with an expectation that "debts" from unpaid dowry will be settled later. We need to add here that this concern does not include some communities where the dowry is set according to cultural expectations and is paid over a span of time for the sake of building community over the years. This is a welcome practice because the two families continue to exchange visits long after the couple is married. The concern here is about unscrupulous demands that the girl's parents may make on the bridegroom that are beyond his ability. Discussion of all of these issues should take place in premarital counselling, before anyone says, "I do."

Family Relationships

The Christian counsellor will deal with questions of in-law relationships, some full of joy, others full of rivalry and resentment. Together, the couple can discuss with the counsellor how whole families can best live closely together, learning to slowly and patiently build relationships of acceptance and tolerance. How will their community support their new marriage, family, and kinship relationships? How will the church provide a home for this new family?

Role Expectations

How do the young couple imagine their future role relationships? What kind of relationship has existed between them so far? Conflicts in marriage often occur when men and women have different expectations about appropriate roles or sets of tasks for the other to fulfil. With urbanization, disconnected communities, and many demands for the empowerment of women in legal, social, and economic arenas,[229] gender roles in Africa need an ongoing, informed, biblically focused redefinition.

What is the role of the father in Africa today? The physical and emotional presence of the father is critical because he is the family leader and as such he is fully engaged in the life of the family. This presence can be understood from the art of shepherding. The role of the father in the past was crucial because he was the one who guided and mediated the age-set system that involved the stage-to-stage initiation of children and the training that went with tribal expectations of behaviour at each stage.

What is the role of the mother? In the past, the role of the mother in Meru life was to be both industrious (*ukirote*) and affectionate (*nkatha*). The former included the mother's ability to use her hands in food production, preparation, and storage for the future, to clothe her family; to care for her husband, including sexual fulfilment; and generally, to provide security for the family. The latter referred to the woman's ability to be physically appealing, to be joyful, to communicate with her husband, and to care for herself physically so that he could be proud of her as the mother of his children. However, sexual appeal in a mother was considered empty without her industry.

Children, Infertility, and Adoption

The Christian counsellor will explore factors regarding fertility and infertility, since in Africa, having children is perceived as a mark of a healthy marriage. For many indigenous communities, offspring "guarantee the continuity of the group over time and help living members to produce the necessary food."[230] What alternatives are there to infertility? With so many orphans in Africa, is adoption an option? Many traditional African communities have absorbed orphaned children within families and such children even receive an inheritance, along with biological members of the families. Is the couple open to caring for an orphan? How much can the church encourage the cultural practice of caring for orphans?

Ethical Issues

The Christian counsellor may also be faced with issues of separation, divorce, remarriage, and polygamy. How will the counsellor respond to a couple planning to be married when the man already has a wife, all are Christians, and all want to participate in the life of the church? Some polygamists want baptism and full church membership. Others desire church leadership. How does the church respond to their requests? Some are willing to pay the price of separation from a spouse in order to serve, while others choose to continue living together because of their responsibility for children born to a particular union. These are difficult issues, which the church cannot avoid. What biblical teaching guides us in making our decisions? Mugambi believes that polygamy is one of the challenges to moral reconstruction in Africa today.[231]

Topics to Discuss

There are many more topics to discuss during a premarital counselling session.

Here is a partial list:

1. **The past**. (Individual past experiences that are likely to impact the current relationship – for example, the kind of family each grew up in and early traumatic experiences.)

2. **Personality**. (The need to take responsibility for one's own behaviour and the grace to leave changing the other person to God.)

3. **Sexuality**. (The commitment to chastity before wedlock. Preparing for marital sex by discussing the biology, psychology, and spirituality of sex.)

4. **Children**. (Desires regarding the number of children, as well as family planning issues.)

5. **Future goals and dreams**. (Further education, training, career changes, and attitudes towards money, property, and investment.)

6. **Money matters**. (Joint or separate bank accounts, personal allowances, budgeting, debt, and insurance.)

7. **Relationships**. (Role of extended family and friends in the marital relationship. Some individuals continue to value friends over and above their partners.)

8. **Residence**. (Where to live? Given the common practice of a wife living in the rural areas while a husband works in the city, will they live separated or together?)

9. **Leisure, rest, and health**. (Diet, exercise, and regular medical check-ups.)

Maritha and Sulaiman

Here is a concrete example of a couple seeking premarital counselling. At a young adult retreat, Maritha met the love of her life. At 26 years of age, having worked for some time, she was ready for marriage. Sulaiman was everything she ever wanted in a male friend: tall, handsome, charismatic, and respectful. She fell in love with him and was happy that her feelings were reciprocated. After the one-week retreat, they continued to call each other, write letters, and visit. Before long, members of their young adult fellowship knew that the two were dating. Within six months, Sulaiman had proposed and Maritha gladly accepted. The next step was to tell their families.

By this time, Maritha had started hearing rumours that Sulaiman was not all that he seemed to be. People dropped hints that he had already broken several engagements and was self-centred – too focused on the impressions he made on people. Maritha was too much in love to listen to these murmurings. After all, she rationalized, these people were jealous of her relationship with Sulaiman. However, she decided to share these rumours with her best friend, Katheki, who advised Maritha to seek the advice of a trained counsellor at their church. Eventually, Sulaiman and Maritha began meeting with the counsellor.

In counselling, Maritha explained that they wanted to explore their growing relationship, as well as what each brought into the relationship. The counsellor reviewed the way Maritha and Sulaiman perceived each other's personalities, family histories, cultural training and socialization, past romantic relationships, hopes for the future, money responsibilities, conflict resolution skills, attitudes towards money and property, work ethics, and spiritual commitment. The counsellor gave the couple individual homework assignments on these topics each week, so that they could discuss them together. Maritha did her part of the work, but Sulaiman always resisted completing his assignments. Then it became clear that Sulaiman had not been like other young men in his tribe. Like many professional men in his age group, Sulaiman's father had decided to bring up his children away from his village and had refused to have them trained and initiated as adults. In addition, he had refused to have his children attend church or Sunday school, declaring that too old-fashioned. Consequently, Sulaiman had had neither a Christian upbringing nor training by tribal elders on the responsibilities of adulthood.

One day, Maritha was shocked to open a letter that read: "Dear Maritha, thank you for being who you are, sweet and loving. I am sorry that I have to call it quits. It's nothing about you. After much heart searching, I have decided that marrying you is not the best thing to do. I wish you happiness. Love, Sulaiman." Maritha was devastated, especially after she learnt that Sulaiman had another girlfriend he had been seeing even while he was proposing to Maritha and attending counselling.

With the help of the counsellor, Maritha began to deal with her feelings of loss and confusion, as well to piece together a more accurate picture of Sulaiman. Over time, she was able to admit that Sulaiman had a controlling nature. He was a poor listener and became angry when crossed. He was so self-centred that he never noticed what Maritha wore or the many ways she tried to please him. Sulaiman's heart was like a deep hole; he never seemed to get enough attention. He had a cynical, criticizing spirit, and had problems with commitment. All this she had not seen before. Maritha mourned her naiveté. A few more meetings with the counsellor and participation in a singles' prayer group helped her to grieve her loss and embarrassment. Maritha's mother remained strong for her daughter and secretly thanked God that Sulaiman was out of the picture.

Courting in African Cultures

In Africa, marriage "is not simply a human or natural institution: it is clearly a cultural and spiritual unit which is at the basis of the religious, economic and social life of the society."[232] It links not only two people but also people groups, enriching the extended family.[233] Indeed, Kenyatta notes that in Africa, "nobody is an isolated individual but everybody is a member of a family group."[234] Many African societies also perceive of marriage as a preservation of the lineage of the family and the tribe.[235] This is why care was taken in choosing a bride, and courtship extended over a lengthy time so as to build relational alliances through ritual and ceremony. When the bride and groom indicated the possibility of a new alliance, the leadership of the people group explored the proposed union, examining bloodlines to make sure that the new union did not endanger the group. For example, marrying into a bloodline was discouraged if it was known to contain psychotic individuals, women who were known to be hostile and oppositional, or men known to be irresponsible and wanton.[236]

Premarital counselling can begin with an examination of the positive aspects of an indigenous culture that can be utilized to support biblical principles about marriage and the family. Take, for example, the fact that ancestors (the living dead) were considered part of the marriage union in many African communities. Thus, children were named after dead relatives in order to carry on the link between the living and the dead.[237] In many African communities, discussions about bride price took a long time, and the engaged couple remained mainly *outside* the negotiations as elders from both sides built their relationship. The Meru labelled this intricate formation between the two families as *gutuma*, "knitting a garment." What was the meaning of this long dialogue and ritual wherein the marrying couple had no voice? Some of these practices may be difficult to understand, especially since very little has been written about the richness of indigenous African cultures in regard to relationships within marriage, family, and the community. Consequently, it is the role of Christian counsellors to be students of the culture within which they are working, so as to learn and teach positive elements that can bring people together and enrich relationships.

Mate Selection

Courtship begins with mate selection. Rarely were marriages arranged among the Meru, except in cases where a man needed help in finding a mate. Since society was organized in age-sets, the age-set that was ready for marriage usually began the process of mate selection at the same time. After young men reached puberty, they would go through an initiation ceremony. The purpose of this initiation was to train the young men in the lore of the tribe, as well as to set them apart as warriors. After initiation, while living in the *gaaru* ("training centre"), the young people knew what to do when the time for marriage came. By then, they would have been known in the community for various accomplishments: leadership abilities, courage in battle, industry, oratory skills, wisdom, kindness and care for others, or the gift of communication through poetry, song, and dance. While still in the *gaaru*, young men owned land, fenced it, and began to grow staple all-weather foods like yams and bananas on their property in order to provide for their families after marriage.

Getting to Know Each Other

Social occasions like evenings of song and dance provided an opportunity for young people to meet. After the young people paired up, young women would be escorted home after the dance. In this way, parents began to know the young man who was courting their daughter. All the way through the courting relationship, strict sexual purity was to be observed. Single women would be expected to leave the dance floor early, before it became dark. Young people themselves challenged any deviation from this rule with songs like:

> *Mukenye uti munyaynya*
> Young woman with no suitor
> *Imbi ugiraga mbiriine*
> What do you seek on the social dance scene?
> *Riua riakara kwegega*
> When the sun begins to wane
> *Ukaanua nuu kaugi*
> Who will escort you home, naughty one?

The purpose of the song was to discourage aimless "hanging out" on the social scene, and to ensure that the beginning of socialization as couples remained focused, intentional, and free from abuse.

Eventually, a young man would initiate visits to the home of a girl. Never would the two meet on the path or in some other place. The suitor also never visited the girl alone. He would always bring a companion, whose purpose was to keep the couple accountable. At the approach of the young men, the girl's mother and siblings would leave the mother's hut to make room for the guests. The whole visit would take place in the mother's hut. Good homes were known by the quality of the mother, one of whose jobs was to make sure that there was enough food for all. The community frowned upon homes where the family did not provide hospitality. In such cases, the mother along with her daughters were labelled *nguutu* or "lazy." With no refrigeration, food served to visitors also had to be freshly prepared to avoid the risk of food poisoning. Such an unfortunate happening would certainly mar the hostess's reputation.

Young women had to learn cooking skills. For example, after obtaining millet from the family granary, the young woman proceeded to wash it, and grind it into flour on a flat stone. Then she mixed it into a thick gruel, prepared it hot, and served it to her suitor and his friend. All of this happened amidst talking and getting to know one another. The young man accompanying the suitor did not participate in the dialogue but remained a quiet observer who could then bear witness that the courtship meeting had been a pure encounter. After eating, the young men would leave for the *gaaru*.

The ability to entertain, and to prepare and serve the food by firelight, were qualities sought after by the suitor. The young woman also looked for a man who appreciated her labour of love and did not take it for granted. Such encounters by the couple would assure the young man that his future wife would be able to combine both the quality of *nkatha* (beauty and an appealing personality) and that of *ukirote* (industry and preparedness to cater to other people). The young woman would also begin to get to know her suitor through these visits, in long evening discussions that dealt with matters of interest to both of them.

Leaving Home and the Bride Price

From time immemorial, the custom of bride price or dowry was practiced across most of Africa, but the exchange of animals or wealth never meant that the woman was "purchased." Indeed, the term *bride price* was changed to *bride wealth* in the years from 1929 to 1931. The exchange represented the sealing of a relationship between one family and another. A woman was never owned by her husband's family. In fact, given the slightest provocation, many women threatened to leave and go back home. Some actually did. Western education has changed many things within the organization of the Meru people, but there are still positive elements that can be adapted and incorporated into training, teaching, and counselling on marriage and the family.

For example, in traditional Africa, spousal abuse was frowned upon, and a man who constantly abused his wife would be punished by people of his age group. He would have to provide a goat to his age-mates. The eating together of the meat would signify both his repentance and a promise to improve his behaviour. This was done after the elders had ascertained the circumstances that led to the abuse, in which case counsellors could be engaged to help the couple with reconciliation. If a lazy woman did not feed her husband, strict counselling by other women would follow. Such an expectation remains to this day: a true Meru woman, educated or not, sees to the physical needs of her husband. In marriage counselling, the counsellor would look for underlying factors in marital problems and seek cultural support systems to deal with problems and to maintain marital wellness.[238]

Christian Perspectives on Marriage and the Family

Whom shall I marry? How do I know what is God's will? What if the man I am interested in is not as good as my dad? What if this woman lacks the skills of my mother? What if I find myself attracted to young people outside my tribe? What if I propose marriage to one of them? What will my family say? Knowing that I must marry within the faith, what if I fall in love with a non-Christian? These and many other anxieties arise in young people regarding marriage. The Bible provides numerous guidelines for marriage and the family to help us to fulfil what God intended. These guiding principles can be part of premarital counselling, and the counsellor should work closely with church pastors to learn their teachings and expectations about marriage.[239]

The People of God

The marriage covenant mirrors God's covenant with us as a people. A key dimension is faithfulness, so we are faithful to our spouses as God is faithful to us. It is possible that generation upon generation of faithfulness in marriage will create a greater possibility of trust in God. Just as Africans are a tribal people, so God has created a tribe and nation that is to reflect his character. It should be obvious from the description of African courtship that the role of the community is critical. As Christians, we honour and respect our original families, and we also consider very important the blessing of the whole Christian community on the new pair.[240]

The Mystery of Covenant

The idea of two people becoming one flesh is a mystery.[241] The meaning of one flesh or body here refers to more than a physical union. The new oneness is the symbol of the whole person, a "communion of life"[242] in which two people are united in a common purpose. Marriage is the unity of a covenant rather than simply a "contract." A covenant is a vow made before God, a promise such as "*till death do us part*." This is a promise that should not be broken. If it is broken, it also breaks the people involved in it. In a contractual marriage, if one partner leaves because the other has not kept the bargain, the pain of a broken covenant may be passed on from one generation to the next. This is one of the reasons why premarital counselling is of paramount importance in Christian counselling. A broken engagement is always better than a broken marriage.

On Meeting

The Bible does not tell us much about selecting mates. However, it does provide guidelines on selecting close acquaintances. Paul admonishes believers not to be "yoked together with unbelievers."[243] Spiritual commitment is a major requirement in mate selection. Under other circumstances, a woman like Maritha might have seen that she and her intended husband, Sulaiman, were not equal. She may have seen his faults, but she denied what she saw, telling herself, "My love will change him." Sulaiman needed help to address problems in his life that would have shown up no matter which person he might marry.

The Christian community has the responsibility of establishing teaching and coaching, so that young adults can see their way into courtship clearly. Mate selection happens best with safe opportunities for socializing. As we indicated above, traditional cultures created such opportunities. What can the church and indigenous communities do to encourage healthy socialization among young adults? Some men are shy and need help in knowing how to approach and talk to a woman. Women with alcoholic or abusive fathers have sometimes married men who are like their fathers. However, a vibrant Christian community offering many different activities and settings in which to meet provides an environment in which healthy couple relationships can be nurtured. When the church is a community of accountability, the observations on the emerging relationship made by wise fellow believers can prevent a marriage filled with pain.

Couples choosing life partners must seek to discover common spiritual ground uniting them. They can do this by spending time together, recognizing mutual spiritual interests, developing appreciation for each other's gifts, encouraging one another, making and keeping commitments, acquiring mutually supportive friends, and negotiating over disagreements. Couples begin building a covenant by talking openly, developing common convictions about money and possessions, and practicing integrity by "walking in the light," that is, living accountably to each other.

On Leaving Home and Separating from Parents

Good marriages build healthy connections between generations, though the couple will need to develop a healthy separation from their parents.[244] Many Africans take it for granted that men do not *leave home*, but stay home to receive the woman, who leaves *her* home after the wedding. Written within a patriarchal culture, Genesis makes it clear that it is the man who mentally, emotionally, and physically separates from his father and mother in order to head up a new family unit. Many problems in marriage occur because some men remain under the control of their parents and never quite leave home. The new couple needs to form a gentle but firm boundary between themselves and the in-laws on both sides, providing freedom to grow more deeply together.

Becoming One

Cleaving, or uniting, is the basis for oneness in marriage, in which two people form an inseparable union. This union is evident in emotional and sexual loyalty. The divine intention for marriage is monogamy, and "what God has joined together, let no one separate."[245] Jesus spoke these words in response to a question about divorce, adding that in a society that had disregarded God's will,[246] divorce was tantamount to committing adultery, and that in the new law, that practice was unacceptable. This is one of the reasons why when a marriage breaks up, the tearing apart of what God had joined together leaves many wounds.[247]

The process of becoming one is built on mutual love and honour between the couple, but the health of the family is also dependent on the health of the community. Hopefully, attitudes of love and honour are passed along to children as they enter the family, and the family obviously impacts the church and community. The union of two whole, separate persons becomes a unit within the wider community. Kisembo, Magesa, and Shorter note that this Christian idea of oneness does not conflict with the traditional concept of marriage within African societies. They add that "the community would mean nothing if the personal aspect [of two separate wholes becoming one whole] were lacking, for the community is the very field of personal relationships; and the person would mean nothing if he or she were not a person in the community."[248]

Mutual Submission

It is easy to insist on the teaching, "wives, submit yourselves to your own husbands as you do to the Lord."[249] But Paul's teaching on submission begins in the previous verse with, *"Submit one to another out of reverence for Christ."* This submission or deferring to the other involves humility, listening to the other, placing oneself second, serving the other, and joyfully celebrating the other.

> *Dr Mwiti*: Speaking about "mutual submission" reminds me of the day a non-Christian man and colleague at work asked me how my husband and I handle disagreements in our marriage. I replied that there are no marriages without disagreements. However, if he meant the kind of disputes where people slam the door and leave in anger, I haven't seen such in my marriage. We have other ways of managing our differences. To which he answered, "Then, one of you must be a weakling." My response was: "Knowing me as you do, would you call me a weakling?" "Never," he answered with a smile. "Then, your husband must be the weakling." "That's very amusing!" I responded. "You know Gershon as well. Would you call him a weakling?" "Certainly not!" he responded. After a pause, he continued, "Then, how do you do it?" "I guess both of us seek all the time to communicate to the other from a kneeling position." "How's that?" he wanted to know. "We both kneel at the foot of the cross, fully aware of our weaknesses before Christ, and ready to be transformed by him in whatever area our differences bring up – and we have many weaknesses. In that kneeling position before God, we are in a kneeling position in regard to one another. This doesn't happen as much as it should, however, because we too can be stubborn. But the point is – mutuality, from a kneeling position." His response: "That's very interesting!"

Care and Wisdom in Daily Living

Paul admonishes us to live wisely, to make the best of every opportunity, and to avoid foolishness. Couples who grow together can set an example for their children to imitate Christ's model for loving relationships. Christians do well to work at their marriages, fully investing themselves in their unions so that opportunities for bettering themselves and their families do not pass them by.[250]

A story is told of a nominal Christian man who kept a log of all the mistakes his wife made from the day they got married. She would break a cup, and he would run to his room and write down, "broke cup," and the date. She would put too much salt in the food, and he would enter, "too much salt," and the date. Not a good example!

Paul admonishes Christians to live a life empowered by the Holy Spirit. He empowers us in all we do, from eating, to working, to loving, to serving. The best gift a husband can give to his children is to love their mother, and the best gift a wife can give to her children is to love their father. Let Spirit-filled living begin at home, long before children hear about it from pulpits and at crusades.[251]

In close relationships like marriage and the family, it is easy to give praise sparingly, or to fail to encourage the dearest and the nearest while we are gracious to strangers. However, as profitable as outside investments may be, we have a responsibility to enrich our own homes and empower members of our own families to achieve their best. This way, we have the opportunity to pass on a lasting legacy and so influence future generations.[252]

Singleness

With all of our cultural preoccupation with couples, we cannot forget those who are single. What if I do not marry? Am I less of a person? Will the church accept me as one with gifts? How can I address feelings of rejection and unworthiness? There are many reasons why people are single: some choose to be single, some are never chosen in marriage, and others become single after divorce or the death of a spouse. Each person reacts differently to being single.

Take Mona, for example. Many of Mona's friends were already married. Indeed, in the past five years, she had attended one wedding after another, but none of them was Mona's. Her friends gave testimonies of God's faithfulness in providing marriage partners and Mona wished that she, too, could say, "I prayed, and he heard my prayer." After all, she had done everything right – she became a committed Christian in high school, lived a pure life, and served the Lord first at church and later in the Students' Christian Fellowship. She had mentored young people and was known as a faithful servant of the Lord. But she was still single. Worst was the loneliness she felt. Her friends were now young mothers, busy with their husbands and with other young families. Mona dreaded visiting them, because she and her old friends no longer had much in common. She also dreaded going home to visit. Her mother did not bother her about her single status, because as a woman of faith, she was confident that God would provide for Mona. However, her aunts were always asking questions like, "Have you come with an announcement this time?" This pressure to end her singleness was ever-present. Mona started to become obsessed with questions such as: "Am I different, Lord?" "How long shall I wait?" "Is my service to you in vain?"

Then there was Peter. At 40, he was one of the most eligible bachelors in the village. He had a good job, a nice car, and a pleasant personality. But he was single.

However, unlike many single men, his singleness did not seem to bother him. Peter was inundated with telephone calls and invitations to dinners. Nothing anyone said seemed to interest him in marriage. His devoted mother was confused as well. After the death of his father, Peter supported his mother and when the question of marriage came up, his answer was always, "*Pole pole ndio mwendo*," meaning: "Mama, do not worry. I want to be slow and sure." However, many wondered whether Peter had other reasons for avoiding marriage that he wasn't talking about.

Kathambi had yet another story. Kathambi had been married for four years to Simon, a young executive with the National Electricity Board. The young man was beloved at the church, at work, at home, and in the community. Everybody remembered the couple's wedding, held back in the village. Hundreds of people had come to celebrate the occasion. As a primary schoolteacher, Kathambi did not earn much, but her husband was paid enough to provide the young couple with a nice house and a car, plus medical benefits through his company. Blessed with two beautiful children, they felt they could not ask for more. All this was shattered overnight, however, when Simon was suddenly killed in a road accident. He had left no will. His family was living in the city in a house with a mortgage. What could Kathambi do? How was she to support the children? A 27-year-old widow? Most widows were old women. How supportive would her in-laws be? Could she marry again? Would her church, the only community she had in the city, know how to minister to the needs of a young, single mother?

Mona, Peter, and Kathambi represent groups of single individuals in the church whose needs are often neglected. The Christian counsellor can help single people in a variety of ways.

1. **Providing acceptance**. Single persons seek self-acceptance, wanting to know that they are they are valued and loved by God and the Christian community. Hopefully, this may lead them to an acceptance of singleness as a status or as a calling. Acceptance releases energy to live a full life at whatever stage of life one might be. For single people, such self-acceptance will come when being single is not considered as a second-class position in church or society. The Christian counsellor can share biblical perspectives on singleness. Paul affirmed singleness as entirely acceptable – but that is easily forgotten in a "married" world. One must take care to make sure that the church does not treat single people as if they do not exist. We must not minimize their needs or fail to hear their often-unspoken cries. Christian counsellors can encourage single people to recognize and affirm their gifts and callings.

2. **Comforting the bereaved**. The church needs a ministry to those who have been widowed, so that they can be reincorporated into the community as single persons who need support and a sense of belonging. The Old Testament places special emphasis on caring for widows, since they are most vulnerable to exploitation and degradation.[253] Some indigenous cultures encouraged "wife inheritance" as a way to care for widows. A surviving brother would care for his brother's wife and children to make sure that the bereaved family did not go uncared for, especially in situations where women could not inherit their husband's property. What is the church's understanding of this cultural practice? Who advocates for women on issues like property inheritance? Could dual ownership of property be taught and practiced, so that a bereaved woman would not have to face two losses: the loss of her spouse and also of all the property they have acquired? How can the church assist in protecting vulnerable widows from greedy relatives?

3. **Assisting in future planning**. Many single people keep waiting for God's answer of a spouse but fail to plan their futures. Singleness does not mean chaos. This kind of strategizing in the midst of emotional pain and sometimes confusion is best accomplished within a coaching relationship. A coach is more a friend than a counsellor. With the loneliness and self-doubt that sometimes comes with singleness, a coach will walk alongside single persons, helping to expand their vision, increase their skills, and maximize their potential.

4. **Encouraging singles to embrace their families**. This may be their biological families or the family of God. This means turning one's focus away from personal needs to the needs of others. Some single people have welcomed their nieces and nephews – or other people's children – into their lives, determined to bless them. In return, the singles have been abundantly blessed as they reached out to others instead of withdrawing from life.

5. **Just as with married people, God invites single people to faithfulness and holiness**. Indeed, authenticity and integrity are ingredients that keep all of us walking with him. His presence comes with blessing and provision for each step of our walk. After all, his promise rings true for all of his children, namely, that "*other things*" are never to be sought because they will be "*added*" if the Kingdom of God is our priority.[254] This great admonition is followed by Jesus's encouragement: "Do not worry about tomorrow . . ."[255]

Conclusion

We have illustrated the importance of the counsellor's role in helping a couple both before and during marriage, as well as in meeting the needs of those who are single. In a fast-changing Africa, whose resiliency is constantly shaken by rapid social changes, marriage has not been spared corresponding upheavals. Cross-cultural and interracial marriages are on the increase, while stabilizing community factors are decreasing. Competition to succeed and achieve more and more leads to stress, and all of these elements corrode marriage relationships.

However, in spite of increasing challenges on the African continent, God's expectations for marriage have not shifted one iota. The joining of a man and a woman continues to be God's idea, one that is of great importance as a foundation for the health of society. It follows that supporting the marriage and family bond is among the most important work that God will ever call upon us to perform as counsellors. Similarly, Christian counsellors support those who are called to singleness, by helping them develop a network of friends. Just as some are called to marriage, God may call others to singleness. African indigenous Christian counsellors, therefore, are faced with the demand for self-care in relationships, whether married or single, and ongoing improvement in their counselling skills. In addition, counsellors will also need to develop the capacity to engage African theologians in struggling with biblical answers to African questions on courtship, divorce, singleness, marriage, and remarriage. Help from these Bible scholars will assist in harnessing positive cultural values that do not negate biblical principles. Africa needs theologians who will continue to provide an understanding of Christian living within an African context. This contribution will support and enrich the marriage and the family. Finally, Africa has a dire need for publications in the areas of marriage preparation and healthy family functioning. All of these and many more challenges and opportunities for marriage building and counselling abound in Africa.

CHAPTER 8

Marriage Counselling

The stability of African families is threatened today by rapid social and economic change, by increased mobility, and by an unclear value system as Western values continue to threaten African indigenous and traditional ways of life. It is no wonder that the African family feels tossed between what was and what is. In this chapter, we will focus on Christian couples, especially the challenges they face and what we can do to guide them. Moving on from premarital counselling in the previous chapter, we now explore marriage counselling from an African indigenous Christian perspective.

When a counsellor mentions the word *indigenous*, some couples are immediately frightened. They ask: "Are scholars asking us to dig up our traditional goblets and imbibe from animal horns? How can we sing traditional songs anymore? Did we go to school to learn in the city only to come back and sit with the old people in the village? What wisdom does my unschooled father have on how I should raise my children in modern Africa? I left him behind and studied in America, and when I came back, I still find him seated on his three-legged stool!"

When the Bible specifies that a "wise son heeds his father's instruction, but a mocker does not respond to rebukes,"[256] there is no indication in the text about whether the father to be honoured is educated or not, lives in a mansion or a shack, is white or black, African or European, drives a Cadillac or pushes a *mkokoteni* (African cart used in the market). Neither is the mocker described as a college graduate, popular televangelist, surgeon, or cardiologist. Whoever does not listen to his father is a mocker. Wisdom comes to those who listen to wise fathers. There is still much wisdom in the African villages among old men seated under a *mugumo* tree, among retired church leaders, and among aging grandmothers. What enabled village couples to survive in earlier years? What makes for healthy, strong couples today?

Dr Mwiti: Family leaders show the way to build community for family wellness. My father-in-law would often send a message that he wanted to see all his children. Scattered around the nation, we would come home to a weekend of eating and feasting. The old man would kill a calf and the women would prepare the food. Men would barbecue the meat and, while the children chased each other in and out of the banana plantation, food would be served. At the end of such a gathering, my philosophically minded husband stood up to thank his father for his wonderful hospitality. Gershon ended his speech with the words: "Baituuru (using the name of respect for his father), we are sure that you called us for some agenda. That is the usual practice in our tribe when a man has a heavy matter to share with his family. We have waited the whole weekend to know why you called us. Could you now disclose the reason for this feast?" The old man's response was a chuckle, followed by these powerful words: "My son, if a father wants to watch his happy family for a weekend, is that too much to ask? Do I need an agenda for that?" Everybody nodded and said, "Indeed, you don't!" And the feasting continued.

In days gone by, marriages survived because African parents had a commitment to keeping the family healthy and strong. With divorce not an option, sheer determination kept some of these families working hard to enrich their marriages. Many Africans have wonderful stories of persevering parents who sacrificed much, and who refused to give in to separation for the sake of family unity. With a society that supported the marital union, marriages survived.

Marriages in Africa were often healthy and committed because they had community support. Since the wedding was a communal affair, the community helped the new relationship to thrive.[257] If the newlyweds made a point of connecting with their community, community members most often reciprocated by helping them navigate the challenges of married life.

Dr Mwiti: As a young couple, my husband and I were often invited to speak at marriage retreats. One such invitation found me very conflicted because I had no one with whom to leave my young children for the weekend. As I struggled with the decision to go or not to go, a friend and older mother called me and said, "Gladys, I hear that you may not go to teach at the retreat because you need care for your children this weekend. You know, I cannot preach or teach, but I can take care of babies very well. Please, bring your children to my house this weekend and take off to do your ministry." And I did. Our children were spoilt with love and care that weekend, and I was at peace as we ministered in the retreat. The church can become an alternative community, especially in urban areas where community resilience is threatened.

African marriages also survived because they had a transcendent perspective. They looked away from the self to the Almighty, visualizing life and its demands as a God-given assignment. Through death and illness, through tears and joy, through periods of poverty or plenty, God continued to sustain. Set alongside such triumphs over adversity, periods of celebration and thanksgiving gained a deep meaning.

This kind of age-old wisdom can be translated into the "modern" context for those who seek help from a Christian counsellor. As the elders knew, if you leave God out, things fall apart. The centre cannot hold in God's absence.

Causes of Marriage Problems

The Bible encourages believers to enjoy positive interpersonal and sexual relationships with their spouses. Finding a mate is described as a good thing that "receives favour from the Lord."[258] However, the book of Proverbs also describes the difficulties of living with a quarrelsome marriage partner. Sharing a house with such a person is like listening to "the dripping of a leaky roof in a rainstorm" and trying to control such a person is as futile as attempting to restrain "the wind or grasping oil with the hand."[259] Some marriage problems can be avoided through ongoing education on marriage and the family within the whole body of Christ.

God does not promise us marriages without tension, and neither do indigenous African traditions. Indeed, Meru culture reminds us: *Maiga jari nyungune imwe jatiregaga kuringana*, meaning "Two stones in the same pot must have some conflict from time to time." This means that "living happily ever after" is more a wish than reality. People walking together will always struggle with the dynamics of that walk. Communication, forgiveness, esteeming the other, and a deliberate decision to keep walking together irrespective of thorns on the way keep marriages safe and fulfilling. However, constant conflict that threatens to tear the fabric of a marriage is often a symptom of something deeper: selfishness, unwillingness to forgive, anger, bitterness, anxiety, communication problems, sexual abuse, drunkenness, feelings of inferiority, sin, or the deliberate rejection of God's will.

Conflict over Differences

We have emphasized the need for a couple to grow together, because each spouse comes into marriage from his or her own unique family system. Our thoughts, perceptions, and expectations are shaped by our experiences in the families we grew up in. Conflict arises when marriage partners are not willing to grow together, to listen to one another, to defer to each other, and to respect the other. Conflict worsens when they are reluctant to change.

Inflexibility

People who are stubborn are not aware of the benefits of brokenness. But marriage is about change and growth. To yield and say, "I am sorry," to prefer the other person, to listen, to change course when wrong, to allow someone else to guide the way – all of these do not come easily. However, such attitudes are the everyday meal, the *fufu* or *ugali*, of marriages. Flexibility lies at the core of growing together, much as with two vines that are supple enough to be twisted together until they grow together, bearing ample fruit, as one.

Oppression

Oppression is certainly one of the main causes of marital problems. There are parts of Africa, for example, where women are not allowed to eat at the same table with men. They cook the food, serve it, and then retreat to the kitchen to eat with the children. Women in such situations may become so bitter at the cruelty and lack of consideration with which they are treated that they refuse to receive Holy Communion from their husbands in church. If such practices are cultural, they contradict the Christian faith, and will not bring needed transformation to African communities.

Spiritual growth is tied to intellectual growth. The husband may go to Bible School while his wife remains at home. She may wish to join him, but some Bible Schools do not allow wives to study for credit. They are encouraged to join the "Pastors' Wives" class to occupy their time while the men attend school. These women are often as gifted as their husbands. They may not necessarily study theology, but they can take certificate courses in their areas of gifting. The needs of the church are vast, and no talent should be wasted. A woman is likely to be a mother, a mentor, and an example for her children. What kind of mentor is kept at home while the man studies, travels, and graduates with an advanced degree? Some individuals may perceive this advocacy as a fight for the equality of men and women. It is not. The African church has a responsibility to motivate growth in the whole body of Christ, in both men and women, and this will encourage healthy marriages and families.

Poor Communication

Poor communication is another cause of marital problems. People are often afraid to tell their spouses what they are really feeling and desiring. No one can read minds. Consider the husband who wishes to have sex with his wife, because he feels both physical desire and also a need for intimacy. He hopes that she will respond to his initiative, but she is tired and not interested at that time. He is frustrated. If he communicates only his expectation of sexual contact and not his underlying desire for intimacy, she is likely to feel criticized by him and pull back even more to defend herself from his anger. Communicating needs and desires is especially important in addressing differences.

Money

We can often point to money as a source of marital problems. One of the obvious reasons is that in Africa, there is never enough money available. A second one is that even when their income is good, people may not know how to use money. A school education prepares people to earn a living, but rarely is anyone taught there how to develop a budget or shown the art of investment. Some marriage partners continue old habits of either overspending or hoarding, depending on what they learned growing up. One partner may have grown up in a poor home and remains stingy in the midst of plenty, while the other partner might have been brought up in household of plenty and knows no limits to spending. Such a couple will need to learn how to adjust if their marriage is to flourish.

A further problem occurs when people retire and their income ends. Often depression, bitterness, and hopelessness follow early retirement.[260] Many are ill-prepared for this change. What role do the church and Christian counselling play in preparing people for such a life change?

Monotony

Monotony, or what young people call "same old, same old," is another problem we often see when a marriage starts to break down. Monotony results from a lack of creativity. Boredom drains marriage of life and laughter. It is a common saying that if you see a couple talking non-stop and laughing together, they are probably not married. Where does the laughter go?

> *Dr Mwiti*: In my own family, I've seen several wonderful examples of how a spouse used creativity to keep a relationship fresh and exciting. My father-in-law used to sing Ki-Meru poetry to his wife. Coming home in the African night, his voice would ring with praises to his bride. When I got married, I

loved to watch the two sit on the green lawn, talking and laughing for hours. My husband, too, sings to me in complicated Ki-Meru poetry, and our children long to know the words and their translations. His response, "Dare you tell your father to read you his love letters to his wife?" With pressures of work, love songs seem to decrease, but should they be allowed to be buried under pressing tasks and committee meetings?

Childlessness

The Christian counsellor will often see couples with marital issues related to childlessness and other pregnancy problems. In Africa, having children is not a choice, but an expectation. The only thing that varies from country to country is how many children people are expected to have and how far apart it is traditional to have them. With childlessness, the married couple waits to have children – and when none are forthcoming, they feel anxious, different, and lonely as their friends celebrate the births of their own children. Many African couples are not quick to seek medical advice in such a situation, and when they do, it is assumed that the wife must go to the doctor first. If she is diagnosed as infertile, she experiences anger, guilt, and despondency. Many women go through a monthly "hope-despair cycle." At the beginning of each month, the woman feels expectancy and hope. However, after much waiting and hoping, she feels despair when the pregnancy does not occur.

Other couples may face Sudden Infant Death Syndrome (SIDS), in which a baby dies suddenly for no apparent reason, often within the first six months of life. Grief counselling will be needed for these parents, so that they can deal with the anger, self-blame, or blaming of the other that they may experience. Another issue that may arise in counselling is the birth to a couple of children with a birth defect. In all these situations, counselling is needed to offer support, encourage emotional expression, and even suggest establishing a memorial when loss is involved.[261] In Africa, it is common for couples experiencing childlessness or SIDS to revert to superstitious ways to try to find out why bad luck seems to follow them. The support of a Christian community and a faith in God's benevolence will keep such couples from losing hope.

Counselling for Healthy Marriages

Counselling for marital problems begins with the Christian counsellor's commitment to what marriage ultimately stands for. Such an inner awareness will provide the motivation that counsellors need to work with troubled marriages. Since marriage is first and foremost God's idea, we can provide hope for a struggling couple. We will look next at healthy communication patterns, sexual satisfaction, and the creative use of anger and conflict.

Communication

To help couples build healthy marriages, we must help them to build healthy communication patterns. This involves helping each spouse to be attuned to the needs of the other, pacing oneself with the partner and seeking to understand the partner's experience. When is the best time to bring up a critical matter for discussion? Early in the morning when people are hurrying off for the day? No. Lack of time to fully deal with the issue may cause a spouse to respond with frustration and irritability, leaving the other feeling unheard and unloved and perhaps spoiling a whole day. The better way would be to wait until evening when both spouses have eaten and rested. Then one can request a time to talk. Finding the best time to communicate involves the emotional side of listening. Listening amounts to more than understanding what people say. It means paying at least equal attention to the way something is said, when it is said, and who is saying it.

We encourage couples to recognize that there are two kinds of communication, verbal and non-verbal. In non-verbal communication, we use gestures, facial expressions, and finger-pointing. Giving the partner the "silent treatment" occurs when one spouse does not talk, sometimes for days, to the other, instead of verbally expressing feelings. Among the Meru, women are often known to use this non-verbal means of communication. In trying to make a silent woman talk, a husband might say, *Ai, niatia waimba ta Kathita?* meaning, "Wow, how come you are swollen like the Kathita River?" Kathita is one of the major rivers in Meru District and flows from Mt. Kenya towards the Indian Ocean. After heavy rains it is swollen with floodwater, so the analogy is made to a woman who is filled with repressed hurt feelings. Sometimes a spouse sleeps facing the wall, as if to say, "I am so angry with you that all I can show you is my back." The late Kenyan psychiatrist Dr Sam Gatere said that this sleep posture is the farthest one can be away from the spouse in the same bed because that person lies exactly 180 degrees distant from the other. Turning either way would necessarily result in an angle of less than 180 degrees.[262]

Verbal communication involves using spoken words to say what one is feeling, to discuss a plan, to ask a question or respond to one, or to use one's spouse as a sounding board to test out new ideas. However, satisfactory verbal response to another requires careful listening.

> *Dr Mwiti*: In the early days of our marriage, Gershon and I practiced listening that involves concentration and putting aside distractions. In particular, I learned the art of listening from my husband – although I am the psychologist! Apparently, learning to listen does not come from book learning, but through commitment and caring. Whenever I talked to Gershon, he would put aside whatever he was doing and listen to me. He would always pause and look me in the eye as I spoke. This helped me to learn to put aside what I was doing whenever he started talking to me.

Sexuality

Counselling includes helping couples to understand the importance of sex in marriage, and the need to talk with each other openly about sexual problems. Failure to talk about sex leads to ignorance and mistaken assumptions. Sexual intimacy was created by God, who looked at the male and female at creation and declared them very good.[263] Sex was given as a gift through which a couple could express love towards one another. The Bible portrays such love as better than wine: "How delightful is your love, my sister, my bride! How much more pleasing is your love than wine, and the fragrance of your perfume more than any spice!"[264] If this kind of adoration radiated out of Christian marriages, the beauty of the Lord would indeed shine in his world more brightly. And this is what sex at creation was meant to be – good.

Choosing to give the other pleasure and joy requires being intentional about learning how one's partner experiences pleasure. Couples are often in too much of a hurry, too unwilling, or too arrogant to learn about their partner's sexual needs. Each spouse must remember that the other is different. Each partner has different approaches, different responses, and different time clocks.

Healthy sex happens in marriages when couples choose fidelity. The fact that a man and woman get married does not mean that they cease to be attractive. Leaving all others and clinging to this one *only* demands a choice to exclude any emotional loyalty to others and to practice self-control that raises one above sexual temptation.

Creative Use of Anger and Conflict

Counsellors can help couples to learn creative ways of handling anger and conflict as they grow together. There is no promise that in marriage, the road will always be smooth. There will be *vikwazo* or "hindrances" along the way. What a couple does with those situations will reveal how determined they are to place the marriage first. The Bible is clear: " 'In your anger do not sin': do not let the sun go down while you are still angry, and do not give the devil a foothold."[265]

Zac found out that his wife had lent some money to her brother without his knowledge. The brother was beginning a new business and had promised to pay the money back as quickly as possible. However, two months later, none had been returned. Zac had hoped to use some of that money to complete a down payment on a piece of land. He was angry and felt threatened that his wife could make such a loan without his knowledge. "What else have you done that I do not know about?" he barked. His wife said she had never done anything like that before, and that her brother had sworn that the money would be repaid with interest.

At least three options were open to Zac. Zac could *fight*, responding with a physical blow or verbal attack. Alternatively, he could walk away and slam the door after himself muttering, "Woman! Your brother has always been a crook, and you know it!" Demonstrating a refusal to face his emotions, this action would be classified as *flight*. Zac might also withdraw emotionally, feeling paralyzed, not knowing how to respond and afraid he might go out of control. This would be *freezing* emotionally.

There are creative ways of dealing with anger, and the ability to grow in this kind of creativity marks a marriage that is growing towards health. First, the marriage partners could individually develop more self-control. Self-control is listed as one of the fruits of the Spirit.[266] Other fruits of the Spirit that help with self-control are love and gentleness. If we love people and are gentle with them, we will not easily strike out against them, however angry we may feel. Individuals need to recognize that anger often flows out of hurt feelings. *Hurt people hurt people.* To prevent hurt from spreading, an offended spouse can communicate his or her disappointment with the other. The purpose would not be to condemn the other, but to explain the impact that the other's action had on the partner who feels hurt.

Dealing with his anger creatively, Zac could have shared his hurt feelings with someone he trusts – something that is hard for many men to do. Then Zac could have worked with his wife to clear up the situation that triggered the anger in the first place. David and Vera Mace note:

> Dealing with anger is one of the best ways of coming closer together. To fight is to alienate each other. To suppress anger and pretend it isn't there is to evade clearing up the situation and also risks an explosion of accumulated resentment later. To get behind the anger to the hurt that caused it and to clear that up is to remove a barrier to closeness and love.[267]

The Story of Mate and Sylvia

Reading the story of a couple named Mate and Sylvia, the reader may note all of the points that might cause problems in their marriage. Later, we will see how counselling can help to resolve some of their conflicts and keep their family intact.

Sylvia and Mate met at their local church, where he had just joined the staff as a new pastor. The day he was introduced to the congregation, Sylvia reports that something happened to her as she looked at this handsome young man. It didn't take long before he noticed her too. Their courtship was brief, and within two months, the couple announced their wedding. As much as people loved Sylvia, they were a bit surprised, because the usual marriage system had hardly been followed.

Tradition expected that courtship allow time for the couple to really get to know one another before making any commitment. The brethren in the church also wanted more time to get to know this new pastor who was courting their "daughter," who belonged to the church and community as much as she did to her own parents and extended family. Tradition also called for the families of the courting couple to get together for ceremonies in order to get to know each other and for the couple to go through premarital counselling. But none of this happened because of the speed of the courtship. Whenever Sylvia expressed concerns about rushing too fast, Mate swept all of her doubts under the carpet, reassuring the young woman of his love. So the wedding took place.

It did not take long for problems to emerge after they were married. Sylvia found that her publicly charismatic, warm husband became something else at home – unpredictable; cold; distant; calculating; and verbally, emotionally, and physically abusive. At first, she thought that all of the problems were her fault and she tried more and more to be the best wife possible. However, the more Sylvia tried, the more Mate complained. After the birth of their second child, he demanded that she quit her job and stay at home to raise the children. Sylvia resisted, pointing out that her mother had worked and raised a family at the same time. However, Mate was adamant, and Sylvia obediently quit her job. When her family and friends asked her why, she told them that she needed more time with her children.

As much as Sylvia tried, nothing she did ever seemed to satisfy her husband. He criticized her cooking, her housekeeping, her child-rearing and even the way she dressed. The couple's two young children were afraid of their father, because he would often burst out in anger for no apparent reason. On one occasion, Sylvia thought she smelled alcohol on her husband's breath. A few months later, Mate demanded that Sylvia reduce the frequency of her visits to her family. He himself did not seem to have any close family.

Mate blamed all of Sylvia's unhappiness on her. He maintained that there was nothing wrong with him, and if she would only try to please him more, they would both be happy. Mate spent most of his time in his office at the Bible School or travelling. Eventually, Sylvia began to accept the blame for all of the problems in her family. The once-vibrant woman became sad and listless. She would have crying spells that would last a week, followed by days of meaningless laughter. She would also pick on one child, beating her at the least provocation. Sylvia's parents watched all of this with concern, and at last decided to talk with their daughter. They urged her to return home with them, but she decided to ask the advice of her senior pastor. Help was near for Mate and Sylvia.

Basic Assumptions in Marriage Counselling

Both marriage and family begin with relationships. In chapter two, we outlined the basic assumptions of a relational model that informs our understanding of persons, especially from an indigenous African Christian perspective. Our relational model begins with covenant and ends with kinship survival. We place a strong emphasis on the fact that resilient communities can create resilient families. Resilient families can help to form resilient individuals. The individual's resiliency comes from a healthy, active connection to God and humanity, seeking on a daily basis to be known and transformed by the Almighty so that one can in turn become a change agent in the community. Couples with this connection bring wellness to themselves, their families, their churches, and their communities, thus promoting relational health throughout society.

Covenant

We begin again with God's covenant of faithfulness to us.[268] When couples are not faithful to their children, the next generation is negatively affected. To love one's partner is to model for the next generation the way God loves us. African indigenous Christian counselling affirms and strengthens the covenant between partners in a marriage. A marital covenant is a relationship that is more than a contract, because it invokes God's name and is relational, based on unity and community, justice and fairness.[269]

Created in God's Image

All members of any family are created in God's image. The counsellor will therefore correctly assume that both marriage partners are thirsting for wellness in their relationship. When their marriage is not harmonious, something somewhere has been broken. Mate believed that his happiness depended on Sylvia's efforts to please him. Sylvia, too, assumed that her identity was wrapped up in pleasing Mate. Each was expecting more from the other than that person could humanly give. Mate was a self-centred man who did not take time to build or nurture relationships. Sylvia was a woman who based her identity on her husband. Counselling in such a case can take the direction of helping the couple to understand how they have made each other into miniature gods, which, of course, has to lead to disappointment.[270]

Relational Brokenness

In counselling Mate and Sylvia, the counsellor explored their connections to their families and to their communities in order to uncover the source of their current problems. As the counsellor listened to Mate, he discovered a scared little child in the pastor's heart. It was revealed that Mate had been conceived out of wedlock. His grandparents had forced his mother to marry his father, a man who already had another wife. The man mistreated Mate and beat him so much in his childhood that his mother had to leave the home in order to save the life of her child. She returned to her family, but Mate's uncles never had a kind word for the fatherless boy. His mother lived at their mercy and eked out a living from a small plot of land given to her by her grandfather. Mate's grandfather hated him and saw in the child the reason his daughter's life was a mess. Caught between a hateful, neglecting father and an angry grandfather, Mate grew up with a cold heart, determined to get the best out of life. He never connected emotionally with anyone – neither his mother, his uncles, his cousins, nor his grandfather.

The counsellor worked with Mate to piece together his painful, disjointed past, and the impact it had on his personality. Mate began to understand the importance of family relationships. With guidance from the counsellor, Mate learned how he could seek out his mother for reconciliation, as well as begin to build relationships with his estranged family. In time, he found that he still had a place in his mother's heart, and that she had long waited for her son to "come back home." At a rural wedding of one of his cousins, Mate talked long into the night with his family elders, and at last a way began to open for reconciliation. As Mate offered forgiveness and made room to embrace his extended family, his hardness towards Sylvia also began to abate.

Since Sylvia had been brought up to aim for perfection in all she undertook, including her marriage, she blamed herself when things did not work out and worried that it was her fault whenever her husband failed to act like the kind of man she thought she married. Sylvia had lived too long with the belief that the success of her marriage depended wholly on her and her obedience to her husband. She saw that this was not working. Every time she hit her children out of frustration, she hated herself and what she was becoming. The more she hated herself, the more helpless she felt. It had never occurred to her that God or the Christian community around her could help. In working with Sylvia, the counsellor reminded her that God loves us *just as we are*, and as a result, we are set free to focus more on the needs of others and less on our own. Sylvia began to offer herself to work in the church's "Adopt a Granny"[271] programme which cared for the church's elderly people who lived without close family members nearby. She organized regular visits to these older individuals and began to create community for them. As Sylvia served, her perfectionist expectations at home relaxed, and she became a happier person to live with.

Inner Image of God

Mate's counsellor sought to know the man's inner image and his perception of God. What kind of God resided there? How did Mate become a Christian? How did he experience God's love? The counsellor learnt that Mate's mother sent him away to a mission school at an early age. There he was introduced to faith in Jesus Christ, and in his loneliness he embraced God's love. However, no one talked to him then about how God could help him to deal with his inner pain. The counsellor worked with Mate to help him to change his beliefs and expectations. Mate felt that his mother owed it to him to make his life happy, after all she had done to wreck it. That was the emotional wound with which he had approached his marriage. Sylvia was a beautiful, good woman who kept his home just the way he wanted it. However, Mate expected her to do the impossible: make him happy. When the image of God in our hearts is distorted, we make others into gods. He saw in Sylvia his mother. She had to succeed in all of the areas in which his mother had failed. She had to be the perfect wife. In this illusion, he could not fathom God as a Father who wished abundant life for his children. Never having tasted abundant life, Mate had no idea what he was missing – or how to get it.

Sylvia, on the other hand, lived with an introjection, a mental image of her mother and a demanding God. As much as she had detested her mother's desire for perfection, nothing the children or her husband did was enough to please her. Sylvia's personality had been constructed by adopting her mother's external behavioural patterns, expecting perfection from Mate and herself, and withdrawing in self-blame when her efforts failed to bear what she considered the necessary fruit. In the same way that her mother blamed her husband for his alcoholism, Sylvia blamed Mate for the unhappiness in their marriage.

Alienation

It was clear that although Mate was a Christian, he lived in a state of alienation from God and from humanity. As the counsellor worked with him, he found that Mate's suffering as a child had left him stunted emotionally and spiritually. For self-protection, Mate had distanced himself from his true self and from others as well. He protected himself by never again becoming vulnerable. Such fear of vulnerability locks an individual in darkness.

As a child, Sylvia was left longing for love from a father who was often emotionally absent due to his drinking, and from a mother who communicated that she could never be good enough. Sylvia externalized these feelings by blaming Mate for his emotional and physical absence, and by demanding perfection both from him and from herself. All of this locked the couple in a relationship that both experienced as destructive, but from which neither could find a way out.

Reconciliation

Mate's counsellor helped him to recognize his part in the problems in his marriage. All of the tears Mate had refused to cry as a boy as he suffered at the hands of his cruel father and other men in his family poured out like a flood. Mate made peace with God, realizing that he had perceived God as an angry taskmaster whom he could never please. This was why Mate was so driven at work, trying to please an angry "Father." Slowly, he came to realize that God could be served not out of obligation, but out of love. Reconciliation with his wife also became possible after Mate realized that he had seen his mother in Sylvia and tried to force the young woman to pay for all of the ways he felt his mother had failed him. He acknowledged that in his relationship with Sylvia, he had demanded of her what she could not give. As soon as his repressed anger began to melt, Mate saw Sylvia for who she really was, a woman who cared for him deeply and needed his love. Reconciled with God, Mate also became reconciled to himself and to his wife. He was determined to look for his mother and ask for forgiveness. And maybe, just maybe, he could be reconciled with his grandparents as well and then even with his father.

In turn, Sylvia's counsellor helped her to recognize her part in the problems of her marriage. Sylvia wept when she realized how much like her mother she had become, and how she had subconsciously hated herself for it. All of her anger against her mother and father came out in counselling. She recognized that she had made a habit of expressing the same anger she had seen in her mother towards Mate, because Sylvia saw in him her father and his drinking. She remembered that she froze in fear the day she smelt alcohol on Mate's breath, and that her sleep that night had been filled with images of her drunken father and her mother's cold disapproval of him. Sylvia was able to receive God's assurance that he loves her just as she is, and she prayed for an outpouring of unconditional love towards Mate. She realized that reconciliation was possible. Sylvia was able to see her parents' love beneath their own struggles and so forgave them for loving her in their own troubled way.

Restoring the Relationship

Mate and Sylvia's healing was a slow process, but it produced delightful fruit. Their joy began to show first in their marriage, and then with their children. A metamorphosis had taken place. Mate became an easier person to work with. At home, there was peace as the two renewed their marriage vows and continued to work with the counsellor. Mate and Sylvia concentrated on blessing each other, setting each other free, improving their communication, and increasing their time spent together. They also learnt how to forgive each other and to avoid harbouring anger or bitterness. The couple increased the frequency of their visits to their parents and were even emotionally mature enough to handle the caustic comments that still came from time to time from Sylvia's mother.

Community Resiliency

Following his own transformation, Mate instituted premarital and marriage counselling for the students at Tema Bible School, and he suggested that a similar programme be adapted by his whole denomination. The Bible School would initiate a continuing education programme for pastors in both premarital and marriage counselling, so that all the church members could benefit. Mate's healing was impacting the whole community. Eventually, Sylvia began to consider training to become a pastoral counsellor. She desired to help others as she had been helped.

Kinship Survival

Tema Bible School enriched the indigenous African church by transforming marriages in the community. Mate, who had not previously honoured cultural celebrations of marriage, was now a proponent of involving everyone from both sides of each partner's family so that, as their culture mandated, marriage was not for individuals but for everyone in the community. Clans, villages, and extended families meet, court, and marry each other through their children. This is the African way. Mate and Sylvia's village celebrated the restoration of marriage that was based on the Christian value system and sensitive to their tribal culture. This celebration of marriage was a communal act that would enrich the couple's current relationships as well as act as a communal means of passing on a legacy to younger generations. This, indeed, is the African practice of ensuring kinship survival.

Christian Counselling for Marriage Problems

Counselling married couples can be emotionally intense, and the competent Christian counsellor refrains from being drawn into taking sides. Before any counsel is offered, fees, if any, should be agreed upon, time should be set aside for information gathering, the nature of counselling should be explained, and any concerns the clients have about counselling should be addressed. Counselling might initially be spread over ten sessions, with the number of sessions depending on the couple's commitment and the nature of the problem.

Creating a Context for Counselling

The first task is to create a good framework within which counselling can occur. The counsellor can do so by determining who is willing to come in for counselling: an "offended" spouse, the couple, the family, the extended family, or significant members of the tribe. Next, if both husband and wife are willing to participate, decisions need to be made regarding where to meet with the couple, whether to see them together or apart, whether the counsellor needs to work alone or with another counsellor, and the length of time the couple wants to commit to the counselling programme Also, one must decide with the couple whether information shared by one counselee in a session with the counsellor may be brought into joint sessions by the counsellor.

Evaluating the Nature of the Problem

The counsellor meets the couple for two to three sessions in order to evaluate the nature of the presenting problem. What does the couple think is the problem? How does each perceive the spouse's role in the problem? Are there symptoms of deeper issues? What is the level of spirituality of this couple? How willing are they to change? How long has the problem been going on? Have they sought help elsewhere? If so, from who? What were the results? As the couple answers each question, the counsellor seeks to provide hope and comfort.

It is important for the counsellor to assess whether it is safe to see the couple together. If there are issues of domestic violence involved, meeting together may put the couple at greater risk for violence, and because of that, the counsellor may not be able to accurately assess the response that each partner has to the other. It may therefore be helpful to have time with each partner individually; this may be the only way to make it safe for a partner to express fears. A simple set of questions can be helpful in this assessment: What happens when you argue? Do things ever get out of control? What does that look like? If the assessment reveals that a spouse's life is in significant danger, the counsellor can encourage that counselee to find shelter with a friend or relative.

Assessing Resources

It is important to discern what strengths or resources the couple brings to the counselling experience. They obviously have a commitment to address the problem in counselling. Have there been good times in their marriage? What strengths does each partner have? Are there role models in their lives for a healthy marriage? Is there an uncle or aunt, pastor or community leader who has taken special interest in the marriage partners? Knowing what resources a couple can count on as they begin counselling is important. At a later time, the couple may need to be reminded of these resources. When issues are deep and difficult, the counsellor could seek the help of those in the couple's support system. Is there an aunt or uncle who could get involved?

If community and family resources are exhausted, and the counsellor senses that the problems are beyond his or her competence, it would be wise to refer the couple to a more experienced psychotherapist. If the counsellor feels that he or she can handle the issues the couple has presented, the evaluation session can be followed with other meetings as the couple needs – as long as all parties involved commit themselves to keeping the appointments and working on assignments given by the counsellor.

Assessing Cultural Issues

Counsellors need to assess any cultural issues that might exacerbate marital problems. For example, in some indigenous communities, a wife may be perceived as "ours." She left her original family and came into the new family to cater to "our" needs, some in the husband's family may think. In keeping with this warped understanding, some young married couples have come home from the honeymoon to find their new marital home full of the husband's relatives, who have come to stay. This may happen in urban areas, as the new husband's siblings hang around looking for jobs or just visiting for weeks. Such early intrusions into a very young marriage may interfere with the couple's ability to bond because of a lack of private time. A new couple needs to be left alone for at least the first two years of marriage – free to love, make mistakes, rest, and entertain without the intrusion of family members. Friends also do well to respect the private space of newly married couples, so that community, as important as it is, does not begin to suffocate a fledgling marital relationship.

We have already indicated that Christian counsellors are students of the culture in which they are living, and that the church is encouraged to remain in dialogue about cultural issues that impact the way people live. Cultural practices that do not meet biblical standards – for example, polygamy or female circumcision – should be sacrificed for the sake of health in the body. Churches that provide this kind of guidance are fulfilling Jesus's call to be responsible shepherds of the flock. People might need re-education on negative cultural elements that might cause stress in marriages. For example, some traditional cultures assume that after marriage, a wife should stay at home helping her in-laws – but this would create considerable stresses for a professional woman. Will a husband encourage such a woman to express her gifts, or will he listen to his parents, who demand that she leave her job to help run the family farm?

Utilizing Indigenous Resources

The Christian counsellor does not limit him- or herself to examining only the problematic impact of the culture on marriage and family life, but also pays close attention to positive cultural traditions that can be used to enrich these relationships. Sue and Sue note that indigenous societies abound in three elements that can be utilized to enrich the counselling process: the community, where a wider group offers support for struggling clients; the use of faith and spirituality to enrich the recovery process; and the utilization of wise people in the community, who can be linked to struggling clients.[272] Elders can support the counsellor with added wisdom, as the counsellor leads the couple to explore and utilize the richness of indigenous cultures for healing, as well as for the prevention of future problems. All of this promotes marriage resilience and health.

Clarifying Goals and Outcomes

It's important that both counsellors and counselees clarify their goals. Goals for marriage counsellors typically include understanding what is causing problems, offering a safe place for the couple to express their feelings and frustrations, providing an opportunity to work together on the marriage, instilling hope, teaching conflict-management skills, and motivating positive change and growth.[273] Counselee goals may include clarifying what each partner is looking for, what they think should be changed, and their levels of commitment to change. Setting mutually acceptable goals will involve an examination of those goals in terms of the general wellness of the marriage. How specific, measurable, achievable, and time-specific are the goals? Finally, counselling will involve charting a course toward achieving the goals.

Intervening in the Family Structure

Over time, couples and families develop structures, patterns of relating. Is there one person in the marriage or family who is consistently blamed when things go wrong, a scapegoat? Are any members of the family close to the point of physical illness because of stress? Is there healthy separation and togetherness? When people get too close, they may cross boundaries that keep others from growing. To escape the suffocation of control from more dominant family members, a weaker person may become ill, whether the illness is imaginary or physical. One young woman had a very dominant, intrusive father. She hated the fact that he demanded to know everything that was going on in her life. To escape his intrusion and never-ending demands, she often went to bed as a defence against his hassles.

> *Dr Mwiti*: Intervention in this relationship would include an exploration of this father-daughter relationship. The father, labelling the young woman as rude and withdrawing, brought her to me for psychotherapy. Could I make sure she behaved better? We explored this relationship by seeing the family together part of the time and each of them separately at other times. As understanding grew, the whole family began to see that their communication patterns needed an overhaul. I remember the young woman saying to me: "Dr Mwiti, it is not me, but my dad who needs to see you more often. He has so many personal problems that keep him from communicating in a sane manner

with anyone. Ask him, does he even have any friends anymore?" Speaking in front of her husband and daughter, the mother said: "Tell them, Dr Mwiti, to learn to communicate with each other. I am tired of being used as a conduit between them." Family counselling helped build open, positive communication patterns in this family, as each individual began to identify and change their negative communication patterns; deal with problematic emotional outbursts; and rebuild connections with each other, family, and community.

Teaching for Wholeness

The Christian counsellor is committed to the prevention of marital conflict through teaching. This can be done through enrichment seminars, couples' retreats, and premarital counselling. Christian counsellors do not wait for marriages to break down and then fix them. On the contrary, they can encourage the church to keep marriages whole through the celebration of wedding anniversaries, sermons addressing marriage, and financial and emotional support for couples in conflict. Indeed, Christian counselling for marriages in Africa needs to be the kind that seeks to enrich matrimony as well as to keep healed relationships from backsliding into brokenness.

Conclusion

We have described in this chapter ways in which we can provide counselling for married couples and their families. This includes helping couples realize that to build healthy marriages, they need to give priority to their marital relationships. This choice becomes a commitment that will release energy to build lasting relationships. The resulting vigour can bring excitement as each couple experiences the mystery of marriage. Children born into such relationships will experience the security that comes from knowing that their parents are committed to one another and are willing to weather any storms to keep their marriage and family healthy. Thus, surrounded with consistency and enduring love, children learn to act consistently themselves and to thrive.

CHAPTER 9

On Counselling Families

Dr Mwiti: Many years ago, a respected professional man, Dr Mari[274], arrived at my office with his 15-year-old son, Kairu, in tow. His opening words were: "I hear that you talk to such as these," pointing to his son. "How long will you take? I want to leave you together and come back later. When will you be through?" "Sessions are usually about one hour," I responded. "Fine, I'll see you later." And with that, he got into his car and drove off. As soon as we sat down, I asked the young man, "What can I do for you? Why are you here?" "I don't know. You tell me! I thought he told you why he brought me to you." He talked; I listened. Then he talked some more. As the session progressed, the boy narrated struggles with his father: the man's poor communication, his anger, his frustration, and his absences from home. Slowly, I realized that my actual client was not in the room. He'd just driven away. Here was a man who, although he had a PhD, did not have the wisdom to manage his own family. He was able to present technical research papers at international conferences, but he could not carry on a five-minute conversation with his son.

Culturally, African young people are caught up in a contradiction. On the one hand, they are supposed to show allegiance to their indigenous cultures, although most are ignorant of the expectations of their heritage. On the other hand, modern culture screams at them from the West – a pop culture that dictates fashion, music, physique, and success. The call of African identity is muffled by ignorance and shame inherited from Western packaging that devalues everything African as primitive and backward. Consequently, African youth may live with an inner devotion to their African roots but with an outward allegiance to some alien cultural standards. However, this Western call is illusive, a mirage coloured by myths created in Hollywood, conventions that contain promises that even Westerners themselves cannot attain. The divide between the two worlds leaves African youth in what we have called a *values vacuum*.[275]

More counselling and education for families with young children and adolescents is one of Africa's greatest needs today.

The call for the restoration of the systematic training of children and young people cannot be ignored. We are all familiar with these biblical texts: "Start children off on the way they should go, and even when they are old they will not turn from it."[276] "Hold on to instruction, do not let it go; guard it well, for it is your life."[277] Who must answer the call to train and educate? Everyone! Parents, the church, the school community, and the wider society – involving art and culture, the mass media, literature, and the entertainment industry. All must assume responsibility.

In the past, African communities had traditional ways of training children and young people. Education in these settings was holistic, incorporating survival skills, spirituality, and values. Therefore, every Christian counsellor is encouraged to understand the system of child and youth training that was used in the community in which he or she works, or in which their counselees were raised. Of course, Africans must not unrealistically and simplistically accept what worked in the past. That which agrees with Christian convictions may be adopted. *The challenge is to remember that Christian counselling and education that builds on biblical and progressive cultural practices already present in society will bear sustainable fruit in the long run.* This is the fundamental assumption of our African indigenous Christian model of counselling. Counselling children, youth, and whole families will be the subject of this chapter.

A Family without Rituals

In the following story, we meet Mr Theuri, a Christian counsellor who was asked to see two brothers, Tim and Karis. Tim was a 17-year-old in trouble for fighting at school. He was a bully who was also a loner and had several times threatened to hurt himself and others. He had never shown any interest in his school performance. He barely made it to high school, saved only by his natural intelligence. His brother Karis was 15 years old, and his primary problem was also poor school performance. He had done well in primary school but seemed to struggle in high school. The boys' mother came with them for counselling, but it was clear that without threats from the school, the mother would not have bothered to seek help from anyone.

At first, Mr Theuri saw the boys' mother alone. She was a quiet woman who sometimes spoke in a whisper that made her difficult to understand. She declared that she was at her wits' end in raising the boys. The brothers appeared to be complete opposites. At the first counselling session, Tim was arrogant and rude, while Karis was sad and withdrawn. Tim lashed out at people in anger, while Karis recoiled at the smallest reproach. While Tim did not care about school, Karis was so afraid of failure that he would not even try to do well. Mr Theuri learned that the family went to church rarely, though the father, a rich man in the community, contributed fairly large sums of money to the church construction fund.

Mr Theuri listened to the boys' mother and began to piece together the family situation. Mrs Matheka, the mother, told Mr Theuri that the boy's father was a hard, domineering man, who had treated the children as mature adults since they were born. "He forced them to work like grown men very early and beat them when they showed any weakness. He operated several stone quarries for his construction business, and he would make the children work in them, cutting stone, every Saturday and over the school holidays. The children also were required to bring home 'A' papers in every subject. A beating would follow if anyone failed to do that."

Mrs Matheka continued: "The boys' father never allowed for any luxury at home. He claimed that an easy life spoiled the children. He had grown up in his uncle's home. No one knew who his father was. His mother had married and left her illegitimate baby with her brother. Although his community made a place for such children, the uncle always reminded the growing young man that, were it not for the uncle's kind heart, he would have been a beggar in the village. The family never went to church.

"Finally, my husband was able to enrol in a trade school far away from home. He vowed that he would never return to his uncle's village. And he didn't. After the two years of training, he sought work at a nearby construction site – and step by step built himself up, until he owned a construction company himself. After we were married, my husband cut off all connections with his uncle and the rest of his family. However, his anger remained, burning inside him. He poured this anger out on our children and filled me with fear."

As Mr Theuri listened, it became clear that the young men were responding as well as they knew how to a very toxic family situation. In addition to the problem of Mr Matheka's anger, this was a family without rituals. They celebrated no birthdays. There were no coming-of-age celebrations. The family attended church events at Christmas and Easter, but there were no celebrations at home later. Sadly, the boys had no friends in the community or in the church.

Not surprisingly, both children were depressed, imprisoned, helpless, and hopeless. However, their symptoms were as different as their personalities.

Because he could not strike back when his father was angry, Tim responded by displacing his aggression and anger onto younger children. Full of guilt at wanting to hurt his father, he was more likely to hurt himself or someone else. Eventually, consumed by fury and guilt, Tim retreated into himself.

Karis, as emotionally wounded as his brother, became depressed and full of self-loathing. He, too, was very angry with his father. However, in his helplessness, Karis was afraid of even trying to succeed, because the older man never recognized anyone's effort and never encouraged his sons to succeed. The cruelty that Mr Matheka had experienced from his uncle was being passed on to Mr Matheka's own children. Mr Theuri was reminded of the biblical text in which the sins of the parents affect the children to the third and the fourth generation.[278]

Due to Tim's threat to hurt himself, Mr Theuri saw him briefly to find out if he had an actual plan to carry out his threat. He did this in an attitude of prayer, asking God for wisdom and guidance. The counsellor obtained a contract from Tim, promising that he would not act on any plan for self-harm. After that assessment, Mr Theuri referred Tim to a clinical psychologist, who would begin treatment and send the young man to a psychiatrist for medication, if necessary. Tim later returned to participate in family counselling sessions.

After referring Tim for treatment, Mr Theuri worked with Karis and his parents. Any benefits of this counselling would also benefit Tim, since he and Karis belonged to the same family system. Mr Theuri began by assessing Karis's depression. From talking to Karis's mother, he became convinced that the young man's depression was not related to a physical condition but was a reaction to stress from the erratic parenting of his father and the passive parenting of his mother. Mr Theuri asked Karis to talk about his life experiences and learned more about the effect of Mr Matheka's poor parenting on the young man. The father had set his expectations so far above what the young man could achieve that his failure was inevitable. While Tim became rebellious, Karis had become sad and depressed. Karis shared that he felt that he had no control over anything in his life. No matter what he did, he could not please his father, and his mother was too docile to protect him from her husband. Several times he had wished that he could run away from home, Karis said, but he did not know where to go. With no relatives in the area, he had no one to ask for help. Isolated and lonely, he had become sad and withdrawn.

Mr Theuri found that counselling could help Karis, since he was willing to talk about his situation and welcomed any guidance that the counsellor could provide. Mr Theuri also discovered that during a Christian Union meeting in school, Karis had become a Christian – but that he had not grown spiritually.

Counselling now included building on this fragile spiritual commitment. The counsellor prayed the young man would experience God's presence within his painful experience.

Mr Theuri noted that Karis always talked of himself as a failure and disappointment to his parents. For example, the young man kept saying, "I am useless. I disappoint my parents." It was necessary, therefore, to confront these thoughts. Mr Theuri offered the sad young man unconditional acceptance in their counselling sessions. Karis was wary at first, wondering whether Mr Theuri would condemn him as his father did, or call him lazy, as did some of the teachers at school.

When Karis again indicated that he felt unloved, Mr Theuri asked Karis if he felt that God loved him. Karis said he did. "How do you know that?" Mr Theuri asked. After they had read Scripture together, Mr Theuri asked Karis to imagine the ways in which God loved him. Karis was eventually able to imagine God as a kind elder, encouraging him rather than beating him. Accepting and relying on God's love, Karis began to grow in self-worth and to remember that God valued him for himself.

When the young man said, "There is *nothing* I ever do right," the counsellor countered by asking, "Is that true? Are there some things that you do right? Or is it your father who says so?" They realized that it was mainly Mr Matheka who used these negative words. Karis was helped to make a list of things he did well: playing soccer, helping around the house, writing good stories, and reading voraciously. Slowly, he began to acknowledge these positive aspects of his life, and he seemed happier each time he came to meet with Mr Theuri. As Karis changed, the counsellor encouraged him to join the school soccer team, which he did. Spiritually, Karis grew phenomenally. He became active in the Christian Union and was part of the club's hospital visitation team, which often visited patients in the AIDS ward.

Mr. Theuri met alone with Mrs Matheka a few times. Before Mr Theuri asked to see Mr Matheka, Mrs Matheka told him that she was so afraid of her husband's anger that she felt helpless to protect the boys from their father. She added that she now realized how damaging her silence had become. With Mr Theuri's encouragement, Mrs Matheka was able to send some village elders to discuss with her husband the damage he was doing to his children. She boldly followed this with a talk with her husband, after a dinner with the pastor in their home.

Later, Mrs Matheka reported to Mr Theuri that she was surprised to find that her husband had some kindness in him after all. He had just hidden it under his long-term resentment, because he had never learnt from anyone how to be gentle. In addition to seeking her husband's support in encouraging their sons, Mrs Matheka began to make regular visits to school to talk to the boys' teachers. This partnership increased her understanding of the school's expectations, and she began to work closely with the boys, encouraging them in their studies.

Eventually, Mr Theuri called Mr Matheka, asking him to come to "help the counsellor with his sons' treatment." This was the only way to convince him to see the counsellor. In sessions, Mr Theuri listened as Mr Matheka told his childhood story of being abused, declaring that he truly wanted to be a good father. Mr Matheka could not understand how the boys had become so unruly. The two discussed which men in the village had been Mr Matheka's role models. He mentioned a favourite uncle, and the counsellor asked him to contact this relative for advice on how to raise the boys.

Mr Matheka's attitude changed after returning home from the meeting with his uncle. His uncle had reminded him that it is not the African way to train children by hitting or demanding, but that a gentle spirit was needed in raising children. However, knowing what to do was not enough. He and the counsellor spent months quieting the impatient and unkind voices in his heart. Ever so slowly, his attitude and behaviour changed.

As therapy drew to an end, Mr Matheka actually thanked Mr Theuri for helping his family. Tim was doing better, he reported, and both boys had more time to spend acting like teenagers everywhere, hanging out with their friends at church or in the community. Mr Matheka proudly announced that he had already bought each of his sons a bicycle, so that as soon as they finished morning duties at the quarry, they could quickly cycle home, attend to other matters, and join their friends.

Mr Theuri ended counselling with a few meetings with both parents, and later with the entire family. They all recounted the gains that Tim and Karis had made, and the positive changes in the family. Tim reported that he was doing well at home, and that he had become more peaceful as his parents became more supportive.

Before ending the counselling relationship, Mr Theuri emphasized the need for continuing family communication, for enriching community links, and for actively participating in the church community. Mrs Matheka joined the local church, as well as the ladies' meetings there. Mr Matheka said that he was still unsure about the church, given his history. Mr Theuri taught the parents and the children how to engage in family rituals, suggesting regular vacations, birthday celebrations, and visits to cousins in the village. He even recommended that the boys spend some school holiday time helping their grandparents. The family was in a better place, well aware that past pains, if not taken care of, continue to hurt people.

The Christian counselling team in Mr Theuri's counselling centre met regularly for peer supervision. They reported progress or failures in therapy, prayed together, and from time to time, invited one of the professional counsellors in the area to discuss his or her work as counsellor. Local pastors valued and supported the counsellors, considering counselling to be a ministry just as important as discipleship, youth work, women's ministry, intercession, and teaching.

As the primary counsellor, Mr Theuri utilized community resources to work with this family. There were referrals to the clinical psychologist and the psychiatrist. He involved the parents, as well as the church. The mother established links with both teachers and community elders. It took a village to bring wellness to the boys and their family.

Growing Up African

Growing up African isn't just about growing up *in* Africa. It has to do with the values that African parents want to impart to their children – standards that are authentic, tested, and tried. This focus then becomes the goal of child training through early development and maturation. This was missing in the Matheka family. So, what elements are involved in bringing up young people who are authentically African? Young people need a type of training that includes the richness of what most traditional African communities provided in the past. This training was cohort-based and involved consistent behavioural expectations that were reinforced through family and community rituals and specific rites of passage. Parents, counsellors, teachers, and pastors can work together as a team to teach behavioural standards that can be ingrained from childhood to adulthood, leaving no doubt about community expectations and standards for living.

Gentle training communicates love and security to young people. Positive peer pressure will come with positive friendships and associations, while negative peer pressure will lead to destructive habits and behaviours. Surrounded with care, young people will find it easier to develop a sense of identity and purpose. Similarly, shame surrounding deviant behaviour will discourage rebelliousness and contribute to the self-discipline that enhances communal health. Under this system, young people will be entrusted early with responsibilities ranging from agricultural work to voluntary community service. These other areas of self-expression will give them experience in contributing to family and community life.

The current reality is that many African children and young people have received no such training. Too many parents hope that the schools will train their children, while they themselves concentrate on earning more money. Villages are often seen as provincial, compared with city life. The village is what one "visits" to see parents and to nostalgically experience again the old rituals – but for many, the village is not considered useful for modern life. Africans today may not recapture the grandeur of past cultural traditions, but cultural themes can be used as a foundation for church and school training programmes for youth.

It may not be necessary to revert to village life to train children, since one can deliberately build new "training" neighbourhoods, using the church as the primary community, whether in the city or a suburb. This idea is not a dream. Some churches in the cities of Africa have already reclaimed rich cultural principles for training their youth. For example, the Presbyterian Church of East Africa in Kenya has a national programme operating in 42 presbyteries, in which hundreds of adolescents meet for teaching in preparation for circumcision for the boys and initiation into adulthood for the girls. As the boys go through the physical "cut," the girls go through instruction for adulthood by older women. In some churches, this teaching is sometimes called the "cut of the tongue," to indicate that although the church no longer practices female circumcision, the training for adulthood that goes with it should not be lost. Accompanied by their parents, the training is provided in the context of a ceremony that recovers cultural rites of passage into adulthood by bringing the reconstructed practices into the household of faith. This is what we mean by building a new Christian community to train the youth.

To help the church in Africa to reclaim and rename this rich tradition of child socialization, it is necessary to consider how African children were trained in the past. Africans have primarily utilized three elements: specific rituals, age-cohorts, and adult mentorship.

Specific Rituals

Among the Meru of Kenya, training of children and adolescents was set within specific rituals designed for kinship survival. Historian M'Imanyara notes that "life was full of rituals and ceremonies relating to adolescence, marriages, death, and achievements."[279] The rituals and training involved the whole community, from parents and children to community and spiritual leadership. Meru culture was founded on the solid ground of discipline, education, and wisdom. Meru traditions included many practices similar to Jewish and biblical customs such as circumcision rites, sacrifices, and oaths. The age-group system was set up in such a way that no one missed out on initiation rites. Those without parents to sponsor them were sponsored by relatives.

Age Cohorts

Formal training among the Meru was based on the age-group system and on membership in the *Ndwato* or *Biama*, the "political and social organizations."[280] *Ndwato* was the name of guilds or organizations for uncircumcised males up to 25 years of age. Circumcision ushered them into *Biama*. Women did not have as many groups as the men but belonged to one social organization called *Kagita*. The main purpose of Kagita was to preserve agricultural standards and protect the environment from degradation, since the community was agricultural. For example, members of *Kagita* made sure that plants like sugarcane and bananas were not interfered with until harvest. This care for crops would not only preserve food for the tribe in times of famine, but also teach good husbandry.

Cohort training ensured that no child was left out. Teaching and training responded to developmental needs at each stage. Girls and boys were nurtured and trained within their age-group setting, and each individual had the responsibility of abiding by the tribal standards of behaviour so that they would not shame their age group. Peer pressure thus created a positive force for accountability.

Adult Mentorship

As young people moved towards young adulthood, they needed older adults who would stay close to them and keep them accountable. Among the Meru, peer accountability was realized within a circle of adult mentorship. Besides general adult coaching, there were specific assignments that were officially recognized in the initiation training system. For example, young women would receive training in topics related to their maturation: developmental issues, behavioural expectations, and peer accountability. Each cohort had to pass this assigned training before its members could graduate to the next cohort. Training for girls was fully integrated into the indigenous society, with parents, especially mothers, entrusted with the training of their daughters and other female family members (for example, orphaned children). In addition to the mentorship of the youth, the young people would also be recognized and rewarded for talents and abilities within a clear system for developing leadership and guiding them to take on responsibilities within the tribe. People occupied positions according to their abilities, from national leadership to the headship of families, subclans and clans, or serving in the judiciary. African cultural training programmes left no room for meandering through life without goals.[281]

Tim and Karis, from our last story, had received no such cultural training.

> *Dr Mwiti*: From childhood, in addition to mentoring within the tribal system, the church was my empowering community. First, the adults believed in my Christian faith. The elders did not doubt that as a child, I could love God and live in obedience to him.
>
> The fact that others believed in me created self-worth and helped develop my identity as an equal partner in the household of faith. For me as an African female child, the church provided more than my tribal group could – because no one in the church ever told me I could not do something because I was a girl. The church also provided mentors, older women who taught me how to mature holistically, taking my place in church, school, and community, and to use my gifts wherever I could. Every holiday, together with others from the Kenya Students' Christian Fellowship, young people attended Christian youth camps where we were trained on everything from responsible sexuality to how to study, relate to our parents, handle leisure time, and live as responsible persons in the community. Teaching was reinforced through rewards and appreciation. It was clear to me that faith is not a prison, but that in living within the boundaries of biblical and cultural expectations, there is freedom. The church community was not devoid of toxic people, mainly older ones who never believed that young people would successfully keep their faith and live accountable lives. However, with my pastors, my mentors, several close teachers, and my family believing in me, I successfully navigated adolescence. This was my community and I dared not let it down.

Restoration of indigenous, biblically oriented and culturally-rooted youth training offers an answer to the values vacuum in Africa. However, we must not *romanticize* the past.

> *Dr Mwiti*: Adult mentors are not always perfect, and neither are villages. For example, my uncle believed that he had the responsibility to raise me, and culturally, that was acceptable. However, he was so exasperating. I had long, beautiful hair and loved to braid it at night. This practice was carried out by

many young women, in order that their hair would be somewhat straight in the morning. My uncle would come home and demand to see my report card. He never commended me for good grades – and there were many. However, he would focus on the classes where I had not done so well. If one of my grades at school did not suit him, he would tell me that if I did not spend all my time braiding my hair, I'd have done better in school. He would add, "And you know, those who braid their hair will never enter heaven." I felt doubly condemned. After the damage was done, my mother would comfort me, telling me that she knew I was doing my best in school, and adding "Hair is not a ticket to heaven."

My uncle continued to poke his nose into my affairs until one day I told him: "You keep harping about my hair and heaven. If perchance you hold the keys to paradise, please don't let me in." Later on, I regretted this sharp remark, but enough was enough. With my mother's encouragement and appreciation, I went on to become an honour student in both high school and college. She loved me and trusted me so much that I couldn't let her down. Her love for Christ also modelled the love of God to me, and as I got to know Christ better, I was ever so careful not to let him down or to bring him displeasure and pain. I started living my life with a desire to please God. My mother's love and acceptance paved my way to love God, to be obedient to Christ, and to serve in God's Kingdom.

The Church as a New Community for Families

From Ur of the Chaldeans to a promised land, to Egypt and back, God was creating a people, a new people who would reflect God's holiness and act as a witness to the world.[282] The African indigenous Christian counsellor must help the church to be faithful to its calling, which includes providing a home for the Christian family. Like the traditional village, the church supports the family as it raises children. In the church, children can be taught the law of the Lord[283] and are not hindered from knowing and loving God. When the disciples tried to keep children away from Jesus, he declared, "Let the little children come to me, and do not hinder them, for the kingdom of heaven belongs to such as these."[284]

When children observe adults honouring each other, they may also learn to honour their father and mother – which is the first commandment with a promise – "that it may go well with you and that you may enjoy long life on the earth."[285] Fathers who learn to be patient with their brothers and sisters in the congregation may also learn to not exasperate their children, but "instead, bring them up in the training and instruction of the Lord."[286] If fathers learn from Jesus what it means to be a servant, then they may choose not to teach and train their children from a position of absolute power, for this only exasperates them.

The Christian community, including parents and Christian counsellors, can learn how to love young people so that major problems can be avoided in their maturation. A Christian community that upholds the extended family creates a web that holds its youth but is also flexible enough to allow each individual young person to stretch. Youth mentoring and coaching does not depend as much on rules as on relationships.

Unconditional Love

Unconditional acceptance by members of a congregation and by parents means communicating to the child that they will love her or him regardless of how badly the child might fail. Unconditional acceptance creates a sense of *security*, in which the maturing adolescent does not have to prove anything to anyone.

A common African proverb states, "If you do not feed your cat at home, it will go to the neighbours in search of something to eat." Similarly, young people starved of love at home will often seek love outside the home. Fortunately, some may find that affection from other adult Christians. However, many teenagers have fallen into sexually exploitative relationships while looking for the love they are missing at home. A young woman once told an Oasis Africa counsellor, "If my dad does not tell me that I am beautiful and loved, I will look for a man outside my home to tell me what I most need to hear."

Recognition

Recognition communicates significance. The church can shine by repeatedly affirming the gifts of children and adolescents. Accomplishments can be celebrated. Musical gifts can be exercised in the church community. Instead of focusing on the wrong that children are doing or the right that they are not doing, a positive approach by adult Christians, including parents, makes a habit of praising children for all of the things they do well. Appreciation must be genuine, because young people have an allergic reaction to lies and dishonesty by adults.

Mark, a troubled young man in therapy, told an Oasis Africa counsellor that in his family's home, communication was so poor that people did not meet or talk to one another. Living in the city and far away from tribal support systems, the family was not only nuclear but also isolated. Families survive within a network of extended family relationships of care and community connectedness.[287] However, Mark's family had neither. Communication in his house was mostly through little notes left on top of the television set or stuck on the refrigerator. No parent was around to listen to his fears about maturation and questions of identity. No one recognized or affirmed his gifts. The young man spent time alone and became depressed. The fact that his parents had poor communication skills between themselves did not help, either. They snapped at each other, and his dad slammed doors whenever he was angry. Mark withdrew more and more into himself. His parents might have been able to help had they understood the young man's need for significance and reached out to affirm it. In the church, too, a youth leader who might have sought Mark out to chat could have made a difference. However, in his isolation, the young man slipped into depression.

Responsibility

Whereas love and acceptance create security, accountability teaches self-control. When children are made accountable, they are able to develop self-discipline and a sense of responsibility. Many parents give in to suspicion, *expecting* their children to do wrong. A young person growing up within an atmosphere of suspicion and lack of trust may very well fulfil those negative expectations. On the other hand, a trusted youth will often work hard to reward that trust.

> *Dr Mwiti*: My mother trusted me so much that I made sure that I proved myself trustworthy. If I went out with my friends, promising to be back by a certain time, I would make sure that I did what I said I would do – because she did not doubt my word. Keeping my word became part of my personality, such that I will remind myself today to do what I promise, and if I cannot, make it clear early enough for the other person to know not to expect me to come through. Young people do not develop self-discipline through parental lectures, but by parents who model self-discipline themselves.

Loving Authority

Authoritative parenting creates a relationship within which parental limits can be set and expectations communicated within a nourishing parent-child relationship. Authoritarian parents focus on control, with little warmth and nurture. Authoritative parenting is positive, while authoritarian parenting is negative and damaging. Authoritarian parents use their power arbitrarily and inconsistently. Authoritative parents are firm and gentle. Parents need to monitor their tone of voice when they set limits regarding bedtime, actions such as hitting, or behaviour during meals. Many children will manipulate their parents' disagreement for their own gain, pitting one parent against the other. However, consistency leads to understanding when a parent has to say "No" or when limits have to be negotiated. Positive parenting is set within an atmosphere of love and concern. A loved child or youth is motivated to work harder, and with reinforcement and appreciation of her abilities, she will blossom towards self-responsibility and responsibility to others. Parenting in Africa is not the sole responsibility of individual parents, but also of any adult in a child's extended family or even within the community of men and women who believe the adage that *it takes a village to raise a child*.

Assessing Parents, Children, and Adolescents

How can the counsellor best assess and address the needs of families with children and adolescents? First, the counsellor can explore the major factors that contribute to holistic health, namely: the physical, mental, emotional, relational, spiritual, and social aspects of the child's life. Also, one can assess the youth's community, neighbourhood, possible presence of grief and trauma, and resources for recovery.

A Family Systems Approach

The Christian counsellor needs to realize that the greatest gains will be made in working with the parents as well as with the child. If both parents are not available, the counsellor can work with the one who is willing to come to sessions. However, if the absent parent is involved in the life of the child in any way, it is advisable to include him or her in the counselling process as much as possible. The child is part of a family system, and in many cases, the child's struggles reflect problems within the family system. Therefore, lasting changes can be made only when the whole family system changes. Another way of looking at this is that if the child is living in a toxic environment, no matter what gains he or she makes in therapy, at the end of the day the child will still return home to the same troubling situation. If neither of the parents is willing or available to come for counselling, with the parent's consent, one can enlist the help of a relative or another adult who is close to the child – and who may also be able to mediate between the child and the parents.

Aunts, uncles, neighbours, parents' workmates, pastors, and schoolteachers may sometimes be used to form a bridge between the child and the parents.

Physical

In evaluating the factors that lead to holistic child health, begin by looking at the physical aspects.[288] Although the counsellor is not a medical doctor, he or she can look for signs of illness and, if they are found, refer the child to a clinic. The counsellor can explore areas of diet, exercise, and sleep patterns. Could the young person be using drugs or alcohol? Is there physical evidence of abuse? Are there fears of an unwanted pregnancy or HIV infection? A young person may have been tempted to become sexually active or may have been forced into sexual intimacy.

Mental

The counsellor can evaluate the child's mental status. Is there evidence of mental retardation or mental illness? For example, some young people who perform poorly in school are often stigmatised by teachers and punished by parents. What really is going on? To clarify the diagnosis and seek help, what resources and referrals are needed?[289] At age 14, Kiambi should be a healthy adolescent running and playing with his friends at home, at school, at church, and in the community. However, Kiambi is short in stature and extremely bow-legged. He talks slowly, with his tongue seeming to fill his mouth. He is slow in class, although he is only a grade below average. It is clear that the child is developmentally delayed. His mother came to see the counsellor at the end of a community event requesting help. Kiambi's mother spoke of her anxiety that her son was failing academically. What could she do? On examining the boy, it was quite clear to the counsellor that Kiambi would not suddenly become an "A" student. What *could* he do? What were some of his strengths that could be developed? Did the mother recognize any gifts in the boy?

Kiambi's mother replied that the young man had gifted hands: he constructed chicken coops for everyone in the village. The counsellor helped the mother to obtain a hospital referral and eventually an operation that made it possible for Kiambi to walk more normally. The counsellor helped him deal with the stigma of being different, explored and reinforced his gift of creativity, and encouraged him to do his best in school. His mother was encouraged to seek vocational training for Kiambi after high school. The counsellor suggested that Kiambi was different, not disabled. He was also a gift to his community, loved by many for his gentle ways. Through counselling, the boy's mother, too, began to perceive her son in a new light. Kiambi's classmates also noticed a new confidence in their friend.

Emotional

The counsellor can determine the child's emotional state. What negative feelings does the child or youth bring to counselling? For example, you may see a child who is consistently aggressive and angry; or another one who is sad, withdrawn, and isolated. One can listen to their stories, evaluate their feelings and emotions, and help them talk things out. It is important to find out what may cause these emotions and feelings to surface. For example: "I feel scared when my dad comes home drunk." "What scares you?" "I fear that he's going to hit my mom."

Relational

Assessment includes exploring the kind of relationships the child or youth has. Does the boy or girl have positive relationships at home, school, and church? How does she get along with her parents, siblings, classmates, and teachers? What feedback does he receive from his relationships? What concerns him most about this feedback? What does she do with negative feedback? Is there love and affirmation in the home? If so, from whom? Is there any relationship that tends to be abusive? What protection does he have from the abuse? Are there government protective services? What is the process of reporting child abuse?[290]

Spiritual

The Christian counsellor will explore any spiritual resources the child or youth may have. Is the family part of an active church congregation? If so, does the child/adolescent participate in activities for children or youth? How does the young person view the Bible? What is the child's perception of God and his love? A child abused by her father may find it difficult to perceive God as a loving Father. Is Jesus's life a compelling example for the young person to imitate? Is the youth able to sense Jesus's love, comfort, and the hope he gives? If the family is not religious, can you sense how God has been present in their family history nonetheless?

Assessment of Family Structure

Nancy Boyd-Franklin, an African American family therapist, thinks that family[291] assessment will examine issues of:

❖ **Boundaries**: who plays a part in the family and how. Healthy boundaries allow individuals to express themselves without fear of judgement, hurt, or disappointment.

❖ **Alliances**: supportive working interactions in which families strive for a common goal.

❖ **Coalitions**: where several family members work against others in the family.

❖ **Power**: the process of decision-making and its impact on the family. How empowered are family members in decision-making? Are there those who abuse power and position by controlling others?

We can illustrate this approach with the case of Mwaura and Ciru. Married for 15 years, Ciru has always complained that her husband is secretive. He seems to spend considerable time away from home, and, when he is home, he hardly spends any time in the evening with his young family. Ciru complains about her husband to her 13-year-old daughter. "What's wrong with your dad? He's always away from home. Doesn't he realize that we need him? Look at Mary, your friend. Her dad is always there when she needs him." The daughter begins to resent her father but is too afraid of him to show her anger. Besides his absences, Mwaura does not share with his wife his business dealings or disclose the identity of his business partners. Mwaura argues that he is busy conducting his business and does not understand Ciru's fuss. Should a man tell his wife everything? What does she want him to do? Sit at home and gossip like a *woman*? After all, as a man, he can do whatever he wants with his life.

At first, Mwaura refused to talk to anyone that Ciru contacted about their problems, whether it was the parents, the best couple at their wedding, or the counsellor. The counsellor decided to see Ciru alone, hoping that maybe Mwaura would come for sessions later when he was home. Some immediate work involved coaching Ciru to live a fulfilled life herself. What constructive things could she do to ward off loneliness when Mwaura travelled on business? Which relationships could she build to keep herself occupied when Mwaura was away?

The counsellor role-played with Ciru positive communication patterns that would communicate appreciation for her husband's work, replacing her grumbling and complaining when Mwaura arrived home. She also worked to break her coalition with her daughter against Mwaura. Making the child take sides was also destroying the child's relationship with her own father and not empowering her to freely express herself. Such unhealthy relationships have the capacity to create unhealthy boundaries. Ciru began to understand the implications regarding her own family. Underlying Ciru's other concerns were fears related to her husband's faithfulness. "Can I trust him in these days of HIV and AIDS?" she asked. Eventually, she was able to confront her fears, and her attitude towards her husband began to change. Finally, he, too, saw the counsellor for some sessions.

As the couple explored their relationship, Mwaura began to see that his own attitude was similar to that of his father, a man who had worked in the city while his wife and children lived in a rural area. Mwaura never saw consistent communication between his parents, and so had no modelling to learn from. He also lived with a cultural understanding that men did not have to tell their wives everything. The counsellor role-played with Ciru in a session with Mwaura, helping the man to learn to value, instead of trivializing, the concerns his wife raised. He began to learn that his power as a man and the head of his family should be used to build others up instead of ignoring and disregarding their needs. At the end of each session, the couple took home assignments on better communicating and spending time together when Mwaura was home. Eventually, they decided to terminate therapy. The counsellor was sure that the couple had learnt new ways of empowering each other that would continue to enrich their marriage. Their main homework was to build alliances that would help the family to work as a unit without alienating anyone. Things were not going to change overnight, but the couple was willing to continue working on their relationships.

Social Network

Social networks increase a family's and an individual's resiliency. Friends, relatives, peer groups, and so on, are crucial aspects of holistic functioning. However, they, too, need to be appreciated, deliberately developed, and nurtured. The counsellor will therefore explore if a child belongs to a social network and what nature of relationships exist therein. For example, how healthy is her peer group? With whom does he socialize? What kind of families do her parents connect with? Is there a need for more connections? Some parents belong to a couples' fellowship group where, on a regular basis, they participate in activities as families. This becomes a healthy way to socialize children as parents proactively identify positive value systems that they will impress upon the growing children.

Neighbourhood

What is the child or youth's neighbourhood like? Some neighbourhoods are destructive and dangerous, providing little safety for the counselee. If the youth lives in such a neighbourhood, what support or protection is available? If a young woman has to walk to and from school through a dangerous neighbourhood, does she have a plan for self-protection? One means of protection that often works for young people is to travel in a group instead of walking alone or in couples. The group also chooses activities to do together, places to visit together, and develops a common way of explaining their values and life principles when confronted. This forms a positive peer group where values are communally owned, protected, and lived.

Community

How does the youth's community celebrate rituals? For example, are rites of passage celebrated? Is healthy development and maturation encouraged? How does the community handle its weakest members? Are they loved and supported, or despised and excommunicated? Traditional communities used to care for weak members. There are those who come from troubled families and may go astray because they were not trained to know better. Does the Christian community care for such as these?

Trauma

The counsellor can determine if there's been a trauma or loss in the family or community. How are people handling the loss and grief? What bereavement rituals does the community observe and what is their significance?[292] What impact has the trauma had on the life of the child or youth? What is the child or youth's earliest memory of the loss? How much of this memory still influences the counselee? For example, children who lose parents early and grow up in poverty may miss important developmental milestones which may be reflected in their personalities. They may act out with aggression, competition, poor table manners, or a refusal to share. Remembering the loss behind the disruptive behaviour may increase the patience of caregivers with the affected child.

Community Resources

Finding out what resources the family and community have to support the counselee towards wellness is important. For example, a healthy church youth programme can provide both socialization and spiritual nourishment. A community library can offer a quiet place for a young person to study away from a chaotic home environment.

Preparing Your Referral Base

Before beginning to work with people needing help in their communities, counsellors should remember the need for teamwork. Counsellors will need to be aware of their limitations and also recognize the kinds of problem families that they work with best. It will be important to prepare a referral list of professional people whom the counsellor trusts. From a holistic perspective, referrals include professionals to assist not only with emotional needs, but also with other necessities including legal services, school support, medical examinations, and the help of government agencies.

Conclusion

The healing of families will come from what Africans have in their hands: willing hearts, God's wisdom, a rich indigenous culture, and the guidance of pastors and professionally trained therapists. With these assets, Africans can create a health-oriented counselling approach that is Christ-centred, holistic, and authentic. Africans can model a methodology that focuses on healing broken families and empowering healthy families. This way, emotional health will begin to flow into African societies, raising up the richness of African culture, to be shared eventually with other nations. Africa has much to offer the rest of the world in terms of a rich value system, although it needs to be clarified, tested, and anointed by God before it can be shared.

CHAPTER 10

Spirits, Demons, and Scourges: Mental Illness and AIDS in Africa

Dr Mwiti: As a doctoral intern in the United States, I worked in a psychiatric ward in a county hospital. It was part of my responsibility to provide psychological testing for patients. Entering the ward to begin assessment of a woman patient named Pat,293 I was warned by the nurses: "Be careful. She bites! She will certainly not cooperate even though you have many hours of training. She refuses to answer our questions or to give us any of her history. Keep the door open and sit near the exit, so that you can run for it if she lunges at you." This was not encouraging preparation, especially for an intern!

I examined Pat's medical chart and realized that she was homeless; no one knew her background since she had been in the area only a few weeks. I then went to meet Pat in her hospital room. She was lying down, apparently fast asleep. I awakened her, introduced myself, and told her that I needed some time for her to help me with something. She followed me into the examining room, where I sat down near the door for a possible quick exit. I told Pat that her medical chart confused me. Over the years, she seemed to have received many and varying diagnoses, from schizophrenia to bipolar disorder, major depressive disorder, and substance abuse. She shouted, "You're right, I am angry at being labelled and pumped with many medications. No one listens to me. I am only a number in their records." She started crying. I let her cry quietly for a while, and then said, "Pat, you seem very sad about something. What is it? What is happening?"

I was supposed to proceed with my assessments and make my diagnoses. It was not to be. I put away my notebook and fixed my attention on the crying, bedraggled woman. She looked at me, "Do you really want to hear my story?" I said, "Yes, Pat. And you have all the time in the world to tell me. I do not have to test you today. We can make another appointment, because your story matters a lot to me."

She sat back, and through many tears, narrated a history of the horrible abuse she had experienced throughout her life. She had lost both parents before she was five and was separated from siblings never to see them again, as each of them was placed in a different foster home. Pat lived in more than ten foster homes before she was twelve, was sexually molested in six of these placements, ran away at 14, and started using drugs to dull the pain.

At the end of a three-hour outpouring of pain and distress, I made an appointment for psychological testing later in the week. The staff did not believe that Pat had cooperated with me. I had simply approached Pat as God would, with compassion, not condemnation.

Mental illness and AIDS are afflictions that must be faced directly rather than denied and responded to compassionately rather than with punishment. That is the focus of this last chapter. We will give an example of a young man who encountered the occult and was traumatized by the experience. Is the Christian counsellor also an exorcist? Then we will examine depression as one form of mental illness. Finally, we address the issue of AIDS in Africa. How can Christian counsellors and the church respond in helpful ways to this scourge?

Those who are mentally ill deserve our compassion rather than our judgement and so we begin with some key biblical texts on compassion versus condemnation. Indeed, the Bible is short on condemnation, but very long on compassion as one of God's characteristics. Condemnation is the opposite of commendation. It means to blame, disapprove, criticize, scorn, and denounce. Condemnation would view persons with addictions and mental illness as hopeless. But condemnation of the wounded is not in God's character. "Do not condemn, and you will not be condemned."[294]

Compassion is the opposite of condemnation, communicating sympathy, empathy, concern, kindness, consideration, and care. Compassion views emotional illness with hope since compassion is important in God's character. The Bible indicates that God has compassion on the wounded. "When he saw the crowds, he had compassion on them, because they were harassed and helpless, like sheep without a shepherd."[295] God seeks to fill the Christian counsellor with this concern and care, so that we can touch the emotionally troubled with God's hand and give them cups of cold water on Christ's behalf.

Schultz utilizes the book of Job to explore two paradigms of caregiving or counselling.[296] He suggests that the attitudes and behaviours of Job's friends offer negative models for counsellors who might preach at or reprimand their counselees. The four men framed Job's experience in a way that made sense to their own theology. There is too much inappropriate "God-talk" in their many words. Schultz contrasts the many words of Job's friends with God's silence. God listens with compassion and does not berate Job for speaking so freely in complaint about his situation.

Job's friends do not find it easy to deal with ambiguity. They compete to find quick answers to this man's suffering. However, God invites Job to contemplate and explore the mysterious nature of creation and suffering.

The Occult, Demonic Oppression, and Possession

We turn first to the problem of demon-possession to illustrate compassionate caring. The mentally ill have often been dismissed as "crazy" by the larger public, and as demon-possessed people in need of exorcism in Christian circles. We begin with a narrative on which to reflect.

Jamba[297] complained to his medical doctor that he had suffered from anxiety attacks and nightmares for almost a month. The doctor tried to treat the symptoms with medication, but that did little to alleviate Jamba's anxiety. Convinced that Jamba's situation had an emotional and/or spiritual basis, the doctor referred him to Oasis Africa for help.

Though only 25, Jamba looked older than his years. He indicated that he was the eldest of seven siblings, and that his parents had died when he was 15. There was no history of mental illness in his family. For the past 10 years, he had functioned as the head of his family, taking over the responsibility of caring for his brothers and sisters. He had dropped out of school and taken many low-paying jobs to support his siblings. Living in a city far away from their relatives, these children in a household headed by their teenage brother were separated from a supportive community. Apart from Jamba, who attended the local Catholic church intermittently, the children did not have any particular faith.

When Jamba came to his session, he indicated that he was married, and that the stress of caring for his new family had increased his exhaustion. To make ends meet, he had started a retail business that began to do well – but this became an additional stressor. Before long, Jamba began to experience sleeplessness and headaches that would not respond to medication.

Finally, someone advised him to seek the help of a traditional healer. Jamba told of his visit to this man's dwelling, an experience that totally changed his life.

The "healer's" front room served as a reception area, where Jamba was asked to empty his pockets and leave all of his belongings as well as most of his clothes. Then he was ushered in to see the "doctor." He found himself in a dark room where he had to squint to see anything. When his eyes became accustomed to the darkness, he saw a wrinkled, clean-shaven man, naked to the waist, sitting on the floor.

The "healer" beckoned to Jamba to sit facing him. Jamba remembered the incantations the man said over him as he danced around Jamba and chanted in a strange tongue. At some point, the rhythm moved Jamba into a hypnotic state. A raw egg was broken over his head and the dancing ended. The man now looked at Jamba in the darkness, with eyes that shone through the hazy light. He told him, "I have cast a spell on you. I know you have a business with a regular income. At the end of every week, I want you to bring me an amount of money. If you don't bring me your money, you will die." Jamba ran, sprinting all the way to the police station to report his frightening ordeal. He even forgot his wallet and clothes. Later, the police escorted him back to pick up his belongings, but all they found was a different man sitting in the front office. The medicine man was nowhere in sight. A policeman gave Jamba a stern warning, "Be careful where you seek treatment, young man."

This incident was the beginning of horrible nightmares and panic attacks for Jamba. He was afraid of falling asleep, because the medicine man always appeared in his dreams. He had headaches, low appetite, insomnia, and a fear that in his condition, he might leave his family and younger siblings with no help.

He also hated walking in the area of town where the medicine man lived and, although the police had told him to report any incidents to them, Jamba feared that eventually, someone would come to him from the "healer" demanding money. His friends and colleagues told the young man that he must have been bewitched by the medicine man, and Jamba believed them. His mind was often filled with thoughts of death, which he assumed was the consequence of disobeying the medicine man. However, Jamba was determined not to give in to his fear or to the threats he had received, although coping with this stress was proving very difficult.

Was Jamba possessed? Should the therapist now become a Christian exorcist and order a demon to leave Jamba? The African indigenous Christian counsellor would not rule out demon-oppression, because the devil "prowls around like a roaring lion looking for someone to devour."[298] The counsellor could respond to the presence of this oppression by sending the counselee to an exorcist, or work with him on aspects of his life that were promoting oppression. In the situations of people like Jamba, there is much controversy as to the cause of their suffering, as well as about appropriate treatment. Christian counsellors cannot evade this debate. Our deliberation centres on four aspects: psychological, physical, theological, and demonic.

Psychological

In Jamba's case, the counsellor examined the impact of losing his parents at such an early age, plus the burden of caring for a whole family of younger siblings instead of enjoying adolescence. Jamba was able to mourn his parents as well as the loss of his youth in subsequent sessions. He and the counsellor also worked together on Jamba's anxiety and panic attacks, using relaxation exercises, and changing his work schedule to include periods of rest and leisure. He became better at self-care and learned the art of delegation, giving more responsibility to his younger brothers instead of continuing on to act endlessly as their "father."

Physical

How much of Jamba's problem might be caused by physical matters including quality and quantity of diet, chemical imbalances, glandular malfunctioning, genetic influences, disease, allergic reactions, and environmental factors? We take this holistic approach because our understanding of counselling in African indigenous cultures is that physical illness and emotional wellness cannot be separated. One impacts the other.[299] This means that the Christian counsellor will consistently ask the question: Is there a physiological cause to this presenting problem? With Jamba, the counsellor began by asking about not only his history, but also his physical condition. Gradually, the counsellor was able to learn what was troubling Jamba. He was exhausted, afraid of becoming sick and failing to support his family – and this made him susceptible to the healer's ministrations.

Theological

From a theological perspective, some people may falsely assume that all emotional problems are a result of individual sin. Therefore, they confront what they think is the "offending" sin and urge the "sinner" to confess. Although it is true that sin is the bedrock of humanity's fallenness, Christian counsellors do not assume that all problems result from specific, individual, sinful behaviour. At an appropriate time, the counsellor explored Jamba's faith, and urged him to imagine Jesus as victorious over the principalities and powers of the air that had oppressed him. The counsellor told Jamba that following Jesus meant that the principalities were overcome, that Jesus understood suffering, and that Jesus was a healer for the sick. Jamba eventually joined a study and fellowship group of young adults in his church, and their support increased the young man's courage to face his fears. In time, the nightmares and panic attacks ceased.

Demonic

Finally, the third category of explanation for mental illness involves the demonic.[300] Some Christians believe that all emotional problems arise from demonic influence, and that treatment must be limited to exorcism and spiritual warfare. However, not all mental and emotional instabilities are demonic in nature, and care should be taken in such diagnoses as well as in this type of intervention. Exorcism was an option for the Oasis Africa counsellor. Indeed, prayer to get rid of the demons that haunted Jamba's life would be appropriate, but in addition, Jamba needed to do the work that left him at a better place emotionally, spiritually, physically, and psychologically. Unless Jamba had done this important work in personal and spiritual growth, his demonic fears might have left for a while only to come back later and take up residence again.[301] A life reformed but lacking in God's presence is also open to reoccupation by the original evil.

Working in a culture that is so highly spiritualized, African indigenous Christian counsellors cannot simply dismiss the demonic as a myth. C. S. Lewis wrote, "There are two equal and opposite errors into which our race can fall about devils. One is to disbelieve in their existence. The other is to believe and feel an excessive and unhealthy interest in them. They themselves are equally pleased with both errors."[302] Hence, we need to avoid both extremes.

The Mentally Ill in African Societies

How is mental illness viewed in traditional African societies? In many an African village, one can find persons struggling with schizophrenia, bipolar disorder, clinical depression, and other types of debilitating mental illnesses. Traditionally, such individuals were not ostracized by the community, but were taken in as part of the group. They could not work but were fed by everybody, stopping to eat wherever their roaming feet carried them. People were kind to these less able members of the community. Little was expected of them, and they offered help when they could.

Dr Mwiti: The following story of Kaba illustrates the way mental illness is often addressed in African society – through building relationships. When I was small, there was a man, Kaba, who was a regular visitor in our village. He was dressed in rags, never took a bath, and was very strong. Some people feared him, but he was never violent except when very angry. In those days there was hardly any psychiatric care for such people, but the community knew how to handle men like Kaba. My mother, in particular, invited these "odd" people (the mentally ill, the developmentally slow, the old, the depressed, and other people like Kaba) to come home to eat and talk to her.

Kaba would enter the village singing at the top of his voice, walking with long strides down the path, and at times, making the earth tremble beneath his feet. However, as soon as he entered the gate of our compound, the "madness" would cease. Mother would welcome him, talk to him as to a special, honoured guest, feed him, and serve him cups of hot milky tea. Since Kaba was muscular, he would often offer to split the wood for fire, so that mother did not have to do it. After eating and drinking, he marched out of the compound and seem to pick up his "madness" at the other side of the homestead, singing again at the top of his voice.

What is mental illness in the African context?[303] Many psychiatrists and psychologists utilize the Western Diagnostic and Statistical Manual (DSM-IV-TR)[304] to classify mental disorders. However, a system of classification of mental illness may reflect the culture in which the manual was created. Two Asian-American psychologists, Sue and Sue, warn that mental health professionals who work with ethnic cultures must work towards multicultural competency by taking into account (a) the prominent means of manifesting disorders (e.g., possessing spirits, nerves, fatalism, inexplicable misfortune), (b) perceived causes or explanatory models, and (c) preferences for professional and indigenous sources of care.[305] It follows that mental health professionals cannot use the DSM-IV-TR carelessly across cultures without understanding how and why certain disorders present as such. The DSM-IV-TR may be the diagnostic manual of the West, but certainly cannot be the diagnostic manual for Africa. However, for lack of anything better, this diagnostic tool continues to be used widely in Africa.

How prevalent was mental illness in traditional Africa?[306] Utilizing Western codes of classification, various studies have reported on the presence in Africa of such disorders as anxiety, phobic disorders, obsessive-compulsive disorders, depression, and various forms of psychosis.[307] Ma Mpolo and the anthropologist

Alfâ Ibrâhîm Sow believe that the prevalence of mental illness was lower in African traditional societies than it is in modern-day Africa. Urban centres continue to present with higher incidences of emotional illnesses than do rural communities. This is partly due to the impact of stress and alienation in urban areas, as well as to the breakdown of communal structures. Nonetheless, mental disorders in Africa are still minor in frequency compared with the major illnesses like AIDS and other communicable illnesses.

African Diagnosis and Treatment

What are some elements of diagnosis and treatment of mental illness in traditional Africa? In our model, before patients present themselves for psychiatric or psychological help, we assume that counsellors have examined appropriate cultural means of diagnosis and healing. It is understood that much that is useful goes on at the grassroots level, both to diagnose and to treat emotional and mental health problems. Further, there needs to be a recognition of the value of local, community-based diagnoses and interventions so that these elements of care and prevention can be integrated into healing.

Since the African cosmology includes both seen and unseen beings, ma Mpolo[308] views these forces as influencing life for good or ill. Therefore, besides environmental and relational factors that can contribute to mental illness (such as conflict, family breakdown, anger and aggression, and stress), traditional Africans would want to learn something about the sociocultural and spiritual significance of an illness by asking the questions "Why?" and "Who?" If the cause of the illness is believed to be broken relationships, restoration and restitution would be sought. Such interventions would be carried out at the family level and would include traditional rituals, psychodrama, exorcism, and other rites of reconciliation with the family (both living and dead), as well as with the community. When the diagnosis indicates wider community involvement, such as a breaking of the rules and customs of the clan, a more communal rite of reconciliation would be sought through palaver.[309] Ma Mpolo says that confessions provided the wider community with an opportunity for catharsis as well as reconciliation.[310]

Preventing Mental Illness

Prevention of mental illness in Africa must look beyond individual diagnoses to community and environmental factors that aggravate negative emotional states. As in the case of Rwanda, violence can be so deeply traumatic and long-lasting that repressed bitterness can be carried from generation to generation. It follows that the mental health professional in Africa is called to the business of conflict resolution and prevention, as well as to the treatment of mental health needs arising from conflict.

With a scarcity of professional helpers in Africa, major investments are called for to develop competent mental health workers who are trained in the diagnosis and care of the emotionally impaired, the prevention of emotional illnesses that are related to stressful environments, and the development of culturally sensitive modes of diagnosis. The contribution of such professionals from Africa could greatly enrich a future edition of the Western-based DSM-IV, resulting in a manual that is more inclusive and sensitive to the African situation.

Counselling Depressed Persons

It is impossible for us to describe all the ways one can counsel persons with mental illness, so we will focus on one common problem: depression. In order to deal with depression, the Christian counsellor needs to understand its nature, symptoms, prevention, and management, as well as misconceptions about depression and difficulties in trying to help depressed people.

Christians, in particular, have been blamed for labelling depressed people as persons lacking in faith. Some go so far as to say that if one walks closely with God, one will never be depressed. Many Christians view depression as a sign of spiritual defeat. Others insist that healing for depression cannot include medical intervention, and that prayer alone is the cure. Anderson argues that Christianity seems to have ignored the fact that the peaks and valleys of emotional life are part of normal living for both believers and non-believers.[311]

The causes of depression are varied. Depression can be related to physical causes, emotional factors, and spiritual aspects. Any attempt to explain away causes or to claim to find a cure-all for depression simplifies a very complex situation. We do know that depression affects the whole individual. We remember the words of David: "All my longings lie open before you, Lord: my sighing is not hidden from you. My heart pounds, my strength fails me; even the light has gone from my eyes."[312]

We need to make a distinction between occasional periods of sadness and clinical depression. Normally, people go through gloomy moods, short periods of discouragement, sadness, and unhappiness, conditions that can last for a few hours, days, or even weeks. When depression starts impacting our daily lives (sleep, appetite, and capacity for work and social relationships) and controlling our responses to life, then clinical depression may be involved.[313] Clinical depression may relate to physical causes with genetic influence a possibility. People suffering from clinical depression may have a relative who suffers from some type of mental or emotional condition. Depression may also be a result of broken interpersonal relationships. Considering the seriousness of depression, it is important not to ignore or dismiss it lightly.

Some types of depression are linked with physical conditions including stress and burnout, thyroid problems, and developmental hormonal imbalances in adolescents. In women it may be a result of hormonal changes: premenstrual syndrome (PMS), changes after giving birth (postnatal depression), and emotional and physical changes following an abortion (postabortion syndrome). Hormonal changes in women during menopause may also be related to depression.

Reactive depression is linked to a specific loss (the death of a loved one, retirement, retrenchment) for which sadness is normal except when it extends beyond a normal grieving period.[314] Unresolved sin and guilt can contribute to depression. This type of guilt represents feelings of wrongdoing and may be a healthy human response where there has been moral failure. Other reactions that accompany guilt include disappointment and self-condemnation. These, combined with feelings of frustration, fear of punishment, low self-worth, and social isolation, can lead to despair. Christians may respond to such negative feelings by seeking forgiveness from God and persons they have wronged, as well as making attempts to right wrongs in reparation. Christian counsellors do well to offer forgiveness to those who ask for it, as well as to facilitate repentance and reconciliation. Through confession, repentance, reconciliation, and restitution, healing can flow into the individual and the community.[315]

Dr Mwiti: Christians need to avoid hiding the state of their hearts. Hiding in defensiveness leads to unresolved guilt and possibly, depression. I once counselled a woman who had a physical condition that did not have any physiological explanation. Her doctor conducted tests for many years and prescribed all types of medication, but nothing helped. The woman, a mother of three married to a Christian man, became more and more depressed, wondering what evil had taken root in her body. In counselling, she unveiled a secret that few of her friends ever knew. She had had an abortion in high school, and the image of her premature baby being disposed of after the birth had never left her mind. She had tried hard to forget the incident and managed to block off these memories through her adolescence and young adulthood.

Yet, after ten years of marriage, she suddenly found herself experiencing physical problems that had no cure. As we traced her history, it became clear that her present symptoms of depression were tied to feelings of guilt from an action that was many years old.

What is needed when counselling depressed people? First, if depression is a *symptom* of a physical illness, providing insight that this phase will pass can provide hope. What the client needs is help, encouragement, and support to recover from the illness. If the depression is a *reaction* to a life event such as bereavement, loss, or terminal illness, the Christian counsellor realizes that counselling may be long and difficult. The counsellor must be careful not to speak of quick solutions or suggest some miraculous spiritual technique to end the pain. The counsellor should not give false hope to the counselee by saying, "All will be well soon," or over-spiritualizing the experience with a statement like, "The Lord must surely be teaching you something." Rather, the counselee can be given the opportunity to retell the story of a loss, explore the role a person who died played in his or her life, perhaps prepare for the pain of anniversaries and birthdays, and address the immediate tasks at hand.

For those who work with the depressed, qualities of compassion, warmth, a non-condemning attitude, and active listening are needed. The role of the counsellor is to affirm hope through listening and a prayerful presence. The counsellor must watch for suicidal thoughts or ideas and for any notions by the counselee about hurting someone else. If the person is suicidal, the counsellor will make a verbal agreement with him or her not to hurt him- or herself, and to ask for help either by admitting him- or herself into a hospital or by calling the counsellor. If there is a threat to harm someone, the counsellor needs take care to protect that person and others who might also be in danger.

Depression in Africa is among many emotional needs that do not receive enough attention due to a lack of diagnosis, ignorance, and a shortage of mental health resources. Consequently, many depressed people are not adequately cared for. Some African countries hold mentally ill people in poorly maintained mental hospitals, while others have them hospitalised under more expensive psychiatric care. Medication is often prescribed, but without the additional help of counselling or psychotherapy. Care for this population in Africa must include a thorough understanding of factors contributing to depression, a diagnosis of each type of depression, family education on caring for depressed relatives, and improved community services. Suicide is often linked to depression, and the community needs to be educated on the signs that point to a possible suicide.

Africa needs to shift away from an exclusive emphasis on a medical model for diagnosis and treatment of mental illness in which all illness is understood to have a physical cause and medication is considered the only legitimate means for relieving symptoms or providing healing. Governments are urged to invest in the development and support of psychology and counselling services. In addition, they can encourage a partnership approach to service delivery, in which medicine, psychiatry, psychology, pastoral psychology, and social services complement one another.

The Christian counsellor in an African setting can do much to help prevent depression by preparing individuals to deal with factors that could result in discouragement and emotional problems. For example, training in expectations about midlife transitions can prepare individuals to know what to expect in later years. Retirement seminars can help aging couples with skills to manage their resources as well as their time after formal employment ends. Pastoral retreats can help full-time church workers to deal with the management of stress and possible burnout. Individuals can learn to recognize stressors that may trigger depressive symptoms and be encouraged to comply with medications that may be prescribed by a doctor to control symptoms of depression.

What about the limitations of the lay Christian counsellor when working with depressed people? The counsellor needs to have a referral list available. As soon as the situation exceeds one's competence, one must refer one's counselee. Damage may done by holding on to a counselee when one offered one's best and reached the end of one's abilities and resources.

Counselling for HIV and AIDS

In this next section, we focus on the scourge of AIDS.[316] Recent statistics indicate that in Africa, there are more than 10,000 new HIV infections per day. By the end of 2003, more than 20 million Africans had died from AIDS and 27 million Africans were living with the virus.[317] One estimate is that 40% of today's 15-year-olds will acquire the infection in countries including Cote d'Ivoire and Ethiopia.[318] These figures may not make a lot of sense to those who do not live with AIDS, but for many African pastors, the first sermon they preach after Bible School graduation is at the graveside of an AIDS victim. To respond to the pandemic, some churches have set aside pastors whose sole responsibility is burying those dead of AIDS.

This overwhelming crisis of sick and dying adults and children places major demands on the church and creates additional problems such as: diminished family resources, compromised communities, reduced resiliency, neglected widows and widowers, exhausted caregivers, and overcrowded hospitals. Above all, AIDS leaves vast numbers of orphans and vulnerable children on a continent where many tribes do not even have a word to describe a parentless child. An orphan and vulnerable child can be defined as "a child below the age of 18 who has lost one or both parents or lives in a household with an adult death (age 18-59 years) in the past 12 months or is living without family care."[319]

In traditional Africa, orphans were immediately absorbed into relatives' families, and often accorded the same treatment as all of the new family's other children. They were not allowed even to consider that their dead parents had left them alone to suffer. Today, with resources stretched thin, children find themselves parenting their siblings, because there often aren't enough adults or orphanages to care for them.

Prevention

AIDS prevention must be a task for all caring adults in Africa today because fundamental problems require fundamental solutions. This task requires a multifaceted strategy, with all Africans and lovers of Africa working on every possible front. All nations must join hands with Africa in a worldwide commitment if this continent is to be saved. Unfortunately, we seem so far more focused on treating symptoms. Sometimes drug companies lead in this kind of half-hearted commitment to disease prevention. Some of these corporations fear that if they deal with the causes of problems, they will lose business. Not so. God will always provide for us if we are intent on meeting people's needs, and so there is a call for boldness to touch the causes of the illnesses we suffer from.

We need to balance our investment in caring for the infected and affected with caring for the remnant: adults who have not yet contracted the virus, as well as the uninfected youth and children. Christian counsellors can work with community leadership to strengthen partnerships in educating the public about HIV/AIDS. Ignorance has destroyed many churches. The counsellor can be an educator on matters regarding HIV and AIDS: transmission, protection, care and counselling, and support for the widows and orphans. Especially since one cause of AIDS is related to sexual immorality,[320] there must be Christian groups continuously discussing the role of the church[321] in HIV and AIDS prevention. The eyes of church members in Africa need to be opened not only to the dangers surrounding them, but also to the resources they have among them to meet the needs in their midst.

The need for understanding and caring mandates that the counsellor collaborate with communities regarding AIDS, helping to train male and female lay health educators in the churches, villages, and cities. In so doing, he or she will equip the lay health educators to offer counselling and other preventive services, as well as to share with other people skills on how to live positively with the pandemic. Some counselling services will need to provide support to chronically ill patients at home, while others support spouses and families of the infected.

AIDS counselling in Africa must reach beyond the individual, embracing the spouse, children, extended family and community, and transforming the culture.[322] Such counselling should partner with community leadership to seek adaptive cultural change and cater to the needs of a new society, without losing the richness of the old value systems.

Cultural Factors in the Spread of HIV and AIDS

Various cultural factors contribute to the spread of HIV infection, many of them very controversial and delicate. For example, in Africa, most of the spread of the HIV virus occurs through sexual transmission involving polygamous marriages or, in a few communities, wife inheritance.[323] However, in many African nations such as Kenya, there has been a marked reduction in risky behaviour as people respond to the message of prevention.[324] Knowing this, the counsellor will continue to concentrate not just on caring for the infected, but also on caring for those not yet infected.

How can marriages remain free of the virus? What messages of cultural transformation are needed? Which people can best bring about change? How can the counsellor work with community and spiritual leadership to mobilize changes that enhance community wholeness, without losing the richness of the African value of connectedness and caring for one another?

There is a positive aspect of wife inheritance. Many communities are concerned that after a man dies, one of his brothers should take responsibility for the widow and children to prevent them from suffering. Nwachuku explains that in Nigeria, wife inheritance provided legitimacy to the surviving widow and prevented the family's children from marrying too young.[325] However, if marrying the widow and having sex with her is part of the arrangement, then an infected widow may pass on the HIV/AIDS infection to a healthy brother. How can the brother facilitate care of his brother's family without having to marry the widow? This issue needs urgent attention by African theologians in view of the fact that in communities where wife inheritance is practiced, there has been an increase in the incidence of HIV infections.[326]

The problem of wife inheritance also involves the issues of property ownership and dying without a will. Do men, healthy or sick, have wills? What fears surround the writing of a will? How can men diagnosed with HIV infection be encouraged to make sure that their spouses and children are legal beneficiaries of property (including land) so that after their death, their families do not become dependent on other people, in a state that creates the potential for abuse? All of these issues require that counselling in Africa reach beyond the individual, encompassing the spouse, children, family, community, and culture.

Another cultural issue relates to sexual abstinence in young people. Author Okoronkwo uses the current youth catchwords "choosing to chill" to describe the struggle African young people are experiencing in keeping themselves chaste. She cites Atieno Okudo's description of how sex outside marriage was once perceived for most African communities:

> In most African traditions, virginity was a virtue to be proud of, especially for girls. The boy who broke the virginity of a girl was fined for breaking someone's daughter's "leg." "Breaking the leg" was symbolic of incapacitating the girl, grounding her and devaluing her. He was forced to marry her.[327]

Much has changed in Africa, because girls are no longer passive players in expressing their sexuality. There are forces, cultural and modern, that affect young people's perceptions of chastity. The counsellor should watch for cultural practices that discourage people from remaining sexually pure, whether single or married. Community education is mandated, so that people develop a healthy perception of sex as pure, lovely, and a gift of God. AIDS contracted through sexual relations means that Africans now reap sorrow upon sorrow and pour this sorrow on the innocent – unborn babies, children, and faithful spouses.

Circumcision is often blamed for the spread of the HIV infection. One hears of dirty knives used by the "village doctor" to perform the operation on scores of young men at a time. Certainly, practices that compromise health should be abolished and alternatives for them sought. Can the community keep the ritual of initiation into adulthood, but use the hospital for the actual circumcision instead of the "village doctor"? Keeping the ritual intact mandates that the counsellor understand the meaning of the practice and explore alternate ways of recognizing what it means to become a man or a woman.[328]

Mobilizing Resources for Children

In 2003, Kindernothilfe, a German Christian childcare organization, sponsored a regional consultation in Nairobi, Kenya, which focused on community-based support of orphans and vulnerable children. Participants noted that "while the sense of common purpose in the worldwide struggle against HIV [and] AIDS has intensified, inadequate attention has been paid to the time bomb of children orphaned and made vulnerable by HIV [and] AIDS."[329] With a 2003 estimate there are 143 million orphans[330] under the age of 18 in 93 developing countries,[331] with 80% of these living in sub-Saharan Africa. The call must be for holistic interventions to rescue these millions of young people.

The demand is urgent, especially given the projections of increasing rather than decreasing numbers of those needing help. Indeed, UNICEF estimates that by 2010, 8 million children in sub-Saharan Africa will have lost both parents to the AIDS pandemic.[332] These alarming numbers must inspire more innovative models of care, reaching beyond the individual children to empowering whole communities to offer sustenance to them. The UNICEF report cites the painful experiences that AIDS orphans face: "lack of love and attention; withdrawal from school; psychological distress; loss of inheritance; increased abuse and risk of HIV infection; malnutrition and illness; and stigma, discrimination, and isolation."[333]

Various statistics emphasize the vulnerability of AIDS orphans in Africa. In rural Zimbabwe in 2002, a household that included AIDS orphans earned 31% less than families not affected by the pandemic.[334] In the United Republic of Tanzania, 71% of children in families with one parent attend school compared to 52% for double orphans.[335] A study in the Congo indicated that 71% of children who had lost one or both parents to AIDS were suffering from psychological problems ranging from Post-Traumatic Stress Disorder to depression and anxiety.[336] Similar studies in Dar es Salaam, Tanzania, and Rakai District in Uganda indicated that orphans reported more emotional problems than non-orphans, with girls more affected than boys,[337] and that orphans reported lowered life aspirations with less optimism than other children about survival and the future.[338] Children react to stress in different ways. Many cannot easily talk about their feelings but internalise them, leading to low self-esteem and depression. Others externalise their negative feelings, abusing drugs or indulging in other antisocial behaviours. Unfortunately, little counselling help is available for the millions of orphans in sub-Saharan Africa.

What is the role of counsellors and caregivers in the care of specific orphans and vulnerable children? Depending on their ages and individual risk factors, the needs of these children are many and varied. Besides basic needs for health care, food, shelter, clothing, security, guidance, and education, these children have emotional and maturational needs that can be met through guidance and counselling, as well as through support to enable them to enjoy growing up as moral and responsible adults. There is also a need to facilitate their socializing with other young people as they mature, through community programmes like camps, sports, and other recreational activities. Older youth will require preparation for adolescence, as well as support for rites of passage that bring them together with other young people of the community.

Besides the work of counsellors, the community as a whole has a critical role to play in the care of orphans and vulnerable children. There will never be enough orphanages to house the millions of orphaned children. Therefore, empowering communities to support these children must be the model for Africa's future in the care and support of orphans.

Critical in this category is special support for children who have been forced to take on the role of the "parent." In many parts of Africa, teenage children have become caretakers for their dying parents, and after the parents die of AIDS, for their siblings. These children's needs become complex because this "parenting" robs them of their normal adolescence. Given their added responsibilities, these young people need assistance with legal protection, issues of property inheritance, vocational training, and special education and perhaps mentoring in entrepreneurship and other ways of earning money.

Counselling those Infected with HIV/AIDS

The greatest challenge will be to help people to live positively with AIDS. How do they tell their families, their friends, their employers? Stigmatization is such a great problem. Who will respect them anymore? What will people say about them? Other issues relate to work, and how long one can remain active with AIDS. Then, there are worries about survival as a person faces a terminal illness. How long will I live? What will happen when I die? These are among the questions counsellors will often hear from those living with AIDS. Individual counselling will begin by developing rapport with counselees, assuring them of confidentiality (except where the safety of self or others is compromised), actively listening, validating the counselee and family as they express their fears and anxieties, and creating a safe place for the counselee's hope to be born and nurtured. Living positively with the illness includes knowledge about nutrition, how to obtain supportive counselling, and the availability of medical treatment for AIDS-related conditions. To help the client with AIDS, the counsellor will need to connect the individual with services available in the community to meet that person's specific needs.

The type of counselling required may be individual and/or family, as well as in a group. Depending on their emotional status, some counselees will need psychotherapy and in-depth counselling. It is the role of the counsellor to gauge the counselee's holistic needs, as well as to help to mobilize other support as the counselee needs it. Continuous education is part of counselling to assist the counselees in responding to issues such as job loss and deteriorating health.

Some counselees with AIDS have thought of taking their own lives rather than facing the shame they feel or of taking someone else's life when they have felt betrayed. The counsellor would ask for more information. Is there a plan? If so, what is the plan? Has the counselee tried suicide or engaged in homicidal acts? Depending on the seriousness of the intent, the counsellor will report to necessary authorities when life is threatened. However, some counselees express thoughts of death as a way of dealing with the shock of learning that they have AIDS, and close monitoring, the presence of caring people around them, and compassion help them to get over their shock and think more realistically.

Individual counselling may involve confrontation when destructive behaviours do not change. For example, a spouse continues to be sexually promiscuous although he or she first tested negative for AIDS. Or a counselee may continue to self-medicate by drinking alcohol. The counsellor can communicate to the counselee that their actions do not facilitate coping.

Group counselling is often used to decrease isolation for HIV-infected people, as well as to provide them with support, encouragement, education, and reinforcement of positive changes for making behavioural changes to live positively with the infection. There are various types of groups: short-term groups, community support groups, counselling groups, and psychotherapy groups. If the Christian counsellor has no previous training in leading groups, he or she can seek training in how to organize and facilitate groups. Short-term groups often have a goal of providing both moral support and information that is relevant for positive living to a limited number of members. The counsellor as group leader can prepare a curriculum for ten weeks providing time for learning, emotional sharing, mutual support and other activities. At the end of the ten weeks, the group closes – although it can reopen, depending on the needs and wishes of the members. Groups have also been formed to offer support for the children or spouses of those with AIDS.

Marriage Counselling

HIV and AIDS within the marital relationship is one of the most painful issues to deal with. The counsellor must remain non-judgemental to facilitate the expression of painful emotions of anger, betrayal, and helplessness. Link the counselee (and perhaps the spouse) to a caring community in the church, the city, or the village that facilitates living positively with HIV and AIDS. Many communities now have Voluntary Counselling and Testing Centres (VCT) that receive and guide people seeking their services.[339] Other NGO's (Non-Governmental Organizations), as well as religious groups, offer services for the AIDS-infected and affected. In a country like Botswana, life expectancy has fallen from 65 years in 1990-1995 to 39.7 years in 2000-2005, "a figure about 28 years lower than it would have been without AIDS."[340] Here multifaceted prevention programmes as well as VCT initiatives are bearing fruit. Although progress reported was initially very slow, these programmes are making rapid progress.[341] It is the role of the counsellor to refer the counselee to such services, and to promote their increased availability.

Youth Counselling and Sexuality

Over the years, it has become generally accepted that in Africa today, abstinence from sexual relationships is the only truly safe way for young people to prevent AIDS infection. It is to this end that the African indigenous Christian counsellor will train youth counsellors to communicate that sexual abstinence is possible.

The counsellor becomes not just the bearer of a message about chastity in singleness, but also an encourager, who connects young people with adults in the community to provide a support system that protects the young sexually. Of importance will be how the youth socialize. Where do young people spend their free time? Who are their friends? What places does the community provide for young people to *hang out*? Who are their mentors?

In many African countries, Christian young people socialize in youth organizations like Scripture Union and Word of Life which have taught chastity for many years. As young women and men take a serious interest in each other, as they build friendships in these organizations, they also take a vow of chastity, and hold each other accountable for it. School holidays can be filled with fun activities like plays, musicals, and Christian concerts. Encouraging young people to seek out such environments will make it easier for the youth to weather the turmoil of adolescence. Young people infected with the HIV virus or sick with AIDS may exhibit anger and guilt as well as facing stigmatization. Counsellors can empathize with them. Empathy is the ability to perceive accurately the feelings of another person, and the ability to communicate this understanding to him or her. We can also create a safe place to allow a young person the freedom to find his or her own way through the problem without judgement or criticism. Counsellors can act as coaches to encourage young people not yet infected with the HIV virus to avoid putting themselves at risk of infection through careless living.

Finally, the counsellor will obtain specific information about youth and AIDS in his or her country to educate youth, parents, and communities. This means that once again, the counsellor must reach beyond the individual young person to the community and break out of the mode of wanting to fix broken people. The Christian counsellor, for example, can emphasize care and respect for women because currently girls and women are 50% more likely to contract HIV than boys and young men.[342] We need to consider what in the community may be placing girls and women at greater risk. How can the counsellor become an agent of change?

Transference and Counter Transference in Counselling

Often the counsellor is the main agent of turning crises and hopeless situations into opportunities for hope and inner healing of self and relationships. Hence, the counsellor is sensitive to the ways that a counselee projects personal problems onto the therapist, and the therapist, in turn, projects personal issues onto the client. Transference refers to the counselee's feelings towards the counsellor that may interfere with the counselling relationship. For example, a woman may have been infected with the HIV virus by a promiscuous husband and, in her deep hurt and betrayal, she finds it hard to respect or trust any men. Consequently, she may find it very difficult to work with a male counsellor, because she projects her anger with her husband onto the counsellor. She may react with resistance to counselling because of this by coming late for appointments or not following through on commitments. Other counselees may sometimes express anger towards the counsellor because the counsellor is HIV-negative when they themselves are HIV-positive.

Countertransference refers to the feelings and perceptions the counsellor may bring to the session. Examples of this include impatience when counselees take too long to change, feelings of anger and resentment when counselees persist in self-destructive behaviours, or anger against those who infect innocent people such as unborn babies and faithful spouses. Finally, there are the personal feelings and perceptions about HIV infection that a counsellor may try to impose on counselees and others involved in the intervention. Separating these personal concerns from responses to individual counselees will help to protect the counsellor against countertransference.

Grief Counselling

So far, no cure for AIDS has yet been discovered, and many individuals with an HIV-positive diagnosis live with a death sentence – even though many live long after diagnosis. It follows that grief counselling can begin as soon as the counselee learns that he or she is HIV-positive. Counselees themselves will begin a grieving process.

First, there may be disbelief or minimization of the news that they are carrying a terminal illness. As the truth begins to sink in, there is anger. "Why me?" "Why now?" The counselee may panic as life is suddenly filled with mental chaos and the thoughts of total disruption that may follow the diagnosis. Slowly there is bargaining with God: "God, let it not be true. I'll do all you want me to do, but please, let it not be true." However, when the counselee realizes the truth, there may follow resignation to having to face life under totally different circumstances – and eventual acceptance of the diagnosis. As individuals face the loss that they know accompanies HIV and AIDS, they may begin mourning the loss of the future including their hopes for seeing children grow up and marry. The counselee may also face the loss of friends to AIDS. The intensity of symptoms will vary depending on many factors at the time of diagnosis, including the stage of the infection, the strength and stability of current relationships, and individual coping mechanisms.

Generally, counselling must be supportive and empowering of both the counselee and the counselee's support systems. It can help the counselee and family to express feelings and explore coping mechanisms related to the illness. It is necessary for the counsellor to develop a comprehensive database of other service agencies that can meet the needs of clients with AIDS. The counselee and family will need regular education to increase coping and maximize functioning. The counsellor also acts as the connection between the counselee and community resources.

Conclusion

The challenges of a fast-changing Africa and the need for relevant and holistic interventions for psychosocial challenges on the continent will be faced by every Christian counsellor working within this context. First, there will be the challenge of avoiding quick fixes to problems that traverse generations and crisscross educational training systems. The professional will need to discern which indigenous practices, methodologies, or contemporary psychological perspectives will be helpful. That is hard work.

Secondly, the African indigenous Christian counsellor who wishes to make a lasting difference in Africa will be an individual committed to study, self-improvement, and professional excellence. In a context where too little is often demanded from professionals, Africa needs Christian counsellors with a profound sense of vocation, a call to meet the needs of the continent with competency and dedication.

A third challenge is to understand the dynamics that underlie symptoms of mental illness in Africa. Assuming a holistic approach to mental health, mental illness, and psychological as well as relational problems, the Christian counsellor will be a student not only of Western psychology, but also of African indigenous psychologies and biblical truth embodied in an African theological interpretation of God's presence with his people. An understanding of the history of Africa's suffering means that the Christian counsellor's approach must involve not only reflecting back a counselee's feelings or changing behaviours, but also advocacy, transformational training, discipleship, and a commitment to both community and individual empowerment and protection for the poorest of the poor.

The fourth challenge is to emphasize the development of holistic approaches to the practice of psychotherapy. In this book, we have stated that like the African three-legged stool, we need a three-pronged approach to the practice of psychology in Africa. We need a balance that considers the wealth of African indigenous cultures together with knowledge from Western psychologies all tested by, and founded on, solid biblical truth. Such an approach will bring not only healing but also a transformational change to Africa. This methodology presupposes that counsellors are aware of their own vulnerabilities and will be Bible-centred and totally dependent on God for their sustenance. They must also recognize, nurture, and utilize holistic community support systems; belong to and serve communities of faith; recognize and safeguard family life; live lives of ethical authenticity; and seek and utilize regular supervision by competent professionals in the fields of pastoral counselling and psychology.

Counselling those with mental illness and AIDS presents some of the most difficult challenges the counsellor will ever encounter, but we believe that no work pleases God more than this. You who do this work are truly helping those most in need with the skills and compassion that define the Christian counsellor in today's Africa.

Discussion Questions

Use these discussion questions to personally reflect on the material presented in each chapter. These questions can also be used by a facilitator in a small group or classroom setting.

Chapter 1. Africa: Dis-Membered and Re-Membered

Challenges and Opportunities

1. Does the story of Shem and Rebekah remind you of challenges in your community?
2. What does it mean to say that in Africa there are value vacuums?
3. What are some African resources for healing? Begin with a reference to your own indigenous culture.
4. What does it mean for Africa to be "dis-membered and re-membered"?
5. What are the forces within and outside our communities that have led to the breaking of connectedness in our communities?
6. What are your thoughts about the influence of the West on Africa? On counselling in Africa?

African Indigenous Culture

1. To which African indigenous culture do you belong? Discuss indigenous African values that helped to build connectedness in your community.
2. What are your own indigenous perceptions on counselling?
3. What form did counselling and training take in your community?
4. Have you ever received counsel from an older person? What difference did it make in your life?
5. Present to the group one example of a training ritual or rite of passage.
6. Was counselling in your culture holistic, i.e., catering to the needs of

the whole person, community, environment, including issues of advocacy, peace, and justice?

7. Translate some proverbs or wise sayings used to train individuals in specific groups from your culture and explain their meaning.

8. Which folk stories do you remember that teach wisdom?

African Indigenous Christian Counselling

1. What are some characteristics of an indigenous African Christian approach to counselling?

2. In what ways was Jesus an example for how we can act as counsellors?

3. How realistic is it to expect the church to recapture Jesus's holism in counselling? Discuss possibilities and challenges.

Chapter 2. Personality and Brokenness

African and Western Cultures

1. What does the word *culture* mean to you?

2. Of which aspects of African culture are you most proud?

3. What does it mean to you that Christianity in Africa is "one song sung in many tongues"?

African Psychology

1. What are your impressions of Western psychology? What is surprising to you about it? What do you agree with?

2. Give examples of African psychology.

3. In your own cultural group, how important is the self in comparison with the importance of the group? Is this understanding changing?

4. In your community, where does self-worth come from?

5. How was counselling part of your home community? How were people healed?

6. Discuss examples of African indigenous spirituality and holism.

7. Discuss ways in which African men and women handle unpleasant emotions. What is the impact on mind, body, and spirit if these emotions are not properly handled?

Brokenness: Relational and Spiritual

1. In what ways is brokenness reflected in your African indigenous culture?
2. In small groups, discuss the challenges faced by an indigenous African Christian counsellor.
3. Can the church be a healing community? How can this happen?
4. As an African Christian counsellor, what aspects of Western psychologies would you integrate in your approach?
5. Are spiritual brokenness and mental illness related? How?
6. Can you think of examples of "broken spiritual cisterns"?

Brokenness: Emotional and Physical

1. Can you give examples of defence mechanisms of denial and displacement?
2. Can you give examples of how the body affects the spirit?
3. On the other hand, can you give examples of how the spirit affects the body?

Chapter 3. Objectives and Characteristics

Introduction to African Indigenous Christian Counselling

1. The African indigenous Christian counselling model includes cultural sensitivity, biblical grounding, and Western psychological insights. Discuss your view of African indigenous Christian counselling and its possible role in restoring wellness in Africa.
2. Consistent with the Kingdom of God, what in your indigenous culture needs to be recovered for healing?
3. As an indigenous African Christian counsellor, how might you work with clients who see their own cultural roots or cultural heritage as a problem to be overcome?

Objectives of African Indigenous Christian Counselling.

1. Has the Kenyan notion of harambee or communal enterprise been present in your community? If so, is it still flourishing? How can the Christian counsellor enhance community connectedness?
2. What kind of wholeness can the counsellor help to create?

3. Can the Christian counsellor facilitate reconciliation? How?

4. What are your thoughts about the story of conflict between the two Christian groups and the funeral of the leader?

Ruth and Maria

1. How did you experience the counselling of Maria by Ruth? What questions did it raise for you?

2. Do you think that Ruth was a good Christian counsellor? In what way?

3. How would you have responded to Maria?

The Character of the Christian Counsellor

1. Where can the counsellor find wisdom? Who has shared their wisdom with you?

2. Do you think you have displayed empathy in your counselling of other people? Can you give an example?

3. Would you be able to recognize possible physical symptoms of an emotional or spiritual problem? Do you think that this is relevant?

4. Sometimes, beginning counsellors are reluctant to hold negative emotions of their counselee. How would this be evident?

5. Give an example of using Scripture unwisely in counselling.

6. How can the Christian counsellor still act as a Christian with a counselee who is not a believer?

Chapter 4. Stress Management

Bishop Samuel and Rachel the Therapist

1. Have you ever gone through a period of stress related to your work? Would you be willing to share your story with the group?

2. What events contributed to the stress? How were you functioning spiritually when you were under stress?

3. How did you relate to your brothers and sisters in the Christian community during this period?

4. Examine your indigenous cultural perspectives on stress and burnout. Begin by translating the words *stress* and *burnout*. Are there direct translations in your indigenous language?

5. What cautions were given by your indigenous culture to prevent stress and burnout?

Symptoms of Stress

1. Can you think of someone you know who might be going through a damaging, stressful period at the moment? Without giving a name or identifying information, tell the group about this person.
2. What events or other factors may be contributing to the stress?
3. Name some symptoms that the individual is manifesting: physical, mental, emotional, spiritual, relational, or social.

Spiritual Disciplines for Managing Stress

1. How would you describe your call to counselling or pastoring?
2. Do you have a sense of priorities?
3. Reflect on the kinds of things that distract you from what is most important.
4. Does your church emphasize the discipline of rest?
5. What keeps you from practicing the discipline of rest?

Psychological Disciplines for Managing Stress

1. Share with your group how you keep yourself physically healthy and fit.
2. Describe ways in which a person can nurture relationships.
3. How do you set limits on your workload? Can you say "no" to new tasks or opportunities?
4. What would you say is the order of your priorities?
5. Do you have a mentor? Name and describe the "trees" in your life.
6. If you are a counsellor, do you have a supervisor?

Chapter 5. God's Benevolence and Mass Suffering

Rwanda and Indigenous Explanations of Suffering

1. Discuss any of your own life experiences that would allow you to identify with the Rwanda genocide.
2. As you listened to the stories, what feelings and thoughts did this evoke? Share with your group.

3. What has been most meaningful to you when you have experienced a crisis or loss?

4. Dr Mwiti explains how mass suffering was viewed in her Meru culture. Consider your own indigenous people group. How was natural calamity explained?

5. Give examples of natural or national calamities that you have heard of or experienced, and the thoughts and feelings that you struggled with.

6. Are there any current situations that cause you to question God's mercy and love?

7. Identify some specific coping skills of the African community in the wake of mass suffering.

Where Is God in Faustina's Suffering?

1. What feelings do you experience at hearing of such brutality in Faustina's story?

2. What questions come to your mind?

3. Which question is the most difficult?

The Christian Counsellor and Suffering

1. What answers are usually given to the question of why the innocent suffer? Do you think the explanations are adequate?

2. Can you think of examples of the methods described in this section?

   a. Assist with coping with basic needs of safety, nutrition, and nurture

   b. Process the denial of suffering

   c. Manage the crisis

   d. Motivate transformation

   e. Rebuild broken trust

   f. Affirm indigenous efforts at dealing with loss

   g. Provide social support

   h. Examine community practices

3. Have you found any of the ways of addressing suffering described in this chapter helpful to you or someone you know?

4. In what ways have you helped others when they have experienced a major calamity?

5. Many African indigenous groups traditionally sought blessing and atonement as a group. They went to the diviner together, sought out the medicine men as a group, and offered sacrifice as a group. How is

this group responsibility still practiced in your indigenous group, for example, after bereavement, or in sickness? How can we strategically encourage such a group expression in Christian counselling?

Chapter 6. Building Resilient Communities

Pastor Mariko and the Maitoni Village

1. Can you give an example of community resiliency?
2. Have you encountered situations similar to those of Pastor Mariko in your own community?
3. How are such situations usually handled?
4. How do you bear the burden of handling such situations?
5. What might ease the burden?
6. Can you give examples of the following factors' leading to resilience in African indigenous communities?
   a. Protection of village unity
   b. Communal wisdom
7. Discuss factors that have led to degeneration in your community.

Encouraging Community Resiliency

1. Give examples of the following factors that led to resilience in African indigenous communities:
   a. Encouragement of industry
   b. Care for the less fortunate
   c. Accountability to God
   d. Accountable leadership

Biblical Perspectives on Community Resiliency

1. What lessons do we learn from the following?
   a. The story of Ezekiel in Ezekiel 3:17; 33:6
   b. The story of Nehemiah
   c. Rwanda genocide
2. Are there any other biblical texts that point to community resiliency? What do they tell you?
3. Give examples of leaders or counsellors who have acted as "watchmen," people who could identify destructive powers.

4. Give examples of scapegoats in your community.
5. How can a Christian counsellor counsel for peace?
6. How can a Christian counsellor advocate for the weak?

Steps for Community Mobilization

1. Give an example of success in identifying a community's resources.
2. Give an example of success in identifying the causes of a community's problems.
3. Give an example how you have successfully initiated a community-based intervention.
4. Give an example of how you have encouraged a community to depend on local resources.
5. How can we safeguard those resources from corruption?
6. Give an example of an approach to evaluating a programme.
7. Do you know of programmes that died for lack of funds? Why did the resources dry up?
8. How would you provide stakeholders with information on a programme's goals, objectives, progress, and so on? What is the value of this kind of communication?

Chapter 7. Premarital Counselling

Topics for Premarital Counselling

1. If you are married, share with your group about how you met your spouse.
2. Did you receive premarital counselling?
3. Did it help? How?
4. Relate some advantages of premarital counselling that you can share with your counselees.
5. What are your views about premarital counselling in general? Consider this list and suggest additional topics that an African indigenous Christian counsellor could cover with the prospective couple.
   a. Wedding plans
   b. Family relationships
   c. Role expectations
   d. Ethical issues
6. What important lessons can you draw from courting traditions in African indigenous culture?

A Case Example: Maritha and Sulaiman

1. How would premarital counselling have helped Maritha avoid a disastrous marriage?
2. Discuss how counselling would have helped Maritha to see Sulaiman for who he really was and understand why such a match might not work.
3. If applicable, share how you met your spouse in a traditional cultural setting, and what traditional observances helped to seal your union.
4. Comment on how you would have counselled Maritha and Sulaiman.

Courtship in African Cultures

1. What patterns of courtship practiced in traditional communities do you think are still useful?
2. To what extent do you think the community should participate in mate selection and/or preparation for marriage?
3. How can two persons desiring to marry truly get to know each other?
4. Is it important that persons who wish to marry have similar educational levels or similar faith?

Biblical Perspectives on Marriage

1. Dr Mwiti suggests these biblical themes. Can you think of examples of a healthy Christian marriage? Do you agree with the themes listed below? Which themes would you add?
   a. The couple as part of the people of God
   b. The mystery of becoming one flesh
   c. Healthy connections between generations, as the new couple leave their parental homes to build a new family
   d. Couple is united with a vow
   e. Mutual encouragement
   f. Mutual submission

Singleness

1. What are the experiences of single persons in your community?
2. What are their specific needs?
3. How can the needs of single persons can be met through your church family, and through your indigenous community?

Chapter 8. Marriage Counselling

Christian Counselling for Healthy Marriages

1. Reflect on your indigenous culture(s). What we can learn from traditional marriages: mate selection, courtship, the wedding, and so forth?
2. Relate some examples of factors that contribute to conflict in marriage.
3. In marriages you have seen that are in trouble, what were additional reasons for the conflict?
4. Why is it so important to resolve marital conflicts?
5. Reflect on and share about oppression in a marriage.
6. Cite specific examples of how you have seen oppression lead to marital conflict.
7. Give examples of how poor communication contributes to marital conflict.
8. Name some ways in which couples hurt each other by speaking painful words.
9. Give specific examples of how you have seen money cause marital conflicts.
10. What would you recommend to prevent monotony in a marriage?
11. Cite specific examples of how childlessness might cause marital conflict.
12. Mention some other factors that might contribute to marital problems in your cultural group.

A Case: Mate and Sylvia

1. Name some barriers to communication. How would you help a married couple to overcome such barriers?
2. What kind of sexual problems do couples have? How can one encourage a couple to talk about and resolve their sexual problems?
3. Is conflict in a marriage always destructive? Can you think of a conflict in a marriage that was healthy?
4. How do you feel about Sylvia and Mate's relationship?
5. What are the critical problems in their relationship?
6. How could the problems in Mate and Sylvia's relationship have been prevented?

Foundational Assumptions in Couple Counselling

1. What is the difference between a marriage that is a covenant and one that is based on a contract?

2. Why is it important to think of the couple as being made in the image of God?
3. Do you believe that early childhood experiences and home environment influence the way adults relate in marriage? Give examples.

Assumptions of Couple Counselling
1. How did Mate's experience of God affect his marriage? and Sylvia's?
2. Have you met a couple who were separated or even divorced, but later were reconciled or remarried? Describe their situation.

Chapter 9. On Counselling Families

African Youth Today and the Matheka Family
1. How would you describe young people today?
2. How have they changed from when you were their age? What reasons would you give that might explain this change?
3. Explain your reasons for wanting to be a youth counsellor.
4. Comment on what you think were the problems in the Matheka family.
5. How do you assess Mr Theuri as a counsellor?

Growing Up African
1. Translate into the present some traditional approaches, such as rites of passage, certain rituals, age cohorts, and community support, which we can utilize to train the next generation.
2. Who or what were the most significant influences in your becoming an adult? Describe two of them.
3. Take some time to review various aspects of traditional training in your indigenous community and make a brief presentation of them.

The Church as a New Community for the Family
1. How can the church as a community that serves as a new tribe act as a resource to adolescents?
2. What rituals could the church create that celebrate the coming of age as an adult for boys and girls? How can such practices incorporate the basic purpose of the circumcision rituals? Which other roles does the church play to enhance family wellness? What more could the church do?

3. Discuss ways to communicate to children unconditional acceptance, basic trust, encouragement, and appreciation.
4. Give examples of how parents function as authoritative, authoritarian, or chaotic.

Assessing Parents, Children, and Adolescents

1. Imagine a family with a six-year-old daughter who was traumatized by a shooting at her school. With a member of your group, role-play interviewing the family about their child. Use the guidelines detailed in the chapter: physical, mental, relational, spiritual, family assessment, social network, neighbourhood, community, trauma, and family resources.

Chapter 10 Spirits, Demons, and Scourges: Mental Illness and AIDS in Africa

Compassion and Demon Possession

1. How might the pastor's wife have handled this case differently, and more compassionately?
2. In the story of Pat and Dr Mwiti, why do you think others could not be compassionate with the patient?
3. Can you remember a time when someone acted compassionately to you?
4. Do you think Jamba was demon-possessed? Do you think an exorcism would have been appropriate?
5. What do you think of Dr Mwiti's approach? If in a group setting, discuss your opinions of Dr. Mwiti's approach together.
6. Of the three approaches to the demonic, physiological, theological, and psychological, do you think only one is the right approach? Why?

The Mentally Ill in African Societies

1. Can you tell stories of how mentally ill people were treated in your local community or tribe?
2. Do you think that the prevalence of mental illness is higher in modern Africa than it was in traditional Africa? If so, why?
3. How do you think mental illness can be prevented?
4. Can you think of examples of other people like Kaba who were cared for in your community?

5. Do you have a friend who died of AIDS? Share your story with the group.

6. What means of preventing the spread of AIDS do you think will be effective?

7. What experience or suggestions do you have regarding how to care for AIDS widows?

Mobilizing Resources for Children

1. Do you know of any other programmes like Kindernothilfe in Africa?
2. How can we best assist persons who are living with AIDS?
3. Have you been involved in assisting them? If so, how did you do so?
4. What would you do if the person you are counselling has AIDS and is suicidal?
5. Could you empathize with an AIDS patient who is angry with God that he or she has contracted the disease?
6. If you have lived through the experience of a friend's dying of AIDS, did he or she go through the stages described in the chapter?

Additional General Questions

1. What lessons can we learn from the Bible about compassion?
2. Suppose you are applying for a job in a community health centre. As an indigenous African Christian counsellor, how would you view mental illness and what approaches would you apply in dealing with clients with mental illness?
3. Discuss various ways in which the community could care for children orphaned as a result of AIDS.
4. Explain ways of dealing with transference and countertransference in counselling.
5. Give examples of the following counselling strategies:
   a. Creating a context for counselling
   b. Evaluating the nature of a problem
   c. Assessing the presenting problem
   d. Assessing cultural issues
   e. Utilizing indigenous resources
   f. Clarifying goals and outcomes
   g. Intervening in the family structure
   h. Teaching for wholeness

ENDNOTES

Chapter 1. Africa: Dis-membered and Re-membered

1 Genesis 37–43. All Scripture quotations, unless otherwise indicated, are taken from the New International Version® Anglicized, NIV®. Copyright © 1979, 1984, 2011 by Biblica, Inc.™ Used by permission of Zondervan. All rights reserved worldwide.

2 Gerald West, "Re-Reading the Bible with African Resources: Interpretive Strategies for Reconstruction in a Post colonial Context," in *The Church and Reconstruction of Africa: Theological Considerations*, ed. J. N. K. Mugambi (Nairobi, Kenya: All Africa Conference of Churches, 1997), 153.

3 Simon S. Maimela, "Cultural and Ethnic Diversity in Promotion of Democratic Change," in *Democracy and Development in Africa: The Role of Churches*, ed. J. N. K. Mugambi (Nairobi, Kenya: All Africa Conference of Churches, 1997), 106.

4 Ibid.

5 Ibid. (italics in original text).

6 UNICEF, *Africa's Orphaned Generations* (New York: UNICEF HIV/AIDS Unit, 2004), 7.

7 Urban Studies, *Slum residence and adverse health consequences linked in Kenya* (Population Briefs 3: The Population Council, 2004).

8 J. F. O. McAllister, "Promises to Keep," *TIME Europe*, March 4, 2005, 11.

9 Susan E. Rice, "U.S. Foreign Assistance to Africa: Claims versus Reality" (June 27, 2005), http://www.brookings.edu/views/articles/rice/20050627.htm.

10 Peter Mwikisa, "Reading the African Palimpsest: Breaking the Silence of the Gods in Modern Africa," in *The Role of Christianity in Development, Peace, and Reconstruction*, eds. Isabel Phiri, Kenneth Ross, and James Cox (Nairobi, Kenya: All Africa Conference of Churches, 1996), 259.

11 Mwikisa borrows the term *palimpsest* from Chantal Zabus who uses the term to describe the nature of African literature in European languages in C. Zabus, *The African Palimpsest: Indigenization of Language in the West African Europhone Novel* (Amsterdam: Rodopi, 1991).

12 Mwikisa, "Palimpsest" (see note 10), 260-261.

13 Ngugi wa Mirii and Ngugi wa Thiong'o, trans. *I Will Marry When I Want* (London: Heinemann, 1982), 114.

14 "Factoids and Frequently Asked Questions" (World Population Awareness, May 27, 2006), http://www.overpopulation.org/faq.html.

15 MBendi Information for Africa, "Africa Mining Overview" (May 6, 2006), http://www.mbendi.co.za/indy/ming/af/p0005.htm.

16 Wilson B. Niwagila, "Our Struggle for Justice, Peace and Integrity of Creation: Quest for a Theology of Reconstruction in Africa," in *The Church and Reconstruction of Africa* (see note 2), 164.

17 Philip Jenkins, *The Next Christendom: The Coming of Global Christianity* (Oxford; New York: Oxford University Press, 2002).

18 J. N. K. Mugambi, "Problems and Promises of the Church in Africa," in *The Church and the Future in Africa: Problems and Promises*, ed. J. N. K. Mugambi (Nairobi, Kenya: All Africa Conference of Churches, 1997), 53.

19 Michael Battle, *Reconciliation: The Ubuntu Theology of Desmond Tutu* (Cleveland, OH: Pilgrim Press, 1997).

20 Edward Steven Mwiti, *Kimeru 1200 Proverbs: Sayings of the Wise (Njuno)* (Nairobi, Kenya: Downtown Printing Works Ltd., 2004), 90.

21 Daudi Ajani ya Azibo, ed., *African Psychology in Historical Perspective & Related Commentary* (Trenton: African World Press, Inc., 1996), 4-7.

22 J. A. Baldwin, "Africa (Black Psychology): Issues and Synthesis," *Journal of Black Studies* 16 (1986): 235-249.

23 Ibid., 235.

24 Na'im Akbar, "African Metapsychology of Human Personality," in *African Psychology* (see note 21), 30.

25 Ibid., 30.

26 The Green Belt Movement, *30 Years of Community Empowerment and Environmental Conservation* (Nairobi, Kenya: The Green Belt Movement, 2005), 11-12.

27 Ibid., 10.

28 Akbar, "African Metapsychology" (see note 24), 30.

29 Byang H. Kato, *Theological Pitfalls in Africa* (Nairobi, Kenya: Evangel Publishing House, 1975), 182.

30 Ibid.

31 See 2 Kings 17:32-33.

32 Wilbur O'Donovan, *Biblical Christianity in African Perspective* (Carlisle, UK: Paternoster Press, 1992).

33 Adapted from Mwiti, *Kimeru 1200 Proverbs* (see note 20).

34 Gershon K. Mwiti, in discussion with the first author, 2005.

35 Ngono cia Nyomoo, *Meru Animal Tales* (Meru, Kenya: Meru Bookshop, Methodist Church, 1975), 1.

36 Malidoma Patrice Somé, *The Healing Wisdom of Africa: Finding Life Purpose through Nature, Ritual, and Community* (New York: Penguin Putnam, Inc., 1998).

37 John 4.

38   Cf. Genesis 24:11.

39   John 4:13-14.

40   John 4:29.

41   John 4:39.

42   Gary R. Collins, *Christian Counselling: A Comprehensive Guide* (Dallas, TX: Word Publishing, 1988), 17.

43   Jeremiah 29:5-7.

44   Nlenanya Onwu, "Biblical Perspectives for Peace, Development and Reconstruction. Its Socio-Religious Implications for the Churches in Africa," in *The Role of Christianity in Development, Peace and Reconstruction: Southern Perspectives*, eds. Isobel Phiri, Kenneth Ross, and James Cox (Nairobi, Kenya: All Africa Conference of Churches, 1996).

45   Leviticus 26:6.

46   Onwu, "Biblical Perspectives" (see note 44), 33.

47   Andre Karamaga, *The Problems and Promises of Africa: Towards and Beyond the Year 2000* (Nairobi, Kenya: Theology Department, AACC, 1993), 34.

Chapter 2. Personality and Brokenness

48   Clifford Geertz, *The Interpretation of Cultures: Selected Essays* (New York: Basic Books, 1973).

49   Derald W. Sue and David Sue, *Counseling the Culturally Different: Theory and Practice* (New York: John Wiley and Sons, 1999), 34-35.

50   Ibid., 35.

51   Ibid.

52   Jan T. de Jongh van Arkel, "Teaching Pastoral Care and Counseling in an African Context: A Problem of Contextual Relevancy," *Journal of Pastoral Care* 49 (1995): 190.

53   Ibid.

54   Ibid., 193.

55   K. K. Kambon Kobi, "The Africentric Paradigm and Africa American Psychological Liberation," in *African Psychology* (see chap. 1, n. 21), 59.

56   Kwame Bediako, *Jesus and the Gospel in Africa: History and Experience* (New York: Orbis Books, 2004).

57   Romans 12; 1 Corinthians 12.

58   Jean Vanier, *Community and Growth* (Bombay: St. Paul Publications, 1991); Gerhard Lohfink, *Jesus and Community: The Social Dimension of Christian Faith* (London: S. P. C. K., 1985); Stanley J. Grenz, *Created for Community: Connecting Christian Belief with Christian Living* (Grand Rapids: Baker Books, 1998). David W. Augsburger, *Dissident Discipleship: A Spirituality of Self-Surrender, Love of God, and Love of Neighbor* (Grand Rapids: Brazos Press, 2006).

59   L. E. Bourne and N. F. Russo, *Psychology: Behavior in Context* (New York: W. W. Norton and Company, 1998), 28.

60   B. F. Skinner, *Beyond Freedom and Dignity* (New York: Knopf, 1971).

61   Judith S. Beck, *Cognitive Therapy: Basics and Beyond* (New York: Guilford Press, 1995); Aaron T. Beck, Arthur Freeman, and Denise D. Davis, *Cognitive Therapy of Personality Disorders* (New York: Guilford Press, 2004).

62   David G. Myers, *Exploring Psychology* (New York: Worth Publishers, 2005), chap. 2.

63   Carl R. Rogers and Sigmund Koch, *A Theory of Therapy, Personality, and Interpersonal Relationships, as Developed in the Client–Centered Framework* (New York: McGraw-Hill, 1959), 351.

64   Michael P. Nichols and Richard C. Schwartz, *The Essentials of Family Therapy* (Boston: Allyn and Bacon, 2005).

65   Philip Cushman, *Constructing the Self, Constructing America: A Cultural History of Psychotherapy* (Boston: Addison-Wesley, 1995).

66   See Andrew Olu Igenoza, "Wholeness in African Experience: Christian perspectives," in *The Church and Healing: Echoes from Africa*, eds. Emmanuel Lartey, Daisy Nwachuku, and Kasonga wa Kasonga (New York: Peter Lang, 1994).

67   Azibo, *African Psychology* (see note 21), 4.

68   The Meru are Dr Mwiti's own people group. Our focus is on the Meru people because we cannot possibly describe the myriad of African people groups. Hence, the illustrations come from the people group best known to Dr Mwiti.

69   John S. Mbiti, *The New Testament Eschatology in an African Background* (London, UK: Oxford University Press, 1971), 130.

70   Zablon J. Nthamburi, "Ecclesiology of African Independent Churches," in *The Church in African Christianity: Innovative Essays in Ecclesiology*, eds. J. N. K. Mugambi and Laurent Magesa (Nairobi, Kenya: Initiatives Ltd, 1990), 44.

71   Azibo, *African Psychology* (see note 21), 30.

72   John 12:25.

73   Matthew 10:39.

74   1 Thessalonians 5:6, 8.

75   1 Timothy 3:2.

76   Titus 1:8; 2:2, 5, 6; 2:12.

77   1 Peter 1:13; 4:7; 5:8.

78   John S. Mbiti, *African Religions and Philosophy* (New York: Doubleday and Company, Inc., 1967), 119.

79   Bishop Jonathan Ruhumuliza, in discussion with the authors, 2005.

80   Nthamburi, "Ecclesiology" (see note 23), 44.

81   Ibid.

82   All persons in stories do not represent real people.

83   Genesis 3.

84   Genesis 4:9.

85   Psalm 42:1; Isaiah 55:1.

86   Acts 20:35.

87   Merle R. Jordan, *Taking on the Gods: The Task of the Pastoral Counselor* (Nashville: Abingdon Press, 1986).

88   John 11:35.

89   Luke 19:41.

90   P. E. Greenberg, et al., "The Economic Burden of Depression," *Journal of Clinical Psychiatry* 54 (1993): 405-418.

91   Edward A. Charlesworth and Ronald G. Nathan, *Stress Management: A Comprehensive Guide to Wellness* (New York: Ballantine Books, 2004).

92   William G. Crook, *Chronic Fatigue Syndrome and the Yeast Connection: A "Get-Well" Guide for People with This Often Misunderstood Illness – and Those Who Care for Them* (Jackson, TN: Professional Book, Inc., 1992), 194-204.

93   Ibid., 200.

94   *Hypothyroidism: Too little thyroid hormone,* http://www.endocrineweb.com/hypo1.html.

95   *Hyperthyroidism: Overactivity of the thyroid gland,* http://www.endocrineweb.com/hyper1.html.

96   Ruth L. Fischbach, "Overview: Loneliness in the Context of Illness," (2004), http://info.med.yale.edu/intmed/hummed/yjhm/spirit2004/loneliness/rfischbach.htm.

97   Andrew Baum and Donna Posluszny, "Health Psychology: Mapping Biobehavioral Contributions to Health and Illness," *Annual Review of Psychology* 50 (1999): 137-163.

98   Sandra B. Hutchison, *Effects of and Interventions for Childhood Trauma from Infancy through Adolescence: Pain Unspeakable* (New York: The Haworth Maltreatment and Trauma Press, 2005), 58.

99   Raymond Hicks, "Doing Member Care in Red Zones: Examples from the Middle East," in *Doing Member Care Well: Perspectives and Practices from Around the World*, ed. Kelly O'Donnell (Pasadena: William Carey Library, 2002), 193.

Chapter 3. Objectives and Characteristics

100 Malidoma Patrice Somé, *Ritual, Power, Healing, and Community* (New York: Penguin Group, 1993), 2.

101 Ibid.

102 Emmanuel Lartey, *Pastoral Counselling in Inter-Cultural Perspective: A Study of Some African (Ghanian) and Anglo-American Views on Human Existence and Counselling* (New York: Peter Lang, 1987); Emmanuel Lartey, Daisy Nwachuku, and Kasonga wa Kasonga, eds., *The Church and Healing: Echoes from Africa*

(New York: Peter Lang, 1994); Emmanuel Lartey, *In Living Color: An Intercultural Approach to Pastoral Care and Counseling* (New York: Jessica Kingsley Publishers, 2003).

103 Jean Masamba ma Mpolo and Daisy Nwachuku, eds., *Pastoral Care and Counselling in Africa Today* (Frankfurt am Main: P. Lang, 1991), 27.

104 Ibid., 28.

105 Kasonga wa Kasonga, "African Christian palaver: A contemporary way of healing communal conflicts and crises," in *The Church and Healing* (see note 102), 49-65.

106 Abraham Berinyuu, *Pastoral Care to the Sick in Africa: An Approach to Transcultural Pastoral Theology* (New York: P. Lang, 1988); Abraham Berinyuu, *Towards Theory and Practice of Pastoral Counseling in Africa* (New York: P. Lang, 1989).

107 Heinz Kohut, *Self Psychology and Humanities: Reflections on a New Psychoanalytic Approach* (New York: W.W. Norton, 1985).

108 Abraham Berinyuu, "Change, Ritual, and Grief: Continuity and Discontinuity of Pastoral Theology in Ghana," *Journal of Pastoral Care* 46 (1992): 147.

109 See also Charles V. Gerkin, "Implicit and Explicit Faith: Practical Theology in Dialogue with Object Relations Theory," *Pastoral Sciences: Interdisciplinary Issues in Psychology, Sociology, and Theology* 7 (1988): 21.

110 Berinyuu, "Change, Ritual, and Berinyuu, "Change, Ritual, and Grief" (see note 108): 149.

111 Matthew 27:46.

112 John 14:2b.

113 Ephesians 2:19-21.

114 Asha Ragin, a doctoral student in Fuller's School of Psychology, assisted in research on this model.

115 In the public domain.

116 Edward P. Wimberley, *Prayer in Pastoral Counselling: Suffering, Healing, and Discernment* (Louisville: Westminster/John Knox Press, 1990).

117 Nancy Boyd-Franklin, *Black Families in Therapy: A Multisystems Approach* (New York: Guilford Press, 1989).

118 For the most extensive treatment of mental health issues for Africans in America, see Reginald Jones, ed., *African-American Mental Health* (Hampton, VA: Cobb and Henry Publishers, 1998).

119 Uichol Kim and John W. Berry, eds., *Indigenous Psychologies: Research and Experience in Cultural Context* (Newbury Park: Sage Publications, 1993); Uichol Kim, Guoshu Yang, and Kwang-kuo Hwang, *Indigenous and Cultural Psychology: Understanding People in Context* (New York: Springer, 2006).

120 Klaus Berger, *Identity and Experience in the New Testament* (Minneapolis: Fortress Press, 2003); William P. Oglesby, *Biblical Themes for Pastoral Care* (Eugene: Wipf and Stock, 2002).

121 Kenneth Gergen, A. Gulerce, A. Lock, and G. Misra, "Psychological Science in Cultural Context," *American Psychologist* 51 (1996): 496-503.

122 Alvin C. Dueck, *Between Jerusalem and Athens: Ethical Perspectives on Culture, Religion, and Psychotherapy* (Grand Rapids: Baker Books, 1995).

123 Acts 2:8.

124 The Kenyan notion of *harambee* is integral to the work of John Perkins, an African-American known for his work in community development. See, Vera Mae Perkins, *Oral History Interview with Vera Mae Perkins* (1987), http://www.wheaton.edu/bgc /archives/guides/368.htm.

125 Matthew 5:48.

126 Romans 15:5.

127 Matthew 8:22 (emphasis added).

128 All persons in stories do not represent real people.

129 Romans 12:15.

130 e.g., Matthew 7:1-5; Ephesians 4:17-32; Philippians 4:8-9.

131 John 8:1-11.

132 Romans 8:1-2.

133 A "Merry-Go-Round" is a common African process among women groups. They meet, often on a monthly basis, from home to home among their members for fellowship and to build community. At the end of sharing a meal, singing, and praise, among other activities, they contribute a fixed amount of money that is given to the host to meet her immediate needs. This way, all the efforts put together can do more than the mere savings of one woman.

Chapter 4. Stress Management

134 All persons in stories do not represent real people.

135 Archibald Hart, *Stress and Your Child* (Dallas: Word Publishing, 1992).

136 Christina Maslach, *Burnout: The Cost of Caring* (Cambridge, MA: Malor Books, 2003).

137 Mark Gorkin, "The Four Stages of Burnout," https://jobs.localjobnetwork.com/a/ t-the-four-stages-of-burnout-au-gorkin,-mark-articles-a749.html

138 Sherwood Lingenfelter and Marvin K. Mayers, *Ministering Cross-Culturally: An Incarnational Model for Personal Relationships* (Grand Rapids: Baker Book House, 1986), 83-84.

139 D. Somasundran, et al., "Natural and Technological Disasters," in *Trauma Interventions in War and Peace: Prevention, Practice, and Policy*, ed. B. L. Green, et al. (New York: Kluwer Academic/Plenum Publishers, 2003), 310-314.

140 Gladys K. Mwiti, "Traumatic Exposure, PTSD, Social Support, and Religious Participation among Adult Survivors of the Nairobi Embassy Bombing" (Ph.D. diss., School of Psychology, Fuller Theological Seminary, 2003).

141 Christina Maslach, *Preventing Burnout in Your Organization* (Stanford, CA: Kantola Productions, 2001).

142 Hans Selye, *The Stress of Life*, rev. ed. (New York: McGraw-Hill, 1984).

143 John 17:4.

144 D. Huggett and J. Huggett, "Jesus Christ," in *Doing Member Care Well* (see note 99), 211.

145 Mark 1:35-38.

146 Lazarus and Lois Seruyange, in discussion with the first author, 2004.

147 John 15:12.

148 John 15:14.

149 Luke 22:15-16.

150 John 17:6-19.

151 Luke 24:16.

152 Mark 1:29.

153 2 Corinthians 3:2.

154 Gary R. Collins, *Christian Coaching: Helping Others Turn Potential into Reality* (Colorado Springs, CO: NAVPRESS, 2001), 269.

155 1 Corinthians 12:27.

156 Hebrews 12:1-2.

157 Hebrews 4:9-11.

158 Kelly O'Donnell and Michèle O'Donnell, "Running Well and Resting Well: Twelve Tools for Missionary Life," in *Doing Member Care Well* (see note 99), 309.

159 Ibid. (italics in original text).

160 1 Corinthians 6:19-20.

161 Philippians 4:8.

162 Philippians 4:8.

163 Romans 12:2.

164 1 Peter 5:7 (The Amplified Bible, Classic Edition [AMPC]. Copyright © 1954, 1958, 1962, 1964, 1965, 1987 by The Lockman Foundation.)

Chapter 5. God's Benevolence and Mass Suffering

165 See Philip Gourevitch, *We wish to inform you that tomorrow we will be killed with our families: Stories from Rwanda* (New York: Farrar Straus and Giroux, 1998).

166 Helen Nyambura, *Kenya Refugees Go Hungry as Africa Aid Needs Mount* (2003), https://reliefweb.int/report/kenya/kenya-refugees-go-hungry-africa-aid-needs-mount.

167 Bernardo Bernardi, *The Mugwe: A Blessing Prophet. A Study of a Religious and Public Dignitary of the Meru of Kenya* (Nairobi, Kenya: Gideon S. Were Press, 1989).

168   Ibid., 115.

169   Alfred M. M'Imanyara, *The Restatement of Bantu Origin and Meru History* (Nairobi, Kenya: Longman Kenya, 1992).

170   Jeffrey Fadiman, *Mountain Warriors: The Pre-Colonial Meru of Mt. Kenya* (Athens, OH: Ohio University, Center for International Studies, 1976).

171   As quoted in Alister E. McGrath, ed., *The Blackwell Encyclopaedia of Modern Christian Thought* (Cambridge, MA: Blackwell, 1993), 195.

172   Barry L. Whitney, *What are they saying about God and Evil?* (New York: Paulist Press, 1989), 94.

173   John S. Mbiti, *Concepts of God in Africa* (London: S. P. C. K., 1970), 37.

174   Ibid., 281.

175   Gwinjai H. Muzorewa, *The Origins and Development of African Theology* (Maryknoll, NY: Orbis Books, 1985), 15.

176   Walter Brueggemann, "The Psalms and the Life of Faith: A Suggested Typology of Function," *Journal for the Study of the Old Testament* 17 (1980): 3-32.

177   Habakkuk 1:1-4

178   Habakkuk 3.

179   Habakkuk 3:17-19.

180   John 9:2-3.

181   See Gladys Mwiti and Gershon Mwiti, *Trauma Counseling: A Community-based Approach for Resiliency, Restoration, and Renewal* (Pasadena: The Integration Press, 2001).

182   A. Ehlers and D. M. Clark, "Early psychological interventions for adult survivors of trauma: A review," in *Posttraumatic Stress Disorder: The Latest Assessment and Treatment Strategies*, ed. M. J. Friedman (Kansas City, MO: Compact Clinicals, 2003), 41.

183   Ezekiel 47:1-12.

184   Mwiti, "Traumatic Exposure" (see note 140), 15.

185   Gladys and Gershon Mwiti, *The Turning Point: A Manual for HIV and AIDS Counsellors* (Nairobi, Kenya: Oasis Counseling Center and Training Institute, 2004).

186   All persons in stories do not represent real people.

187   Bishop Desmond Tutu, "The Theology of Liberation in Africa," in *African Theology Enroute*, eds. Kofi Appiah-Kubi and Sergio Torres (Maryknoll, NY: Orbis Books, 1977), 162.

188   Ibid., 163.

Chapter 6. Building Resilient Communities

189   N. Baron, S. B. Jensen, and J. V. T. M. de Jong, "Refugees and Internally Displaced People," in *Trauma Interventions in War and Peace: Prevention, Practice, and Policy*, eds. B. L. Green, et al. (New York: Kluwer Academic/Plenum Publishers, 2003), 247.

190 Stefan Vanistendael, *Growth in the Muddle of Life: Resilience. Building on People's Strengths* (Geneva: International Catholic Child Bureau. ICCB Series, 1996).

191 For more details of the Disaster Theory and the Crunch/Release Model, see P. Blaikie, et al., *At Risk: Natural Hazards, People's Vulnerability, and Disasters* (London: Routledge, 1994); and P. Venton and B. Hansford, *Reducing Risk of Disaster in Our Communities* (Teddington, UK: ROOTS, Tear Fund, 2006), 1-13.

192 Bernardi, *The Mugwe* (see note 167), 13.

193 Ibid.

194 Ibid.

195 Gershon K. Mwiti, "Christian Intellectuals in Church Leadership in the Methodist Church in Kenya" (D. Missiology, Fuller Theological Seminary, School of Intercultural Studies, 2004), 110.

196 Baituuru M'Rinchuni (Meru Village Elder), personal communication, Meru, Kenya, 2000.

197 Mwiti, "Christian Intellectuals" (see note 195).

198 Bernardi, *The Mugwe* (see note 167).

199 Gershon K. Mwiti, "Contextualization as a Method: Synthetic Model" (paper submitted to School of Intercultural Studies, Fuller Theological Seminary, 2004), 28.

200 Ezekiel 3:17 (see also 33:6).

201 Ephesians 6:12.

202 Walter Wink, *Unmasking the Powers* (Philadelphia: Fortress Press, 1984).

203 Ibid., 7.

204 Gerard Prunier, *The Rwanda Crisis: History of a Genocide* (Kampala, Uganda: Fountain Publishers, 1995), 51.

205 Walter Wink, *Naming the Powers: The Language of Power in the New Testament* (Philadelphia: Fortress Press, 1984), 100.

206 Ibid., 5.

207 R. E. Allen, H. W. Fowler, and F. G. Fowler, eds., *The Concise Oxford Dictionary* (Oxford: Clarendon Press, 1993), 1077.

208 Mark 5.

209 Wink, *Unmasking the Powers* (see note 202), 44-47.

210 Ibid., 45.

211 Ibid., 48.

212 Wink, *Naming the Powers* (see note 205), 103-158.

213 Prunier, *The Rwanda Crisis* (see note 204), 142.

214 Art Beals with Larry Libby, *Beyond Hunger: A Biblical Mandate for Social Responsibility* (Portland, OR: Multnomah Press, 1985), 199.

215 Psalm 82:3-4a.

216 Abdul Rahman Abu Zayd Ahmed, Nigel Twose, and Benjamin Pogrund, *War Wounds: Development Costs of Conflict in Southern Sudan* (Washington: Panos Institute, 1988).

217 Matthew 5:39.

218 Ronald J. Sider, *Rich Christians in an Age of Hunger: Moving from Affluence to Generosity* (Dallas: Word Publishing, 1997).

219 David M. Beckmann and Arthur R. Simon, *Grace at the Table: Ending Hunger in God's World* (New York: Paulist Press, 1999), 133.

220 John Lukwata, *Integrated African Liturgy* (Eldoret, Kenya: AMECEA Gaba Publications, 2003), 188.

221 C. E. Nwaka, *The Power of Africentric Celebrations: Inspirations from the Zairean Liturgy* (New York: The Crossroad Publishing Company, 1996), 83.

222 J. N. K. Mugambi, *African Christian Theology: An Introduction* (Nairobi, Kenya: Heinemann Kenya Limited, 1989).

223 Luke 4:18-21.

224 Leviticus 25:8-55.

225 NIV Study Bible, 1545.

Chapter 7. Premarital Counselling

226 For an African perspective see Aggrey and Naomi Ayiro, *The Singles and the Married* (Nairobi, Kenya: Moreland, 1996). For a Western perspective see Robert F. Stahmann and William J. Hiebert, *Premarital and Marital Counseling: The Professional's Handbook* (San Francisco: Jossey-Bass, 1997).

227 Ngugi wa Thiong'o, *Moving the Centre: The Struggle for Cultural Freedoms* (Nairobi, Kenya: East African Educational Publishers, 1993), 57.

228 Setri Nyomi, *African Christian Families in the 21st Century: A Guide* (Nairobi, Kenya: All Africa Conference of Churches, 2000), 19.

229 For a resource calling for equal gender opportunities with a case for women, especially those living in developing economies, see D. B. Rao and D. P. Rao, *Women Challenges and Advancement* (Darya Ganj, New Delhi, India: Discovery Publishing House, 1999).

230 A. K. H. Weinrich, *African Marriage in Zimbabwe* (Gweru, Zimbabwe: Mambo Press, 1982), 104.

231 J. N. K. Mugambi, *Christian Theology and Social Reconstruction* (Nairobi, Kenya: Acton Publishers, 2003), 51. In his book Das discusses family structures in Nigeria, Tanzania, Somalia, Swaziland, and Libya, with a special exploration of the effect of change on traditional marriage and family systems in Africa. See M. S. Das, *The Family in Africa* (New Delhi, India: M.D. Publications Pvt. Ltd., 1993).

232 Remy Beller, *Life, Person and Community in Africa: A Way towards Inculturation with the Spirituality of the Focolare* (Nairobi, Kenya: Pauline Publications Africa, 2001), 19.

233 Aylward Shorter, *African Culture and the Christian Church: An Introduction to Social and Pastoral Anthropology* (Ann Arbor, MI: University of Michigan, 2005), 163.

234 Jomo Kenyatta, *Facing Mount Kenya* (Nairobi, Kenya: Heinemann, 1978), 309.

235 Benjamin Kiriswa, *Pastoral Counseling in Africa: An Integrated Model* (Eldoret, Kenya: AMECEA Gaba Publications, 2002), 112.

236 Rabecca Baituuru, personal interview with author, Meru, Kenya, 1999.

237 M. Y. Nabofa, "Erhi and Eschatology," in *Traditional Religion in West Africa*, E. A. Ade Adegbòola (Ibadan, Nigeria: Sefer, 1998), 312.

238 We need to note that indigenous cultural societies were in no way perfect. However, in this publication, we have emphasized that in many cases, Western education systems discarded both the good and the bad aspects of African traditional value systems. The duty of the Christian counsellor is to value, reclaim, and help African people to own any good practices that have been lost.

239 See Jack Balswick and Judy Balswick, *The Family: A Christian Perspective on the Contemporary Home*, 2nd ed. (Grand Rapids: Baker Books, 1999).

240 Rodney Clapp, *Families at the Crossroads: Beyond Traditional and Modern Options* (Downers Grove, IL: InterVarsity Press, 1993).

241 Ephesians 5:31-32.

242 Benezeri Kisembo, Laurenti Magesa, and Aylward Shorter, *African Christian Marriage*, 2nd. ed. (Nairobi, Kenya: Paulines Publications Africa, 1998), 45.

243 2 Corinthians 6:14.

244 Genesis 2:24.

245 Mark 10:9.

246 Deuteronomy 24:1.

247 Let us note that there are cases where divorce may be justified. However, we recommend all should be done to save the marriage and that the church pastor and community be involved in counselling and guidance right through the process, whatever the end might be.

248 Kisembo, Magesa, and Shorter, *African Christian Marriage* (see note 242), 46.

249 Ephesians 5:22.

250 Ephesians 5:15-16.

251 Ephesians 5:18.

252 Ephesians 5:19-20.

253 See Deuteronomy 10:18; Psalm 68:5.

254 Matthew 6:33.

255 Matthew 6:34.

Chapter 8. Marriage Counselling

256 Proverbs 13:1.

257 Nyomi, *African Christian Families* (see note 228), 19.

258 Proverbs 18:22.

259 Proverbs 27:15.

260 Nyomi, *African Christian Families* (see note 228), 48-49.

261 J. R. Kok and A. E. Jongsma, *The Pastoral Counseling Treatment Planner* (New York: John Wiley and Sons, 1998).

262 Dr Samuel Gatere, in discussion with the first author, 1998.

263 Genesis 1:31.

264 Song of Songs 4:10.

265 Ephesians 4:26-27.

266 Galatians 5:22-23.

267 David and Vera Mace, *When the Honeymoon's Over: Making the Most of Your Marriage* (Nashville: Abingdon Press, 1988), 59.

268 Walter Brueggemann, "Covenanting as Human Vocation: A Discussion of the Relation of Bible and Pastoral Care," *Interpretation* 33 (1979): 115-29.

269 Gordon Paul Hugenberger, *Marriage as a Covenant: A Study of Biblical Law and Ethics Governing Marriage, Developed from the Perspective of Malachi* (New York: E. J. Brill, 1994), 11.

270 Jordan, *Taking on the Gods* (see note 87).

271 Jordan, *Taking on the Gods* (see note 87).

272 Sue and Sue, *Counseling* (see note 49).

273 Collins, *Christian Coaching* (see note 154), 417.

Chapter 9 On Counselling Families

274 All persons in stories do not represent real people.

275 Mwai J. Ndirangu, *Youth in Danger: A Handbook for Teachers, Students, Parents, Pastors, and Community Workers* (Nairobi, Kenya. Uzima, 2000), 57.

276 Proverbs 22:6.

277 Proverbs 4:13.

278 Numbers 14:18.

279 M'Imanyara, *Restatement* (see note 169), 128.

280 Ibid.

281 See Gladys K. Mwiti, *Moving on Towards Maturity: A Manual for Youth Counselors* (Nairobi, Kenya: Evangel Publishing House, 2005), 110.

282 See Rodney Clapp, *A Peculiar People: The Church as Culture in a Post-Christian Society* (Downers Grove, IL: InterVarsity Press, 1996).

283 Deuteronomy 4:9.

284 Matthew 19:14; Mark 10:14; Luke 18:16.

285 Ephesians 6:2-3.

286 Ephesians 6:4.

287 Kiriswa, *Pastoral Counseling* (see note 235).

288 Counsellors should remind parents that some children may misbehave because of neurological problems. Child assessment by qualified child psychologists or psychiatrists can rule out the neurological contribution to child misconduct.

289 Mwamwenda discusses the growth and development of African children. He introduces the term *precocity*, an infant developmental behaviour that is more advanced than would be normal for that age. Citing studies in Uganda, Senegal, Kenya, Botswana, Nigeria, and Zambia, he indicates that an infant's development is a product of cultural expectations and that African children indicate faster accelerated growth than European children. This approach would form a base for future research in child development in Africa, providing an Africentric basis for child assessment and treatment modalities. [T. S. Mwamwenda, *Educational Psychology: An African Perspective* (Sandton, South Africa: Heinemann Further and Higher Education Ltd., 2004).]

290 Unlike Western countries, the process of reporting child abuse is not very clear in many African nations, nor is the punishment for perpetrators clarified legally. However, reports should be made to the relevant authorities: the police for penal offences, social services officers, children's officers, as well as non-governmental organizations working on children's issues. For more information on this topic, refer to Mwiti, G. K. *Child Abuse: Detection, Prevention and Counselling* (Nairobi, Kenya: Evangel Publishing House, 2006).

291 Boyd-Franklin, *Black Families in Therapy* (see note 117).

292 Maurice Eisenbruch, "Cross Cultural Aspects of Bereavement: A Conceptual Framework for Comparative Analysis," *Culture, Medicine, and Psychiatry* 8 (1984): 283-309. Also, see G. M. Humphrey and D. G. Zimpfer, *Counselling for Grief and Bereavement* (London: Sage Publications, 1996).

Chapter 10. Spirits, Demons and Scourges: Mental Illness and AIDS in Africa

293 Details have been changed to protect confidentiality.

294 Luke 6:37.

295 Matthew 9:36.

296 Karl Schultz, *The Art and Vocation of Caring for People in Pain* (New York: Paulist Press, 1993).

297 Details have been changed to protect confidentiality.

298 1 Peter 5:8.

299 Diane B. Stinton, *Jesus of Africa: Voices of Contemporary African Christology* (Maryknoll, NY: Orbis Books, 2004), 75.

300 Roger K. Bufford, *Christian Counseling and the Demonic: Resources for Christian Counseling* (Dallas: Word Publishing, 1988).

301 Luke 11:24-25.

302 C. S. Lewis, *The Screwtape Letters* (Glasgow: Collins-Fontana Books, 1942), 9.

303 Alfâ Ibrâhîm Sow, *Anthropological Structures of Madness in Black Africa*, trans. Joyce Diamanti (New York: International Universities Press, Inc., 1980).

304 American Psychiatric Association, *Diagnostic and Statistical Manual of Mental Disorders: DSM-IV-TR*, 4th ed. text revision (Washington, DC: American Psychiatric Association, 2003).

305 Sue and Sue, *Counseling* (see note 49), 208-232.

306 Jean Masamba ma Mpolo, "A Brief Review of Psychiatric Research in Africa: Some Implications to Pastoral Counseling," in *Pastoral Care and Counselling in Africa Today*, eds. Jean Masamba ma Mpolo and Daisy Nwachuku (Frankfurt am Main: Peter Lang, 1999), 9-33.

307 Sow, *Anthropological Structures* (see note 303).

308 Mpolo, "A Brief Review of Psychiatric Research in Africa" (see note 306), 23.

309 For a deeper understanding of the African palaver and its role in healing of broken relationships, as well as its recommendation as a tool for conflict resolution, see Kasonga wa Kasonga, "African Palaver: A contemporary way of healing communal conflicts and crises," in *The Church and Healing* (see note 102), 49-65. See also Bénézet Bujo, *Foundations of an African Ethic: Beyond the Universal Claims of Western Morality*, trans. Brian McNeil (New York: Crossroad Pub., 2001).

310 Mpolo, "Kindoki as Diagnosis and Therapy," in *Pastoral Care* (see note 306), 94. In this chapter, ma Mpolo discusses the use of *kindoki* or bewitching as serving positive purposes by externalizing diagnoses and so taking the focus off an individual as mentally ill and placing healing under the responsibility of the community and its healers. .

311 Ray S. Anderson, *Self-Care: A Theology of Personal Empowerment and Spiritual Healing* (Pasadena: Fuller Seminary Press, 2004), 54.

312 Psalm 38:9-10.

313 Edward A. Charlesworth and R. G. Nathan, *Stress Management: A Comprehensive Guide to Wellness* (New York: Ballantine Books, 2004), 213.

314 Don Baker and Emery Nester, *Depression: Finding Hope and Meaning in Life's Darkest Shadow* (Portland, OR: Multnomah Press, 1983), 123.

315 Matthew 18:18. See John Dawson, *What Christians Should Know about Reconciliation* (Kent, UK: Sovereign World, 1998), 28.

316 Mwiti and Mwiti, *The Turning Point* (see note 181).

317 Jonathan C. Brown, Didem Ayvalikli, and Nadeem Muhammad, *Turning Bureaucrats into Warriors. Preparing and Implementing Multi-Sector HIV-AIDS Programs in Africa. A Generic Operations Manual* (Washington, DC: Global HIV/AIDS Program of the World Bank, 2004), 1.

318 Ibid.

319   Family Health International (FHI), "Implementing AIDS Prevention and Care Project," *Conducting a Participatory Situation Analysis of Orphans and Vulnerable Children Affected by HIV/AIDS: Guidelines and Tools* (Arlington, VA: FHI, 2005), 1.

320   Donald S. Clarke, *AIDS: The Biblical Solutions* (Nairobi, Kenya: Evangel Publishing House, 1994), 20.

321   Mwiti and Mwiti, *The Turning Point* (see note 181), 26. Counsellors may want to contact MAP International in Nairobi, Kenya for publications on the role of faith-based organizations in the fight against the HIV and AIDS pandemic. For example, MAP International, *The Role of Faith Based Organizations in the Fight against HIV and AIDS* (Nairobi, Kenya: MAP International, 2005); MAP International, HIV and AIDS FBO Directory (Nairobi, Kenya: MAP International, 2005); and MAP International, *Scaling Up FBO Response to HIV and AIDS in Kenya* (Nairobi, Kenya: MAP International, 2006).

322   For more resources on AIDS counselling, see H. N. Tabifor, *The Dignity of Human Sexuality and the AIDS Challenge* (Nairobi, Kenya: Alpha and Omega Centre, 2000).

323   For more information on wife inheritance practices in Africa, see "Human Rights Watch: Women's Property Rights Violations in Sub-Saharan Africa: Illustrated Case." (New York: Human Rights Watch, 2006). https://www.hrw.org/legacy/campaigns/women/property/qna.htm.

324   Republic of Kenya, AIDS in Kenya. *Trends, Interventions, and Impact* (Nairobi, Kenya: National AIDS and STI Control Programme, NASCOP, 2005), 22.

325   Daisy N. Nwachuku, "Family Life Patterns and Christian Counselling in Contemporary Africa: The Nigerian Case," in *Pastoral Care* (see note 306), 121.

326   Nyomi, *African Christian Families* (see note 228), 96.

327   Stella Okoronkwo, *Facts about Sex for Youth: "Choosing to Chill"* (Nairobi, Kenya: Uzima, 2005), 36.

328   Counsellors may want to contact Oasis Africa for youth training materials that respond to this need. For example, Gladys K. Mwiti, *Moving on Towards Maturity* (Nairobi, Kenya: Evangel Publishing House, 2005).

329   Eliab Seroney Some and Karl Pfahler, *Community Based Support of Orphans and Vulnerable Children: A manual for frontline workers in Africa* (Germany: Kindernothilfe e.V, 2004), 1.

330   Joint United Nations Program on HIV/AIDS and World Health Organization, *AIDS Epidemic Update* (Geneva: UNAIDS/WHO, December 2004), 1.

331   H. Rui, L. E. Fulginiti, and W. F. Peterson, *Investing in Hope: AIDS, Life Expectancy, and Human Capital Accumulation.* Paper prepared for presentation at the Meetings of the International Association of Agricultural Economists, Durban, South Africa, August 2003, Abstract 1.

332   *The Framework for the Protection, Care and Support of Orphans and Vulnerable Children Living in a World with HIV and AIDS*, ed. UNICEF (UNICEF and UNAIDS, 2004), 9.

333   Ibid., 9.

334 Zimbabwe National Vulnerability Assessment Committee in collaboration with SADC FANR Vulnerability Assessment Committee, "Zimbabwe Emergency Food Security and Vulnerability Assessment," in UNICEF, et al., *The Framework for the Protection, Care and Support of Orphans and Vulnerable Children Living in a World with HIV and AIDS* (New York: UNICEF and UNAIDS, 2004), 9.

335 United Republic of Tanzania, "Demographic and Health Survey," in UNICEF, et al., *The Framework for the Protection, Care and Support of Orphans and Vulnerable Children Living in a World with HIV and AIDS (see note 334)*, 9.

336 J. Makaya, et al., "Assessment of Psychological Repercussion of AIDS next to 354 AIDS Orphans in Brazzaville," in UNICEF, *Africa's Orphaned Generations* (New York: UNICEF, 2004).

337 V. Makame, C. Aniand S. Grantham-McGregor, "Psychological Well-being of Orphans in Dar es Salaam, Tanzania," *Acta Paediatrica* 91 (2002): 459-465.

338 J. Sengendo and J. Nambi, "The Psychological Effect of Orphanhood: A Study of Orphans in Rakai District [Uganda]," *Health Transition Review* 7 (1997): 105-124.

339 Republic of Kenya, *AIDS in Kenya. Trends, Interventions, and Impact* (Nairobi, Kenya: National AIDS and STI Control Programme, NASCOP, 2005), 29.

340 AVERT, *HIV and AIDS in Botswana*, http://www.avert.org/aidsbotswana.htm, l.

341 M. Grunwald, *A Small Nation's Big Effort Against AIDS: Botswana Spreads Message and Free Drugs, but Old Attitudes Persist* (Washington, DC: The Washington Post Foreign Service, 2002), December 2, 2002. Cited in AVERT, *HIV and AIDS in Botswana*, https://www.avert.org/professionals/hiv-around-world/sub-saharan-africa/botswana.

342 The World Bank, *Youth Development in Kenya. A Report on Economic and Sector Work*. Draft Report (Nairobi, Kenya: The World Bank, May 2005), 38-49; and Musa W. Dube, "'Woman, What Have I to Do With You?' A Post-colonial Feminist Theological Reflection on the Role of Christianity in Development, Peace, and Reconstruction in Africa." In *The Role of Christianity in Development, Peace, and Reconstruction*, (see note 44), 244-258.

OASIS INTERNATIONAL

Satisfying Africa's Thirst for God's Word

Our mission is to grow discipleship through publishing African voices.
Go to oasisinternationalpublishing.com to learn more.

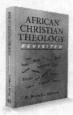

HIGHLY FAVOURED: OUR POWERFUL GOD'S COVENANT WITH YOU
Stuart J. Foster
The God of the Bible is not unreliable or inaccessible like the spiritual beings in African traditional religions. He chooses to have a covenant relationship with his people and we do not have to earn God's favour.

AFRICANS AND AFRICA IN THE BIBLE
Tim Welch
This book shows the presence and the participation of Africans in the biblical text, helping demonstrate that Christianity is not a "white man's religion" and that Christianity has deep roots in African soil.

AFRICAN CHRISTIAN THEOLOGY REVISITED
Richard J. Gehman
For all African Christians, *African Christian Theology Revisited* is a powerful plea to think through your faith in African contexts under the authority of the Word of God.

PARENTING WITH PURPOSE & AFRICAN WISDOM
Gladys K. Mwiti
This practical guide for Christians is a relevant, thoughtful presentation on the characteristics of parenting that delivers results.

ANSWERS FOR YOUR MARRIAGE
Bruce and Carol Britten
Offers practical insights to marriage issues and facts on sex, pregnancy, family planning, child-raising, money issues, adultery, HIV, and sex-related diseases. If your marriage is in despair, look to this book for some answers for your marriage.

LEARNING TO LEAD
Richard J. Gehman
With its discussion questions and practical applications, this book will guide you to obtaining character and skills, and help you become an effective Christian leader. It was written from the living experience of African leaders, and it has been shaped by 36 years of training church leaders in Kenya.

HABITS OF HIGHLY EFFECTIVE CHRISTIANS
Ron Meyers
In today's world of rushed deadlines and hurried lives, it's easy to forget that the Bible holds principles that provide a proper foundation for living. Learn about 17 habits that can help you lead a more fulfilling, healthy life both professionally and personally. Challenge how you think about the way we live in the 21st century.

BIBLICAL CHRISTIANITY IN MODERN AFRICA
Wilbur O'Donovan
Biblical Christianity in Modern Africa describes the major issues facing the church in Africa and offers suggestions on how these problems can be overcome.

OASIS
INTERNATIONAL
PUBLISHING

oasisinternationalpublishing.com | oasisinternational.com

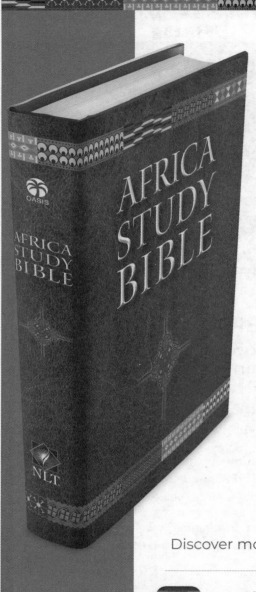